The Films of Michelangelo Antonioni

The Films of Michelangelo Antonioni provides an overview of the Italian director's life and work and examines six of his most important and intellectually challenging films. *L'avventura, La notte,* and *L'eclisse,* released in the early 1960s, form the trilogy that first brought the director to international attention. *Red Desert* was his first film in color. *Blow-up,* shot in English and set in swinging London, became one of the best-known (and most notorious) films of its era. *The Passenger,* starring Jack Nicholson, is the greatest work of Antonioni's maturity. Rather than emphasizing the angst and alienation of Antonioni's characters, Peter Brunette places the films in the context of the director's ongoing social and political analysis of the Italy of the great postwar economic boom and demonstrates how they depend on painterly abstraction for their expressive effects.

Peter Brunette is Professor of English and Film Studies at George Mason University. He is the author of *Roberto Rossellini* and coeditor of *Deconstruction and the Visual Arts* (Cambridge, 1994) and has written extensively about film for the *New York Times, Boston Globe, Village Voice,* and the webzine Film.com.

CAMBRIDGE FILM CLASSICS

General Editor: Ray Carney, Boston University

The Cambridge Film Classics series provides a forum for revisionist studies of the classic works of the cinematic canon from the perspective of the "new auteurism," which recognizes that films emerge from a complex interaction of bureaucratic, technological, intellectual, cultural, and personal forces. The series consists of concise, cutting-edge reassessments of the canonical works of film study, written by innovative scholars and critics. Each volume provides a general introduction to the life and work of a particular director, followed by critical essays on several of the director's most important films.

Other Books in the Series:

Amy Lawrence, *The Films of Peter Greenaway*
Peter Bondanella, *The Films of Roberto Rossellini*
Ray Carney, *The Films of John Cassavetes*
Sam B. Girgus, *The Films of Woody Allen*
Robert Phillip Kolker and Peter Beicken, *The Films of Wim Wenders*
Scott MacDonald, *Avant-Garde Film*
James Naremore, *The Films of Vincente Minnelli*
James Palmer and Michael Riley, *The Films of Joseph Losey*
Scott Simmon, *The Films of D. W. Griffith*
David Sterritt, *The Films of Alfred Hitchcock*
Maurice Yacowar, *The Films of Paul Morrissey*

The Films of
Michelangelo
Antonioni

Peter Brunette

CAMBRIDGE
UNIVERSITY PRESS

PUBLISHED BY THE PRESS SYNDICATE OF THE UNIVERSITY OF CAMBRIDGE
The Pitt Building, Trumpington Street, Cambridge, CB2 1RP, United Kingdom

CAMBRIDGE UNIVERSITY PRESS
The Edinburgh Building, Cambridge CB2 2RU, UK   http://www.cup.cam.ac.uk
40 West 20th Street, New York, NY 10011-4211, USA   http://www.cup.org
10 Stamford Road, Oakleigh, Melbourne 3166, Australia

© Peter Brunette 1998

First published 1998

Printed in the United States of America

Typeset in Sabon 10/13 pt, in Penta™ [RF]

*A catalog record for this book is available from
the British Library.*

Library of Congress Cataloging-in-Publication Data
Brunette, Peter
The films of Michelangelo Antonioni / Peter Brunette.
p.   cm. – (Cambridge film classics)
Filmography: p.
Includes bibliographical references and index.
ISBN 0-521-38085-5 (hb). – ISBN 0-521-38992-5 (pb)
1. Antonioni, Michelangelo – Criticism and interpretation.
I. Title. II. Series.
PN1998.3.A58B78   1998
791.43'0233092 – dc21   97-51311
CIP

ISBN 0 521 38085 5   hardback
ISBN 0 521 38992 5   paperback

All stills are from the Museum of Modern Art Film Stills Archive.

To Ab, Barbara, Gerry, and David
and the pleasures of friendship

Contents

Illustrations

Acknowledgments

Thanks go to Ray Carney, series editor, and Beatrice Rehl, of Cambridge University Press, who first asked me to do this book, and who must have thought at least once during their long, long wait for it that they had made a mistake; to Anne Sanow of Cambridge for the tea and cookies in Manhattan; to Vicky Macintyre, for her sensitive and indefatigable copyediting; to Mary Corliss of the Museum of Modern Art Film Stills Archive, for her usual cheerful and efficient turnaround of an impossibly last-minute request for photographs; to the Italian Cultural Institute in Washington, D.C., for the embarrassingly long-term loan of some crucial books on Antonioni; to Sante Matteo and Gavriel Moses, whose invitations to speak on the director led to the first formulation of the approach to his work that is embodied in this book; and to my wife Lynne Johnson, whose patience surpasseth all understanding.

Introduction

Michelangelo Antonioni, who first gained prominence on the international cinema scene in the 1960s, has become the very symbol of that increasingly rare form, the art film, and of all that the cinema has ever sought to achieve beyond mere entertainment. Along with the films of Ingmar Bergman, Federico Fellini, the directors of the French New Wave, and a few others, Antonioni's films were, during the 1960s, absolutely essential to the cultural life of the educated elite around the world. His work, especially, has carried both the cachet and the condemnation of being particularly "artistic" – that is, symbolic, indirect, metaphysical, and even downright confusing.[1]

Antonioni's early interpreters saw his films primarily as an expression of "existential angst" or "alienation." (Pierre Leprohon, for example, speaks of "the anguish of existence.")[2] In the mid-1960s this was undoubtedly the appropriate tack to take toward films that insisted, in what seemed to be an entirely new manner, on dealing overtly with a certain philosophically inflected *Weltanschauung* in a popular, commercial medium.

Now, however, we can see that this manner of regarding Antonioni's films as transhistorical artifacts is itself not transhistorical but is typical of critical response to the art-film milieu of the period. In other words, his films came to be viewed in this way not only because of their own inherent features, but also because of the period's interpretive frame – at least as posited by critics whose primary interest was aesthetic or formal, rather than political. This focus can also be explained historically by the fact that in the late 1950s European existentialist philosophy, as popularized by Jean-Paul Sartre and others after World War II, began to filter down to more popular artistic forms such as the movies.

I am not saying that these themes are *absent* in Antonioni's films. Many of them are concerned with the essential loneliness of individual human beings and the difficulty of adapting to a relentlessly changing technology that at times seems utterly antihuman. Though these themes are far from irrelevant to the present age, the times now are different, and if the themes of alienation continue to be emphasized to the exclusion of all else, Antonioni's films will quickly become museum pieces, historical artifacts documenting, at best, a certain moment of film and European cultural history. (My students, dumbfounded by this pervasively negative critical attitude, ask me why everybody was so depressed in those days. It is not a bad question.) Therefore the time has come to rethink these films. One way to do that is to examine more closely the errancies of their textual particulars and to pay less attention, at least for a while, to the "big picture." These films continue to be vital precisely because their other themes have more immediate bearing on the present historical situation as the world moves toward the new millennium. Ironically, their relevance becomes clearer when one considers the historical particulars that the "alienation" thesis has tended to overlook.

This rethinking might take several paths. One approach might be to reconsider the rhetorical force of these films' visual metaphors and the way they always exceed whatever rational meaning an audience may attach to them. Another might be to resituate the films in the economic, social, and cultural context in which they arose. We too often forget that directors by and large need to make financially successful films in order to continue their work; the long periods of enforced silence throughout Antonioni's career provide eloquent testimony to this fact of life. Instead of glossing over this commercial and popular context, as is often done in dealing with "art films," we need to explore the precise ways in which such films came to be made in the frame of the Italian film industry and what they "meant" to that industry as an alternative paradigm to more blatantly commercial product.

One might ask how such a challenging, formally demanding film as *L'avventura* (The adventure), could be financed in 1959 and, even more surprisingly, how it managed to break even at the box office in Italy? (*La notte* [The night], which followed in 1961, did even better, showing a substantial profit.) Unfortunately, such questions turn out to be much easier to ask than to answer. Before beginning my research on Antonioni, I knew, from prior experience, that the bulk of Italian film criticism – all of it deeply auteurist – was either formalist, philosophical, or political in nature. But I was taken aback to find that only one slim volume, a book by Vittorio Spinazzola called *Cinema e pubblico: Lo spettacolo filmico in Italia 1945–*

1965 (Cinema and its audience: Film in Italy 1945–1965), published in 1974, even attempted to answer questions similar to those I had begun to pose. Spinazzola's treatment of Antonioni is also rather skimpy; given the limited scope of the present book, I cannot claim to have gotten much further in providing the sociocultural fact-finding that I now believe is necessary to contextualize the formal and thematic analysis of any film.

In addition, the very necessity of resituating these films historically leads to a whole set of other problems that arise in the context of what has come to be called cultural studies. All too often, cultural critics have, in their desire to establish firm connections between political and social events and cultural products, unconsciously resorted to crude metaphors of "reflection," as in "this film reflects the governmental crisis of 1960." But what does it mean to say that a text "reflects" some historical event? What metaphors of seeing and vision are unconsciously at work here, and what is their effect on the analysis?

Even more important, in the rush to establish this relationship between the textual and the supposedly extratextual (that is, History or "the way things really are [or were]"), it is often forgotten that history and even "the real" are themselves texts that must be read, and that the meaning of past events or present reality is never given directly but is always constructed after the fact. This is common knowledge, of course, but sometimes it is more convenient – because more "productive" – to forget it. Above all, cultural critics sometimes tend to forget that the cinematic texts themselves must always be *interpreted*. Reading, in the fullest sense of the word, is a labor that cannot be dispensed with, and thus no matter what political claims, or clandestine truth-claims, are made for or about a text, they will always be situated within a host of limiting, interpretive frames.

I take it to be axiomatic that Antonioni's films – like *all* films, like all *texts*, for that matter – are by definition impossible to dominate. Their recalcitrant particulars, the gritty, diverse, innumerable, even contradictory, facts of their being refuse to give in gracefully to overpowering master narratives that claim (usually only implicitly) to control or subjugate them. In fact, nothing ever really seems to add up in these films, nothing, that is, beyond a vague sense of uneasiness and alienation, and thus most critics have taken this to be what they are about. Such apparent unanimity, however, is only arrived at by means of a certain violent epistemological gesture of transcendence, a gesture that moves one quickly and painlessly from the supposedly "superficial" (and certainly confusing) level of the film's particular, material details to a "higher," more synoptic level where things can be made to cohere.

3

This hermeneutic operation is probably inevitable in all forms of sense-making, for all works of art, for all books, and, of course, for all films. What is especially interesting about Antonioni's films, however, is that this process is itself often, or even always, foregrounded. In other words, these films seem self-consciously to present such a plethora of particular, unreconcilable textual details that critics are unable to escape a confrontation with the fact, the procedures, and the consequences of interpretation. The emphasis, visual or aural, on which viewers rely in most films to help them locate the "important" textual details is often missing or, what amounts to the same thing, present everywhere. Emblematic for me is the moment at the very beginning of *L'eclisse* (The eclipse, 1962) when Vittoria (Monica Vitti) sits at a table idly looking through some empty picture frames. By so doing, she and the director point to the constant necessity and inevitability of framing, that is, of reading within a context, whether the frame is visible, as here, or invisible, as it is in the rest of the film (though everything one sees is, of course, always "within" a frame, the film frame). The question then becomes, what is the proper, or better, most productive, context for reading these films?[3]

Antonioni's films continually offer the promise of meaning, like the gaping garment of French theorist Roland Barthes, tantalizing the viewer and yet always withholding any unambiguous signification. The necessity of interpretation is already obvious when the critic confronts such complex films as *L'avventura* (1960), say, or *Il deserto rosso* (Red Desert, 1964), or the other films of this period; later, however, in *Blow-up* (1966) and *The Passenger* (1974), the interpretive operation is itself foregrounded as part of the plot and incident of the films. There, the hermeneutic work of the audience has been introjected into the characters themselves, as the photographer in *Blow-up* and the journalist in *The Passenger* are actively forced to interpret the texts – and the world – that surround them. (Actually, even as early as *L'avventura*, in the search for the missing Anna, the films' narratives replicate this epistemological problem of making or discovering meaning.)

The vast majority of Antonioni's films thus can be seen as collections of signifiers that turn out to have ambiguous signifieds (which is not a bad description of the world, either), and this impetus, this need to interpret, to make sense of experience, occurs even on the level of the shot. Important narrative or even cognitive information is often withheld, and the constant visual mysteries that result also contribute to a certain "hermeneutic pressure" that is always present.

So, too, whatever seemed to remain of the "natural," the "real," and the "direct" has been evacuated from the world, as Antonioni's characters learn. All is necessarily offered up to an active interpretation that, both for character and for audience, is a never-ending activity; the films thus re-hearse what the Italian philosopher Gianni Vattimo has described as the "infinite interpretability" of reality.[4] As cinema historian Gian Piero Bru-netta has pointed out, in Antonioni's films, "things, in their totemic pres-ence, become signs of signs."[5] Things thus take on the presence and mystery of the film's characters, and the characters themselves take on the rigidity, but also the symbolic signifying potential, of things.

One of the consequences of the interpretive operation I have been de-scribing is that the very ambiguity of these films causes them to become vast blackboards on which individual critics scrawl their own desires and obsessions, thinking all the while that they are describing the films, and only that.[6] (I do not exclude myself from this self-deluding process.) The critic seems earnestly to believe that she or he is attending to the specific particulars of the text, scrupulously avoiding the merely impressionistic, but the exact nature of this negotiation between the critic's position outside the text and the text's inside – terms that are easily reversible – is seldom considered. As such, the details of a film come to resemble the elements of Morse code, or better (because that implies something too systematic), a bunch of apparently unrelated visual and aural signifiers that the critic rearranges and reformulates to send her or his own conscious or uncon-scious message.

This vast uncertainty or undecidability concerning the films' meanings sometimes leads critics to postpone a close engagement with the particulars of any given film by attempting a comprehensive description of what might be called the *world* of these films. It is important to keep in mind, however, that this Antonionian world, even more obviously than the real world, is always a textual one and thus is subject to the same "incoherence" that is inevitably found in all texts. One localized version of this world-making comes in the insistent treatment of *L'avventura*, *La notte*, and *L'eclisse* as a trilogy – which Antonioni scholar Seymour Chatman and others expand to a tetralogy with the addition of *Red Desert*. Although it is true that these films have much in common, having been derived from the same cultural matrix by the same director, continually lumping them together also has the effect of erasing their considerable differences. In general, it seems pro-ductive to efface boundaries between films, or at least to recognize the inevitable permeability of such boundaries by trying to understand the films intertextually. (For example, the character that Monica Vitti plays in *L'avventura* clearly affects the reading of her character in *La notte* and the other films in which she appears.) In this way, the metaphysical tyranny of the rigid logocentric separation between outside and inside, and thus between discrete texts, can perhaps be rethought and rewritten; there is no logical reason for the individual film to be the sacrosanct, basic unit of interpretation.

But regarding these particular films as a trilogy (or a tetralogy) does not have the effect of rewriting the inside/outside opposition or questioning the notion of boundaries. Rather, such a gesture often merely reconstitutes these cinematic texts *as a larger textual unit*, which in turn leads the critic to attempt to produce a more inclusive, more synoptic reading of *that* text. In other words, the individual films do not become texts whose boundaries are permeable and whose meanings as individual texts are thus forever dispersed because they cannot ever be kept "inside," but rather they become a kind of megatext that the critic may then proceed to interpret in essentialistic terms, in a more or less conventional manner.

Consider now the kind of misleading exclusions that have resulted from the overinsistence on the themes of alienation and anxiety described earlier. I am thinking here of the specific political content of these films ("political" in the largest sense of the word, that is, including social critique) that most film commentators, especially Anglo-American and French, have systematically repressed. It is all too often forgotten that Antonioni was, like every other artist, responding to specific social, cultural, and moral problems that had arisen as part of *il boom*, Italy's amazing fifteen-year economic recovery from collapse at the end of World War II. Pierre Leprohon, who, ironically, was a chief architect of the "alienation" thesis, was almost alone among earlier critics of Antonioni in also insisting that both *L'avventura* and Fellini's *La dolce vita*, which appeared the same year, were "first and foremost testimonies on their period." He also stressed the "particular social circumstances" behind the "sexual crisis" in Antonioni's film.[7] It may be true, in other words, that Antonioni's characters are alienated, but this alienation seems to be an effect of a specific social organization, rather than a generalized response to the difficulties of something called "modern life."

Armando Borrelli, in his *Neorealismo e marxismo* (Neorealism and Marxism), published in 1966, provides a good example of the ambiguity with which earlier political critics greeted these films. Borrelli grants that Antonioni is interested in modern Italian reality but believes (along with many others) that he is finally more concerned with the ontological fate of man than with any specific political struggles. Thus Borelli castigates the director for the ambiguity of his social portraits because he allows spectators to draw from these films conclusions that are *either* critical and Marxist – in other words, that say it is not life in general that is meaningless, but this particular form of social life under these particular historical conditions – *or* religious, in their emphasis on the inevitability of human unhappiness.[8] Borrelli's ultimate judgment of Antonioni, though, is a positive one. Although contemporary alienation is not always expressed as concretely as one would like – as it is, say, in *L'eclisse*, Antonioni's most explicit attack on capitalism – Borrelli believes the director has done his part by examining the crisis in this society with scientific precision, leaving it up to the spectator to take from these films a sense of the necessity of creating a different world in which "man makes the decisions that affect his life," a world in which he is not inherently alienated from reality.[9]

In assessing the political aspect of Antonioni's films, one should also remember that they often contain explicit, detailed depictions of class and class relations. For the most part, the director focuses on the middle class, and the absence of other groups can make viewers forget that they are, in fact, examining the foibles and failings of a particular class of people. The director himself is very conscious of this aspect of his films, once saying in an interview:

> Inasmuch as I am the product of a middle-class society, and am preoccupied with making middle-class dramas, I am not equipped to [give solutions]. The middle class doesn't give me the means with which to resolve any middle class problems. That's why I confine myself to pointing out existing problems without proposing any solutions.[10]

Not surprisingly, the director has been attacked by many leftist Italian critics for focusing on the middle class, but film historian Lino Miccichè has rightly seen this as one more example of Antonioni's political agenda. Having realized, perhaps unconsciously, that the bourgeoisie had "won" (for example, in the person of Piero, the flamboyant stockbroker of *L'eclisse*), Antonioni "became interested in the 'winner' because he wanted to x-ray the 'disease' that resulted from the apparent spread of the dominant ideology."[11]

The problem is that by investigating the bourgeoisie, the class that, as Barthes explained in *Mythologies*, refuses to name itself in order to appear more natural, it may seem that Antonioni is offering, once again, a "universal" portrayal of Man, when it is actually a particular portrayal of men and women bound to a specific class. Unfortunately, Antonioni's interest in exploring class dynamics is perhaps most overt in earlier films, such as

Cronaca di un amore (Story of a love affair, 1950), *I vinti* (The vanquished, a controversial, clearly self-conscious social document made in 1952), *Le amiche* (The girlfriends, 1955), films that are rarely seen nowadays, and most important, in *Il grido* (The cry, 1957), whose protagonist is a worker. It is true that this character, Aldo (played by Steve Cochran), suffers from a kind of nebulous melancholy, a psychological depression whose metaphysical roots go beyond the emotional disappointment that motivates the plot, but Antonioni also explores his feelings in the context of a specific possibility of collective political action that he, for reasons that are never made clear, explicitly refuses.

American critic Richard Roud agreed, some thirty-five years ago, that it was important to stress this sociopolitical aspect of Antonioni's films. In a survey of the director's early career, written after the release of *L'avventura*, he said that "throughout all Antonioni's work, one finds unsentimental illustrations of his belief that the emotions are often conditioned by social factors and tastes." In this way, Roud sought to counter the prevailing view that any investigation of emotional life must inherently be a middle-class (and therefore apolitical) project; characteristically, he also felt compelled to add that "whenever Antonioni's social preoccupations gain the upper hand, however, his work seems to suffer."[12]

Another theme that is cast in a different light once one moves beyond the prevailing "existential angst" thesis is Antonioni's resolute focus on women. In this he may have been inspired to some extent by his compatriot Roberto Rossellini's obsessive concentration on his wife Ingrid Bergman in his films of the late 1940s and early 1950s; in any case, the emphasis is unmistakable. This particular interest is often regarded as a function of Antonioni's view that women are "more sensitive" than men, and therefore that they are better exemplars of the alienation that contemporary society has foisted upon *all* human beings. In other words, whatever attention Antonioni pays to women is usually seen as part of a more general critique and not as a specific concern with women as women. He himself has said that "reality can be filtered better through women's psychologies. They are more instinctive, more sincere."[13] Besides its essentializing of certain so-called feminine characteristics (and its covert, but familiar strategy of associating women with the body or the animal through the use of words such as "instinctive"), Antonioni's statement also implies that this filtered reality is ultimately the same for everyone, irrespective of gender: its essence, he might say, is just better shown by filtering it through women.[14]

What this reductive view of the portrayal of women in Antonioni's films misses – in other words, what Antonioni himself misses – is just how probing their examination of gender dynamics frequently can be. These films not only document the difficulties that attend any emotional relationship, as most critics have pointed out, but they also offer a specific analysis of the situation of women in contemporary Western society of the 1960s, an analysis that presents a sustained attack on the patriarchy (whether consciously or not is not ultimately relevant here), and this attack is surprisingly, for its time, sympathetic toward women as women.[15]

Antonioni is concerned in large part with the male way of being in the world. In *L'avventura*, for example, men voraciously watch women from beginning to end. The spectacle of thousands of aroused males following Gloria Perkins (a British prostitute who says she writes in a "trance" and wants to make films) and her torn, slit skirt – an incredibly overt, and thus purposely ridiculous, symbolic exteriorization of female genitalia – is only the most grotesque moment of this scenario. The male obsession with sex is hardly an uncommon theme in Italian cinema (Fellini made a whole career out of it), but here the obsession assumes truly monumental and ugly proportions. Similarly, when in the same film Claudia is momentarily left alone in the Sicilian town of Noto, she is entrapped by a large group of men, who surround her in an intensely threatening manner. It is more than just the supposedly playful "boys will be boys" theme promoted by too many Italian films; Claudia seems truly frightened for her personal safety, in a way familiar at least to American women in the 1990s, and to a degree that can make the "existential anxiety" she supposedly manifests seem remote and almost laughable by comparison. The world here is completely male controlled, in the most physically palpable way, and any slight autonomy that women might have wrested from men in the more sophisticated urban centers by 1960 has evaporated in this Sicilian town. In *Il grido*, the working-class protagonist Aldo beats up his common-law wife, Irma, in front of the entire village, and no one comes to her aid. Later in the film, he is accompanying another woman, Elvira, when she is physically attacked by a group of men. In both of these films, and elsewhere, the patriarchy shows itself in raw, ugly, physically threatening terms.[16]

If the films *do* seem to be about the complexities of the heterosexual relationship, this, too, must be seen in a historical perspective. Thus when Leprohon privileges the normative "unity of the couple" that is, according to him, at times assailed in the films and at other times fostered, in hindsight such a putative "unity" will almost always appear asymmetrical, given the power structures that exist in patriarchal society. And given the fact that feminist film theoreticians have elaborated a complex theory concerning the film's positioning of the male spectator who gazes at the female on screen –

Figure 1. The rapacious Sandro (Gabriele Ferzetti) makes his first amorous moves toward Claudia (Monica Vitti) in *L'avventura*

a theory continually being rewritten over the past twenty years – Antonioni's films are also enlightening in terms of what has been called his "feminine temperament." What is the nature of the apparently contradictory relationship between such a temperament and the phallic, penetrating power of Antonioni's camera, that technological stand-in for the male gaze?

Perhaps the most intriguing aspect of these films is that this often unnoticed social critique is held in tension with a rigorous formalism that was utterly new to mainstream cinema in 1960. That is, the films depicted interiority (e.g., interior emotional states) externally on the screen, in the form of gestures, expression, and – most important – abstract means such as line and color.[17] Even more radically, in film after film, the audience is led to react to the characters as *graphic expressions* as well as humans with whom they identify emotionally. Psychological realism ("What would a character with such and such a personality say or do in a situation like this?") is rarely Antonioni's goal. Rather, his characters can be seen (and to some extent, must be seen, in order to make any sense at all) abstractly as *textual elements*, as much as fictional representations of "real people."

In this regard, Antonioni's formalist project is reminiscent of that undertaken by the American painter James MacNeil Whistler as long ago as the 1870s. In painting after painting, Whistler carefully portrayed specific, easily recognizable people in an unproblematically representational manner, yet he always insisted on giving these paintings abstract titles that foregrounded what was for him their true subject matter. The public (as well as the curators, to judge by the wall labels in museums that exhaustively detail the sitters' biographies) seem to want to see paintings such as *Arrangement in Grey and Black, No. 2: Thomas Carlyle*, or *Arrangement in Grey and Black* (more familiarly known as *Whistler's Mother*) principally as representations of specific people, whereas Whistler apparently wanted to see them at least as much, or more, as arrangements of line, color, and shape.[18]

The perception that Antonioni's characters are not to be understood in traditional ways is abetted by the director's stated view of the role of the actors in his films:

> Inasmuch as I consider an actor as being only one element in a given scene, I regard him as a tree, a wall, or a cloud, that is, as just one element in the overall scene; the attitude or pose of the actor, as determined under my direction, cannot but help to effect the framing of that scene, and I, not the actor, am the one who can know whether that effect is appropriate or not.[19]

The point is that, despite appearances, Antonioni's films are much more formal, graphic experiences, say – almost like animated paintings with characters and narrative – than they are typical film stories to which the viewer responds by identifying with the characters in all the conventionally "human" ways.[20] (It is also significant perhaps, that the period in which *L'avventura* and the other films were made was also the height of the U.S. art movement known as abstract expressionism,[21] and that the male ethos critiqued in Antonioni's films of this period was a salient, even celebrated, aspect of that movement.) In addition to line and shape, color comes into play, even in his early black-and-white films, for as French theorist Pascal Bonitzer has pointed out, *all* the colors in Antonioni's palette, including the blacks and whites, are *ideas* rather than just ornamental, emotional, or psychological features. As with all abstract art, the problem comes when one tries to determine precisely what these ideas, or even emotions, are.[22]

Clearly, the relation between the films' social critique and their involvement in expressionist abstraction provides a tension that activates much of what is most powerful in them. Yet these poles must not be regarded as irreconcilable opposites, either. An argument can be made that it is pre-

Figure 2. Giuliana (Monica Vitti) confronts husband Ugo (Carlo de Pra) and friend Corrado (Richard Harris) in her abstractly smeared shop in *Red Desert*

cisely when Antonioni is at his apparently most formal that he is also at his most political. According to Lino Miccichè, Antonioni's work is comparable (and preferable) to that of the more overtly political Italian filmmakers:

> It is doubtless true that in the Italian cinema, often enough, the loud militancy acts as noisy cover and clamorous industrial subjection to an expressive acquiescence badly masked by striking ideological rigors, to an unlimited faith (mysteriously enough based, it's true) in the possibility that progressive "ideological subject matter" can, without paying or losing anything, be born from regressive formal models. All the films of Antonioni . . . bear witness to the refusal of this handy alibi and to the positive choice of the primary political engagement that one should demand of a filmmaker: that of being "politically" responsible for his or her own expressive means.[23]

Critics have, in addition, found it difficult to understand that Antonioni's "political" vision extends far beyond the field normally covered by that term. For he is also trying to grapple with huge technological changes that are perhaps altering human beings at their very core, and his documentation and analysis of these changes transcend the easy binaries of left and right but are no less politically charged for all that. (This effort is perhaps best exemplified in *Red Desert* [1964], a film that Antonioni sees quite differently from his critics.) He believed that "a great anthropological transformation is occurring that will ultimately change our nature," in the same way that increasing knowledge about the sun, for example, has made us regard it differently. After buying a telescope that enabled him to see the rings of Saturn, he remarked:

> I get out of this a physical perception of the universe which is actually so upsetting that my relationship to the universe can no longer be the same as it was before. . . . [S]ome scientific notions have set in motion a transformational process that will end up changing us too – that will lead us to act in a certain way and not in another, and consequently will change our whole psychology, the mechanisms which regulate our lives.[24]

These will not be merely political and economic changes, the director insists; rather, human beings will themselves be utterly altered. These transformations will also have important, if vague, formal consequences for his own work:

> If what I say is true, I must look at the world with different eyes, I must try to get to the heart of it by routes other than the usual ones. This changes everything – the narrative material I have at hand, the stories, their endings – and it cannot be otherwise if I want to bring out, to express, what I think is happening.[25]

Furthermore, Antonioni's decision to accentuate the productive ambiguity of his films can be seen as being, in the widest sense, political. As Roland Barthes has pointed out in his essay "Cher Antonioni," the director's subtlety of meaning is politically decisive because "as soon as meaning is fixed and imposed, as soon as it loses its subtlety, it becomes an instrument of power. To make meaning more subtle, then, is a political activity, as is any effort that aims to harass, to trouble, to defeat the fanaticism of meaning."[26]

Barthes also praises Antonioni's ability to make the object "vibrate, to the detriment of dogma," and this notion of a vibrating object – which obviously has its graphic features – also leads inevitably to a more overtly philosophical inquiry into the classic problem of the relation between the object and its perceiver, the subject. Here I follow the lead of the Italian critic Lorenzo Cuccu, who describes Antonioni's complicated investigation of vision in such books as *La visione come problema* (Vision as problem, 1973) and *Antonioni: Il discorso dello sguardo* (Antonioni: The discourse of the gaze, 1990). Antonioni has often been accused of heavy-handed visual symbolism (a question that will be discussed in greater detail in the specific context of the films), but Cuccu provides an inkling that the source of this perception lies in the overwhelming pressure that the director can put on individual images, "the problematic and dynamic tension internal to an *image* that cannot be reduced to being a mere illustrative function of the story."[27]

From the beginning, according to Cuccu, Antonioni saw the camera not as "a passive and indifferent instrument, but as a concrete expressive function" (p. 20). In this, his approach departed from the prevailing aesthetic of neorealism, as seen in the work of such major figures as Roberto Rossellini, Luchino Visconti, and Vittorio DeSica. For Antonioni, "the cinematic operation is creative not because it reproduces a creatively elaborated [prior] material but for what it adds, in meaning and artistic elaboration, to this material" (p. 21). Narrative and poetic functions thus coexist in Antonioni's images, and these correspond to the metonymic and metaphoric functions of language that have been identified and catalogued by linguists and semioticians. From this perspective, Antonioni's famous long takes can be seen as a product of the disruption, by the metaphoric level, of the metonymic or narrative level. Nevertheless, these poetic images are necessary to fill out the meaning of the narrative (p. 34).

Cuccu also describes Antonioni's vision as "estranged," "a form of vision whose structures or spatiotemporal articulations follow a function which might be called 'self-representative,' in the sense that they serve to render perceptible . . . *the visual experience that the author is having regarding the visible world*" (p. 137). Antonioni's self-conscious philosophical exploration of the nature of his own vision becomes clearly political in *The Passenger*, in which he considers the possibility of approaching reality through the visual media, in the explicitly political context of revolutionary Africa.

In exploring the nature of vision, Antonioni also examines the nature of the perceiving self, or subject, which is usually thought of as fixed and in command, visually at least, of all that it surveys. Both the object ("vibrating" or not) and the subject come to be portrayed as ambiguous and insubstantial in the films under study; in this light, Antonioni can be regarded as the most postmodern of directors. And in describing this relation, Antonioni adds to its complexity by always questioning as well his own inevitably compromised subject position as filmmaker.

Antonioni was born in 1913 to a middle-class family, in Ferrara, a medium-size town north of Bologna known principally for its Renaissance school of painters whose work tended toward the expressionistic. After graduating from the University of Bologna and dabbling for a while in painting and semiprofessional tennis, his first connection with the movies began in 1935 as a film critic for *Corriere Padano*, the Ferrara newspaper to which he also contributed short stories. Late in the 1930s, Antonioni tried to make a documentary on the inmates of a mental asylum and, to judge by his moving account of the experience some twenty years later, it troubled him profoundly. When the bright lights necessary for filming were turned on, Antonioni recounts,

> for an instant, the inmates remained absolutely stationary as though they were petrified. I have never seen such expressions of total fear on the faces of any actors. The scene that followed is indescribable. The inmates started screaming, twisting, and rolling themselves over the floor. . . . In no time at all the room became an inferno. The inmates tried desperately to get away from the light as if they were being attacked by some kind of prehistoric monster. The same faces that had kept madness within human bounds in the preceding calm, were now crumpled and devastated. And this time we were the ones who stood petrified at the sight. The cameraman didn't even have the strength to turn on the motor, nor I to give an order. It was the head of the asylum who yelled "Stop, lights off!" And as the room became silent and subdued, we saw a slow and feeble movement of bodies which seemed to be in their final stages of agony.[28]

What later came to be recognized as one of the director's most characteristic artistic traits, a certain tentativeness regarding the "investigative" or "penetrating" power of his camera, may have stemmed, at least in part, from this experience.

In 1938 Antonioni left the provinces for the greater opportunities of Rome and, for a while, worked on the Esposizione Universale Roma (EUR), the World's Fair scheduled for 1942, which, owing to the outbreak of World War II, never took place. (The section of Rome that was to be the site of the fair, now associated with Mussolini's grandiose dreams for a new Roman Empire, is the futuristic, alienating setting for *L'eclisse*.) Antonioni spent a few months writing for *Cinema* magazine – an important source of ideas and personnel for the neorealist movement – which was, curiously enough, presided over by the Duce's son, Vittorio Mussolini. Then, in 1940, he enrolled for a few months in the Centro Sperimentale di Cinematografia, the prestigious film school that had been recently established by Mussolini *père*.

At the Centro, Antonioni made a short film about a prostitute who blackmails a well-to-do lady. Apparently the most interesting thing about the short, now lost, was that he used the same actress for both parts; Antonioni is said to have been very proud of the invisible cut that makes the lady's approach to the prostitute seem to consist of a single, impossible shot. The future director next collaborated on Roberto Rossellini's patriotic film, *Un pilota ritorna* (A pilot returns), in 1941, a film that so embarrassed Rossellini that he rarely spoke of it in later years.

In 1942 Antonioni was drafted and, like virtually everyone else connected with the Italian film industry at this difficult time of divided loyalties, he did everything he possibly could to avoid being sent to the front. Since Italy was fighting a losing battle on Germany's side, this reluctance was more than understandable. During a period of leave, Antonioni signed a contract with Scalera, a well-known Italian production company, and went to Paris (then under Nazi occupation) to work as assistant to the great French director Marcel Carné on *Les visiteurs du soir*. His unstable army situation forced him to return to Italy, however, and thus he had to turn down additional film offers from other French masters such as Jean Cocteau and Jean Grémillon.

About the same time, he wrote favorably in *Italia Libera* of the most revolutionary new film of the era, Luchino Visconti's *Ossessione*, which so displeased Fascist censors with its gritty, startling portrayal of working-class life that it was banned within a week of its release. In the winter of 1943, with the help of the Istituto LUCE (which had been busy making propagandistic documentaries on the "successes" of the valiant Italian army), Antonioni shot his first documentary, the completely nonpolitical *Gente del Po* (People of the Po Valley), a strongly realistic yet intensely poetic ten-minute film based on a treatment he had published in *Cinema* in April 1939, about life on the river that ran through his hometown.

It is during this period that Antonioni's special fascination with vision and the nature of the look seems to have ripened. (Significantly, his *Cinema* article, "Toward a Film on the River Po," contained nine photographs, four of them half-page in size, even before the film was shot;[29] in the finished documentary itself, information is often conveyed in purely visual terms, rather than through the more conventional means of the voice-over.) Antonioni later told an interviewer that once he began looking at objects with the intention of making a film, everything changed:

> The things themselves were claiming a different attention, acquiring a different significance. Looking at them in a new way, I was taking control of them. Beginning to understand the world through the image, I was understanding the image, its force, its mystery.
>
> As soon as it was possible for me to do so I returned to those places with a camera. This is how *People of the Po Valley* was born. Everything that I did after that, good or bad as it was, started from there.[30]

When the southern half of the country was liberated by the Allied forces in mid-1943, effectively dividing the country in two, Antonioni had to put the film aside. He was finally able to finish it in 1947, but only after 70 percent of the footage he had shot was accidentally destroyed during the developing process.

Immediately after the war, Antonioni worked for a while as a translator, film critic, and scriptwriter (he wrote two unproduced scripts for Visconti) and made a magnificently photographed nine-minute documentary called *N.U. – Nettezza Urbana*. A study of the men who clean the streets and gather the garbage in Rome, the film poetically documents the magnificence of early morning in the city. It won an important critics' prize in 1948.

Next followed several other shorts such as *L'amorosa menzogna* (Lies of love, 1948–9), a film that humorously and ironically describes the gap between the glamorous lives of photoromance stars – all the rage at the time – and their real lives, and *Superstizione* (Superstition, 1949), which documents the superstitious customs still to be found among rural folk. About the same time, he wrote a treatment for *Lo sceicco bianco* (The White Sheik), based on the same idea as *L'amorosa menzogna*, which was made into a film by Fellini in 1952. Three more made-to-order shorts came in 1949 and 1950, including a documentary on the production of rayon, another on the cable car that runs to Cortina d'Ampezzo in the Dolomites skiing area, and a third on the Villa dei Mostri, a Renaissance garden featuring grotesque figures carved in the rocks.

The urge to document everyday life that appears in all of these films is not surprising given the fact that Antonioni came into his cinematic maturity during the heyday of neorealism, the most famous movement in Italian cinema history. Visconti's little-seen 1942 film *Ossessione* was a forebear of the movement, but although it wallowed in the grit and dirt of everyday life, a look that was to become a staple of neorealism, it lacked that sense of social concern for the downtrodden as a group that would also come to characterize neorealism. By general agreement, the first "real" neorealist film was Roberto Rossellini's *Open City*, which came out in 1945 and was followed by such cinema classics as Vittorio DeSica's *Ladri di biciclette*, (Bicycle Thief, 1948) and Visconti's *La terra trema* (The earth shakes, 1948). The movement began to lose steam in the early 1950s, owing to an exhaustion of creativity and attacks by government ministries fed up with seeing Italy's "dirty laundry" advertised around the world.

Even at the height of the movement, however, few of these films were successful with the Italian film-going public, who were, not surprisingly, tired of the misery of their everyday postwar lives and anxious to see comedy and fantasy on the screen. As a cliché of the time had it, right after the war "one made films either about the people or for the people."[31] According to Vittorio Spinazzola, the crucial weakness of neorealism was that it failed to alter in any significant way the relationship between the audience and the cinema, thus giving free play to the political powers aligned against the movement. Unsupported by the public and restricted to what Spinazzola calls "the radical wing of the bourgeois intelligentsia," most neorealist directors suffered a crisis of confidence and severely altered their approach as the years went on.[32]

Given his emphasis on poetic expressiveness, it now seems clear that Antonioni was never a neorealist. Yet, like all other postwar Italian directors, he cannot be understood except in reference to the movement, as an oppositional background, the way that neorealism itself cannot be understood without reference to its opposite, or what it posed as its opposite, conventional Hollywood narrative cinema. His early documentaries, so concerned with the feeling of place and the specificity of fact, obviously were conceived within the terms of a dominant neorealist aesthetic. But whereas neorealism was "obsessed with the visible," as Italian film historian Guido Fink has put it, Antonioni has always been at least as interested in the *not-seen* as in what is realistically *there*, before the camera.[33]

In 1958 Antonioni himself wondered aloud: "Am I a neorealist director. I really couldn't say. And is neorealism over? Not exactly. It is more correct to say that neorealism is evolving." He stressed the necessity of an *interiorization* of the neorealist project, taking DeSica's masterpiece, *The Bicycle Thief*, as his example. He pointed out that now filmmakers needed to go beyond the stolen bicycle, which was almost the center of DeSica's film, in order to enter the protagonist's heart and mind.[34] It is unclear exactly how interior states might be shown, except through a simultaneous process of *exteriorization*; obviously, it is just this tension that so brilliantly animates Antonioni's best films.

In more thematic terms, and in the context of the features that the director began making in the early 1950s, Gian Piero Brunetta has outlined Antonioni's relation to neorealism in an admirably succinct fashion. Brunetta points out that although neorealism always regarded reality from a decidedly anthropocentric viewpoint – whatever meaning or coherence reality can be said to have stems from the central place of human beings in that reality – "the Antonionian man is no longer either center or measure of space and of reality. He moves and acts in a relationship of inadequacy in respect to others and to his surroundings."[35] Even more than the neorealist films, which typically accentuate the heavy tragic destiny of common people (rather than their inherent political power, through group solidarity, to *actually change things*, which is what leftist critics understandably wanted filmmakers to emphasize), these early features, according to Brunetta, "insist on the chain of necessity with which the flux of existence pushes the individual from error to error, right up until the final collapse, without the resources of the individual subject ever being able to bring him out of himself to establish a relation with his kind."[36] Although this is an accurate assessment of the way these early films outdo the negativity of most neorealist films, it leaves open the central political question: Is this sad state of affairs the result of something inherent in human fate or human nature, or is it the product of a particularly dysfunctional social formation?

This deterministic trajectory is especially evident in Antonioni's first feature, *Cronaca di un amore* (Story of a love affair, 1950), starring Lucia Bosè and Massimo Girotti, the smouldering leading man who had first come to wide notice in Visconti's *Ossessione* in 1942. It is a dark tale of illicit passion and fateful encounters that in fact strongly recalls the brooding atmosphere and iconography of the Visconti film. This film also shows early signs of certain Antonionian mannerisms, such as the use of extreme long shots of empty spaces to convey emotion, as well as expressive lighting and striking black-and-white compositions. The director's focus on a female protagonist is also noteworthy here; it is a focus that will persist for more than fifteen years.

His next film, *La signora senza camelie* (The lady without camelias, 1953), once again features Lucia Bosè in the lead role. It is a bitter look at the complications of love and human relationships (note the ironic reversal of the title of Dumas's novel and play, *La dame aux camélias*), filled with dark, expressive streets and duplicitous noirish men, with the world of the film industry as a backdrop. Significantly, the emphasis on the woman's perspective is even stronger in this film, and the director is clearly sympathetic to her, for he emphasizes the way she is dominated and mistreated by the selfish and inconstant men who surround her. Neither she nor the director, however, at least in 1953, seems able to imagine a life for her without a man.

Though it was actually begun earlier than *La signora senza camelie*, Antonioni's next film, *I vinti* (The vanquished), had its premiere six months later, in September 1953, at the Venice Film Festival. Originally titled *Uno dei "nostri figli"* (One of "our children"), the film, composed of three separate episodes shot in three countries (Italy, England, and France) and in three languages, was to prove one of the director's most controversial projects. Based on true stories, it is an earnest European version of the "troubled youth" movies that were popular throughout the developed world in the 1950s. Both the British and the French episodes were banned in their respective countries because the portrayed families objected, and the censor's permission to shoot the Italian episode was withdrawn at the last minute and another story substituted.

The French part of the film tells of some young people who kill a friend for his money; the Italian episode concerns a young man from a good family who smuggles cigarettes and dies from injuries suffered in a fall that occurs while he is running away from the police; the English section recounts the story of a young poet who kills a prostitute to get his name in the newspaper. The emphasis on documenting a particular historical moment betrays the neorealist context in which this film was conceived, but the long shots of empty streets also show the director's desire to exteriorize internal emotions, and to move toward a stylization that, apart from Visconti's *La terra trema*, was rather rare in neorealism. And although the entire film is filled with a bitter postwar world-weariness that questions the status of all heretofore "eternal" values, the very impulse to describe a particular social problem, precisely *as* a problem to be solved, seems to carry with it some sense of politics, and even a sense of hope.

A crucial document, both in terms of Antonioni's work and of more theoretical questions in general, is "Tentato suicidio" (Suicide attempt), Antonioni's segment of *L'amore in città* (Love in the city), a compilation film released in November 1953. The director used some fifteen actual survivors of suicide attempts brought about by failed love affairs to tell their stories to the camera, in the semblance of a police inquest. Four of the stories are "re-created" by their protagonists, raising tantalizing questions about the relation between reality and its "fictional" representation.

Antonioni's next major film was *Le amiche* (The girlfriends), which opened in 1955. Based loosely on a novella by Cesare Pavese called *Tra donne sole* (translated in 1959 as *Among Women Only*), it tells a group of interlinked stories of young, glamorous women and their loves and careers. It is surprisingly advanced in its examination of feminist issues such as conflicts between love and career or between "femininity" and sexual independence; class differences are also explored. Most important, perhaps, *Le amiche* resolutely, and unapologetically, focuses on women. Though it won the Silver Lion prize at the Venice Film Festival, it did poorly at the box office.

Il grido was the director's next film, and the one that proved to be his entrée onto the international scene. Shot during the winter of 1956–7 in and around the Po Valley, where Antonioni had grown up, the film is especially important because its protagonist, for once, is a worker. Women seem at first to be the locus of power in the film, as the worker, Aldo (played by the American actor Steve Cochran), is thrown into a deep depression after the woman he has been living with for seven years, Irma (Alida Valli), decides to leave him for reasons that are never explained. The balance of power is more than reestablished, however, by his harsh treatment of the other women in the film. In a kind of road movie that reprises characters, situations, and imagery from both DeSica's *Bicycle Thief* and Visconti's *Ossessione* (down to the sexual dynamics at a forlorn gas station in the Po Valley), Aldo wanders from place to place with Rosina, the daughter he has had with Irma, revisiting old women friends and trying to pull his life together. In the midst of labor unrest and an attempt by the government to throw the farmers off their land, Aldo can think only of Irma; the director explicitly shows him rejecting the group solidarity that motivates and gives hope to his fellow workers. Eventually, he gives in to despair and dies when he falls off (or jumps off) the tower on which we first saw him at the beginning of the film. *Il grido* is punctuated by the trademark Antonioni long shots, denuded landscapes, and fog-enshrouded scenes that lead naturally into the triumphant formalism of the great films to come.

At the box office, none of these early films was very successful (*Cronaca di un amore* earned 175 million lire, *La signora senza camelie* 140, and *I vinti* 129, all ridiculously small sums). Even *Le amiche*, which grossed 260 million lire – because, according to Spinazzola, it had a story by the famed writer Cesare Pavese, a recognizable plot, and several well-known actresses in it – nevertheless finished only fortieth in box office receipts the year it was released. *Il grido* – the most formally challenging and most "depressing" of all the pretrilogy films – made the least of all: it ended up grossing only 100 million lire, of which only 25 million came during its initial release.[37]

And then in 1959–60, which is often described as the *annus mirabilis* of postwar Italian cinema, everything changed, for Antonioni and for the entire Italian film industry. Films such as Fellini's *La dolce vita* and Antonioni's *L'avventura* leave the war and antifascism behind, finally, and begin to focus, for really the first time, on present-day middle-class mores. Strangely enough, both of these films are serious works of art of a high intellectual nature, quite "trying" according to conventional standards, yet both were deeply appreciated by the public as well as the critics, in the provinces as well as the major cities.

The entire Italian industry, in fact, experienced a powerful upswing at this moment. According to Gian Piero Brunetta, by 1959 Italy was number one in Europe and second only to the United States in the number of spectators and size of box office receipts; amazingly, there was one theater seat for every nine people in Italy. In the meantime, Italian film production jumped from a robust 140 films in 1958 to an amazing 246 in 1962.

Brunetta attributes this huge change to a number of factors:

> The birth of a center-left government, new lifestyles, the rapid process of industrialization, the rise in mass consumption, the new distribution of leisure time, the maturation of a new social and political conscience, the change in sexual behavior and in social habits, the phenomenon of mass emigration from the south toward the large industrial centers of the north: all of this finds, in the cinema, a terrain that reacts immediately. Precisely in 1960 Italian cinema – like an extremely sensitive seismograph – notes and registers, with perfect timing, all of the processes of transformation in the economic, social, and political life of Italians. And, at the same time, it aims at a complete renewal of its own framework, offering very wide possibilities to a few directors who had come to the fore already in the 1950s, attempting to demonstrate how also the auteur film could translate into both a commercial and critical success.[38]

In 1960, according to Brunetta, Italians began wanting to see a *specific* film, rather than just go "to the movies." This situation was to last until private television came on the scene in the mid-1970s.[39]

For Antonioni, the critical success of *L'avventura* (notwithstanding the hostility it aroused at the Cannes Film Festival) and of the other films that quickly followed – such as *La notte*, *L'eclisse* and then, his first film in color, *Il deserto rosso*, – was a personal vindication for the initiator of a brilliant new style of filmmaking. These films focus relentlessly, almost exclusively, on female protagonists and, in their apparent aimless indirection, explore human relationships and the meaning of human existence using narrative and formal techniques that the cinema had never before attempted. Since the bulk of this book is devoted to these four films, I will forgo further comment on them here.

Antonioni's next effort was a twenty-five-minute segment of a compilation film entitled *I tre volti* (The three faces, 1965); Antonioni's not very interesting section stars Princess Soraya as herself and is called "Prefazione: il provino" ("Preface: The screen test"). But it was *Blow-up* (1966) that made Antonioni the internationally known figure that he remains today. Released by Metro-Goldwyn-Mayer (MGM), set in sexy, "swinging" London, and shot in English, the film, despite its enigmatic (and to some, laughably "arty") exploration of the connection between reality and its photographic representation in the guise of a photographer who accidentally captures a murder on film, became a huge hit. It is discussed in depth later in the book.

Antonioni went on to make *Zabriskie Point*, the second film in a three-picture deal with MGM (produced by Carlo Ponti) and released in 1969. Set in the Berkeley of the student rebellion, the film is burdened with an implausible plot and inexperienced actors whose weak delivery greatly detracted from what could otherwise have been a very interesting film.[40] The problems go deeper than that, however, for Antonioni's uncritical portrayal of the supposed innocence of his youthful protagonists (and the corresponding, one-note depiction of the policemen and capitalist land developers as completely evil) seemed naive even in 1969. Furthermore, in its celebration of a hippie orgy in the desert – no matter how magnificently composed, visually and aurally – the film also serves as a tacky and embarrassing record of the fifty-six-year-old director's own presumed sexual liberation (or wish-fulfillment). In an interview with *Look* magazine at the time, Antonioni said:

> America has changed me. I am now a much less private person, more open, prepared to say more. I have even changed my view of sexual love. In my other films, I looked upon sex as a disease of love. I learned here that sex is only a part of love; to be open and understanding of each other, as the girls and boys of today are, is the important part.[41]

Despite its failure, the film displays moments of brilliance, especially in its initial, documentary-like depiction of a political discussion concerning the possibility of revolutionary action undertaken by middle-class white students, and in the complicated abstract visual designs that reappear throughout.

Antonioni next undertook, at the invitation of the Chinese government and the RAI, the Italian television network, a documentary on contemporary life in China. Shown in 1972 on Italian, French, and American television, "Chung-kuo China" seemed to most Westerners a rather straightforward depiction of the Chinese Communist attempt to build a "New Man," but Chinese officials reacted violently against the film, citing its "distortions" and attacking Antonioni for "imperialistic cultural espionage." The Chinese threatened to break diplomatic relations with any country that showed the film, but a shortened version was eventually shown again later in the United States, with additional commentary.

The Passenger, Antonioni's third and final film in his three-picture contract with Ponti and MGM – and, in my view, one of the best he ever made – was based, for the first time in the director's long career, on a script written by others. Starring the already well-known Jack Nicholson as a television journalist who exchanges identities with a man he barely knows who has died of natural causes in their hotel in the Sahara, the film returns to the themes of the trilogy but with a new depth and historical specificity (and a sharpened political edge) that made it feel thoroughly up to date when it was released; it, too, is treated in detail later in the book.

Next came *Il mistero di Oberwald* (The Mystery of Oberwald, 1980), a weird experiment in color for Italian television that was based on a play by Jean Cocteau and starred Monica Vitti. Set in an unspecified Mitteleuropa country in the nineteenth century, the film tells the melodramatic story of a reclusive widowed queen and a young assassin who becomes her lover and, finally, her murderer as well. Antonioni seems to have agreed to the emotional, somewhat silly project in large part because he had not made a film in five years and because it allowed him to play creatively with the television equipment, changing colors, improbably but expressively, for each character, through purely electronic means.

His next theatrical film was called *Identificazione di una donna*, which was shown at the New York Film Festival in 1982 under the title *Identification of a Woman*, but which never received U.S. distribution. The film has its partisans, but the subtle connection that reigns in films such as *Blow-up* and *The Passenger* between the director and his alter ego, the protagonist, is here made completely obvious and thus infinitely less interesting. The main character is now a *film director*, no less, involved in an obsessive search for two women. Many of Antonioni's typical themes reappear, as well as his trademark formal techniques, bundled together with passionate and revealing sex scenes that seem to overwhelm the rest of the film. *New York Times* film critic Vincent Canby, a longtime partisan of the director, called it "an excruciatingly empty work,"[42] but the best analysis was provided by Andrew Sarris in the *Village Voice*:

> Antonioni has always been up there on the screen, but we tended to mistake his reflection for a portrait of Modern Man with all his wires disconnected. Yet now that the director stands at last nakedly before us, the absence of a plausibly compelling narrative drains his confessional film of the necessary tension to sustain our interest.[43]

Improbably, this connection between character and creator was to become even more blatant in the eighty-four-year-old director's most recent film, *Beyond the Clouds*, made with German filmmaker Wim Wenders, whose presence was necessary for the film production company to obtain completion insurance. (Antonioni suffered a serious stroke in the late 1980s and is no longer able to speak.) In this film, which was shown at the 1996 New York Film Festival and elsewhere and opened commercially in London in early 1997, the film director character, played by John Malkovich, mouths inane dialogue that includes some of Antonioni's bons mots from various interviews he has given. An uncompelling vanity production populated by the crème de la crème of contemporary European cinema (Fanny Ardant, Jean Reno, Sophie Marceau, Jeanne Moreau, and the late Marcello Mastroianni), the film tells several stories of lost love and misunderstanding that seem nearly to parody the director's greatest works in that vein. More charitably, Anthony Lane, writing of *Beyond the Clouds* in the *New Yorker* recently, had this to say:

> I don't happen to believe that Antonioni's work *is* profound, but the illusion of profundity is so spooky, and so exquisitely managed, that it will do just as well. . . . The world of Michelangelo Antonioni throngs with sick souls, and we may be slightly sick of them by now, but I wouldn't want them to get better.[44]

As of this writing, according to the trade journals, the apparently indefatigable, still speechless Antonioni is soon to begin shooting another film, entitled "Just to Be Together," this time with that most Antonionian Canadian director, Atom Egoyan (*The Adjuster, Exotica, The Sweet Hereafter*), as guarantor-sidekick.[45]

Whatever else it may accomplish, this study does not aim to provide a master narrative of Michelangelo Antonioni that purports to "explain" him and his films once and for all. Besides the obvious complexity and ambiguity of the films themselves, the sheer volume of criticism in French, Italian, and English (to name only the most obvious sources of commentary) is itself impossible to master or to give any adequate accounting of.

What I hope to achieve in the following pages is a more modest goal, an "exploration" of what I judge to be Antonioni's "central" films. (Even choosing which films to concentrate on, of course, is already an act of interpretation.) I have decided to focus on *L'avventura, La notte, L'eclisse*, the films of the so-called trilogy; *Red Desert*, the director's first film in color; *Blow-up*, his first "international" film; and, finally, *The Passenger*, the most artistically successful film of his maturity. For considerations of space, I have had to skip over all of the director's earlier films; I especially regret having to omit *Il grido*, since it is the entry film for the themes of the trilogy and beyond. However, the other omitted films are, to my mind at least, clearly secondary efforts.

Some will question the very viability of an "auteur" study focused on an individual director, and whether anything of value can be achieved using such an "old-fashioned" method. Film history of the 1970s and 1980s taught us to look suspiciously upon the auteurist claims that had naturally arisen in the 1960s, when film was struggling in the academy for the acceptance that other art forms already enjoyed. The argument then was – and in large part still holds true – that, perhaps more than any other art form, film is marked by its collaborative nature. Nevertheless, it is also true that Antonioni's films, like those of his countrymen and European filmmakers in general, were created in the context of an auteurist aesthetic that has always valued personal expression – even in such an obviously commercial, "compromised" form as film – above all else.

The auteurist approach was also dealt a serious blow by the writing of French theorists Roland Barthes and Michel Foucault, who loudly, and convincingly, proclaimed "the death of the author" in favor of a new emphasis on the interpretive work of the *reader* in making sense of texts. Jacques Derrida has also raised doubts concerning the possibility that the artist can ever express him or herself in a noncontradictory fashion, given the fact that consciousness, like everything else, is inherently divided. Then there is the question of ideology. In many ways, of course, it is true that the unconscious ideology of any society is always speaking, using the author as its often unwitting mouthpiece, in every text. Yet as Robin Wood has pointed out in a seminal essay on Hitchcock, (now twenty years old but still valuable), "It is only through the medium of the individual [artist] that ideological tensions come to particular focus."[46]

It is also the case that if one's own critical writing about film or anything else is to be coherent – and no publisher I know has become sufficiently "postmodern" to forgo those demands – it must have some principle of design. If that is so, then *any* form of organization – by period, theme, country, whatever, as well as by author – will implicitly depend upon an essentializing process that, by definition, will "deform" its object of study.

Ultimately, since there is before us the hard existential fact that these particular films would never have come into being without this particular author, maybe then it is just as valid to consider these films in terms of their author as any other way. In this regard, I am encouraged by Antonioni's simple but incontrovertible response to an interviewer who innocently asked whether the director's assistants chose the locations: "The location is the very substance of which the shot is made. Those colors, that light, those trees, those objects, those faces. How could I leave the choice of all this to my assistants? Their choices would be entirely different from mine. Who knows the film I am making better than me?"[47]

I
L'avventura (1960)

The birth of *L'avventura*, one of the most celebrated films in Italian cinema history, was not an easy one. From the very beginning, the production was beset with enormous problems. The island that served as the cast and crew's base of operations was without electricity or hot water, and the bad weather caused so many delays that scenes set in the summer ended up being filmed in the winter. The actors in particular found these hardships difficult to bear. Lea Massari, who plays Anna, suffered a heart attack during shooting and was in a coma for two days. The weather also made the crossing to Lisca Bianca, the deserted rocky island where much of the film was shot, a frightening "adventure" of its own. One evening, the area was threatened by a tornado, and when the sea became too rough, some of the company had to spend the night in the makeshift fisherman's hut – as do the characters in the film – while the others huddled in the few available tents.

There were problems of a different sort as well. The firm providing the financial wherewithal, Imeria, suddenly went bankrupt, and after five weeks without a paycheck – the owner of the hotel and restaurant refused to let the groups leave the island until their bill was paid – the crew went on strike. Then, the yacht on which several of the scenes were shot was retrieved by its owner before the shooting was completed, and a replacement was not found until many weeks later. The new yacht was three times larger than the original, however, and Antonioni apparently had a difficult time matching the shots taken on the two boats.[1]

Even after the film was completed, the problems did not stop. *L'avventura* was given a boorish reception when it premiered at the Cannes Film Festival in 1960, which hardly seems believable in view of its present canonic status. Penelope Houston, an early supporter of the film and the long-time editor of the venerable British film journal *Sight & Sound*, re-counted the mayhem:

> To see *L'Avventura* at the London Festival was a revelation. At Cannes, at least during the second half, attention had to be agonis-ingly divided between the screen and one's neighbours. A long love scene set off a fusillade of angry jeering, and one wondered whose moral susceptibilities were being outraged; a reiterated shot of a girl running down a corridor brought bellows of "cut"; and the last scene went through to derisive howls of "He's crying! Look, he's crying!" It was an ugly and unforgivable reception, compounded in about equal parts of moral indignation and boredom, and it effectively wrecked concentration by the rest of us. . . . It was the public, not the film, that got out of hand.[2]

What could possibly have caused such outrage?

First of all, the film, at 145 minutes, was much longer than almost any other in recent cinema history and obviously required a level of patience and concentration to which contemporary critics were unaccustomed. An-tonioni also chose to shoot the film more or less in real time, avoiding the ellipses of "unimportant" actions (such as walking from a door to the center of a room). Part of standard film practice, ellipses are intended to speed things up. Here, Antonioni was directly following the lead of his predecessor, Roberto Rossellini, who, in his films with Ingrid Bergman in the early 1950s, had begun experimenting with cinematic "dead time" as part of his exploration of a realist aesthetic. The technique massively slows things down and makes the viewer attend to the resonance of visual and aural details that are usually lost in the sweep of the narrative. On the other hand, *L'avventura*'s story or narrative line itself *is* filled with ellipses where they had not been used before. Much exposition is forgone, in the best modernist fashion, and this contributes importantly to its unconventional narrative feeling.[3]

Antonioni himself has said that he began making films in this manner in order to "rid myself of much unnecessary technical baggage, eliminating all the logical narrative transitions, all those connective links between se-quences where one sequence served as a springboard for the one that fol-lowed. The reason I did this was because it seemed to me – and of this I am firmly convinced – that cinema today should be tied to the truth rather than to logic."[4]

Leaving aside for the moment Antonioni's implicit claim to be seeking "truth" (a claim that is now, for better or worse, rather out of fashion –

and one that he might think better of were he making these films today), it is clear that he consciously set out to alter conventional cinematic storytelling methods. However, this is not the same thing as saying, as some critics have, that these films are "narrated visually." It is easy to overemphasize Antonioni's apparent departure from conventional storytelling and to assume, as Seymour Chatman sometimes does, that the burden of each film's drama is conveyed through visual composition. This is never more than partly the case.[5]

Nevertheless, it is true that much of Antonioni's effect does come from the visual track of his films (as opposed to dialogue, plot, character, and so on), and nowhere more than in his endings. In the last few superbly choreographed minutes of *L'avventura*, for example, Claudia's hand, which has been individuated a bit earlier in close-up, framed by her white pillow, almost becomes a synecdochic character on its own. We see the bench, the surrounding emptiness, the sobbing Sandro; the entire world becomes focused on the whiteness of her hand as it touches his back and then hesitantly, almost reluctantly, touches the back of his head, her hand now framed starkly against the blackness of his hair, in an act of almost cosmic pity. In the same moment, the sound track softly resounds in quiet, sympathetic harmony (as the bells did earlier, on the rooftop of the church), and for an instant an apparent wholeness is achieved in the perfect juncture of the visual track and the sound track. (This moment of "unity" – which everything else in the film works to deny – has been brilliantly prepared for by a moment of *contradiction* between the two tracks a few minutes earlier: in her hotel room, Claudia mugs comically in the mirror, while the sound track carries a ponderous, sad score.) Antonioni's gift for visual telling will achieve its greatest form in the final shots of *L'eclisse*.[6]

But if the visual track does carry a great deal of meaning, the film also denies the possibility of achieving, through visual means (or any means, for that matter), a full presence that is equated with "reality"; it denies, in other words, the commonplace notion that what is is what is visible. Everything is *always* in focus in an Antonioni image (except when he is deliberately playing with focus, as in *Red Desert*), and one of the minor pleasures one gets from his work is not having to experience the constant lazy rack-focusing of contemporary films. Thus on one level *L'avventura* seems to offer itself as an apotheosis of the visible; at the same time it never ceases to critique neorealist aesthetics by demonstrating that reality is always *more* than what can be seen. As Guido Fink has remarked about Anna's disappearance in *L'avventura*, "Someone is absent: hardly an apt situation for classical *neorealismo* which . . . was mainly concerned with an extension of filmic visibility."[7]

Nevertheless, the absences in this film are not transcendental, nor do they mark something "inexpressible." Rather, they lead to the negation, or better, the calling into question of a prior, unproblematic, completely visible presence. The sense of "mystery" that arises as a result of this suggestive absence as well as from the oddness of Antonioni's narrative seems to be a completely nonspiritual one that speaks to the deep ambiguity of the relation of human beings to reality, rather than to a hankering after the otherworldly.

On a less exalted level, this sense of mystery is linked to the Barthesian idea of the hermeneutic code, the code of interpretation, by means of which we are led by every narrative, stupidly perhaps but crucially, to the solving of a riddle or puzzle.[8] Our will to interpret, to make sense of things, parallels the characters' search for Anna, as they ask, for example, whether another boat was heard, in order to try to make sense of things. The film tantalizingly proffers its meaning to the viewer, just as various female characters are often teasingly put forward visually, in a kind of perverse game or riddle, in order to cause us, momentarily, to misidentify them as Anna. Anna is never found, just as our interpretive work never comes to a definitive end.

But suddenly, about halfway through, the film takes an even more unsuspected turn when Anna's friends simply stop looking for her. This, in fact, is the true scandal of *L'avventura* and may be what actually bothered contemporary viewers the most: what French critic Pascal Bonitzer calls "the disappearance of the disappearance of Anna."[9] This double disappearance creates a gaping hole in the film, an invisibility at its center, which suggests an elsewhere, a nonplace, that remains forever unavailable to interpretation and that destroys the dream of full visibility.

This formal threat to presence and vision obviously meshes easily with a thematics of angst and alienation, and, as pointed out in the introduction, this is where much of Antonioni criticism has tended to reside since *L'avventura* first appeared. But this film, and the films that were to follow, have also functioned, and continue to function, as social criticism, however disguised. Some of it pertains specifically to the Italian context, and some of it is intended as part of a more global criticism about contemporary life in general. Thus *L'avventura* and the other films are obviously concerned with the difficulty of relations between the sexes. Putting it this way, however, can imply once again that Antonioni's theme is primarily an existential or metaphysical one – for example, that the sexes are perhaps natural enemies, that they can never understand each other, and that the force of love, while irresistible, leads inevitably, in our fallen world, to a great deal of unhappiness as well. It is Antonioni's special ability, though, to work on the particular and the general level at the same time, to provide a contemporary social and cultural critique while undertaking larger philosophical explorations.

As already mentioned, men chase women throughout this film: in Messina, thousands of crazed males follow the British woman Gloria and her split skirt. They also physically threaten them: Claudia is menaced by hordes of glowering men in Noto the moment she is left alone. But this threat comes not only from strangers; the first manifestation of this male predatory quality comes when Sandro begins to intimidate Claudia sexually (to her complete surprise and dismay, at least at first), soon after Anna disappears.

Sandro willingly participates in the earlier mob scene in Messina – a scene that is so out of control that it would be funny if it were not so nasty – and in fact he is the lucky one who actually gets to sleep with Gloria Perkins at the end of the film, unlike the other obsessed males who must content themselves with fantasy and the sexual symbolism embodied in this woman with the awful British accent (in Italian) who towers over them. He is also presumably more sophisticated than the men who sexually threaten Claudia at Noto, but his fondness for pushing people around and his general way of being in the world are really only a scaled-down, more subtle urban version of their less inhibited approach. A bit later in the film, Sandro and Claudia survey the rooftops of Noto from the roof of the church, as Sandro explains his various frustrations to Claudia. Most critics have taken his "failed-architect" self-evaluation at face value, even attributing his crisis to a failure of "creativity," which is certainly the interpretation of his life that he himself seems to have constructed.[10] But Claudia's solicitous attention to Sandro at this moment, which helps to cue our own sympathy, can also be seen as just one more manifestation of the female's expected submission to the male and his priorities, in other words, an attempt to understand herself as a function of his needs. Sandro can also be read in more general terms. The Marxist critic Borrelli, for one, has clearly seen the political edge behind Antonioni's portrayal: Sandro, he says, "is a typical character of the Italy of the [economic] miracle."[11]

Though Antonioni will sharpen the focus on the creative male figure in later films such as *Blow-up*, making him seem somewhat more sympathetic, the portrait here seems utterly negative. Sandro is little more than a weakling who pushes old men around, drives like a maniac (early in the film, Anna grimaces after one particular difficult curve), and aggressively preys on women. He whines about the loss of his creativity (though it has been willingly exchanged for a great deal of money), and then petulantly overturns the bottle of ink on the young man's drawing of the church window.[12] When he gets back to the hotel room, his frustration leads him to want to make love to Claudia immediately, in a quite violent way that prompts her to say, "I don't know you." He replies that now she can pretend that she is having an affair – another "adventure," he says – with a different man, a prospect that shocks her. On the train, he has told Claudia: "I don't have the slightest desire to sacrifice myself. Why? For whom?" and the audience has absolutely no reason to doubt him. Sandro complains to *both* Anna and Claudia, at different times, that they think too much, that they rely too much on words. This only confuses things. (It is a nice reversal of the conventional gender division of rational words versus intuitive feelings, but one that does not necessarily endear Sandro to us any more strongly.)

The pharmacist whom Claudia and Sandro encounter on their search for Anna is also sex-crazed, as though addicted, and his wife (of three months!) is inordinately bitter. The man is ugly and in the scene outside seems physically gnarled and unpleasant, even making a small play for Claudia. The couple are so hateful toward each other that they cannot even agree on the facts of his alleged dalliance. Regionality, a common theme in Italian cinema, is also relevant here: in a clear reprise of an important motif of Rossellini's *Stromboli* (1949), the pharmacist's wife complains that she is from Viterbo (in other words, the more sophisticated and presumably more liberated North), and that she hates backward Sicily. But this is ultimately no contest between equals, and when the dispute becomes a standoff, the man invokes his socially sanctioned physical superiority and orders her back into the house. (Interestingly, this scene has begun with a tight shot of the wife's scowling face, before we even know who she is, as though the director means to articulate an emotion and suggest a theme even *before* placing the situation narratively. This technique reappears frequently in his later films.)

Throughout *L'avventura*, in fact, the life of every couple, married or not, is portrayed as a living hell. Corrado and Giulia, on the boat and on the island, pick at each other in the same vicious, dispiriting manner as the married couple seen briefly, but memorably, in Ingmar Bergman's *Wild Strawberries* (1957). Though here both Corrado and Giulia seem to be at fault, Corrado is often gratuitously cruel, and the males in this film seem to come in for harsh criticism from Antonioni. He genuinely seems to have mixed feelings toward men as men, toward the male way of being in the world. (Or do we read the films this way because feminism has altered our interpretive frame? Certainly our reading of *L'avventura*'s gender dynamics would have been different in 1960.) When men become the central characters of the films beginning with *Blow-up*, the critique becomes subtler and more conflicted, but it does not disappear.

In the face of this male aggression, a great deal of female solidarity is expressed in *L'avventura*, both covertly and more openly, and often women do not even need to exchange words to understand what another woman is thinking. When Anna and Claudia change clothes on the yacht, Anna confesses to Claudia that her story of being threatened by a shark was entirely fabricated. But why has she done this? On the one hand, it could be just another example of a bored rich girl looking for new kicks (let us not forget the wilfulness she shows when, early in the film, she deliberately makes Claudia, her best friend, wait while she and Sandro make love); on the other, it seems like a genuine longing for some inchoate sense of freedom on her part (certainly her dialogue at the beginning of the film suggests that this is what she seeks, however awkwardly). Somehow, her claim to have seen a life-threatening animal allows her to gain more control over events. She does not know what she wants, she says, but she does know what she does not want, and that is conventional marriage in this society. ("Non lo so" – "I don't know," an important motif in the film – can have a completely different meaning for an audience thirty-five years later, but even in its contemporary context the suggestion is clear that she is rejecting marriage per se as a limitation of her freedom.) She is the bored rich kid, yes, but she also seems to be trying out different subjectivities in order to find one that fits more comfortably than the one society seems intent on supplying her. She is looking for what in 1960 would have been termed an "authentic existence," an identity apart from her husband's (and her father's), but in this society that is impossible, so she merely disappears, both from the society and from the film, which, thirty-five years ago, would have been equally incapable of suggesting solutions for her dissatisfaction. Her disappearance is thus an expression of autonomy, however self-destructive it may be. As such, it parallels one other moment of autonomy at the beginning of the film, when Anna directly expresses female desire by taking her clothes off, indicating to Sandro her desire to make love. For an American audience that had rarely been shown such "unnatural" desire, this must have been a bracing scene.

Another aspect of many of the female encounters in the film is their strong undercurrent of homoeroticism, especially those encounters between Anna and Claudia. This is especially the case when they are changing

34

Figure 3. Anna (Lea Massari) disrobes for her lover Sandro (Gabriele Ferzetti)

clothes on the boat, and they and the camera are claustrophobically close to one another. The suggestiveness of the scene is so clear that even when the film first appeared, a commentator such as George Amberg could read it in a homoerotic fashion, though interpreting it narrowly as a sign of incipient and pathological lesbianism in Anna (he never actually uses the forbidden word). If we posit lesbian desires for Anna, according to Amberg (his description is "the intimation of an inverted sexual tendency in Anna's psychological makeup"), "it explains the seemingly irrational behavior toward her lover, the incongruously aggressive love scene in the beginning [*sic*!], the sudden changes of mood, the false alarm of the shark incident, the peculiar hints about an indefinite period of separation from Sandro and, most conclusive of all, her refusal to marry him."[13] For Amberg, the open expression of female heterosexual desire (let alone the homosexual variety) and a refusal to marry can only demonstrate that something is wrong with *her*. Once again we see to what extent critics reveal themselves when they think they are only revealing Antonioni. Later Amberg hastens to assure us that these "inverted" proclivities (in this film and in other Antonioni films

35

he points to) "are unconscious, or at least undefined, in the minds of the characters affected" and concludes that the "sexual ambivalence is no more and no less than a plausible metaphor for the desperate isolation of the individual."[14] In other words, sexual ambiguity and a refusal to follow society's strictly heterosexual family script also get rewritten as manifestations of angst and alienation.

The thematic exploration of women and their sexuality is also readily apparent on a formal level, for example, in the great number of shots in this film showing women from *behind*, a phenomenon that several critics have remarked upon. One of the factors that distinguished Antonioni's film in 1960 was that his point-of-view shots often *included* the observer (both female and male), rather than using the standard shot/reverse shot system of conventional filmmaking, which shows the character looking, and then what he or she is looking at, without including the character in the second shot.[15] According to some critics, notably Seymour Chatman and Naomi Greene, the many shots that include women looking are indicative of the autonomy that Antonioni accords to the *female* gaze (as opposed to the male gaze, both within the film and without, that, according to much early feminist film theory, was the primary or even sole addressee of virtually all mainstream films). It does sometimes seem that, in the visual situating of a certain point of view, the female gaze is being privileged. Yet at other times the turning of the woman's back seems more like a subtle sign of resistance to the penetrating male gaze of the director and his stand-in, the camera, a resistance that Antonioni is explicitly thematizing.[16]

More important, these shots of women taken from behind, far from being signs of their empowerment, are more frequently related to that dynamic of sexual vision found, for example, in Ingres's *Baigneuse*. What is primarily in evidence both in Ingres and Antonioni is the pleasure that men have always taken in representing women's bodies from behind, especially because of the unconventional abstracting effect that deindividualizes the body when viewed in this manner. These backs are gorgeous, and the muted sexuality of this part of female anatomy (as opposed to the front) can be more easily justified, classically, because it allows for both a formal appreciation of the abstract beauty of line and shape and the beauty of the body *as such*, rather than as sexual object. Given the power dynamics of sexual looking, though, this is a distinction that cannot be maintained in practice.

This gender-inflected dynamic of vision explicitly ties in with the question of female representation throughout history, which is directly thematized in *L'avventura* when, for example, we discover that the young painter-prince's room visited by Claudia and Giulia is filled with female nudes. The young man, as part of a bravado display of sophistication, claims that women love to pose, to "show themselves," that they have a "natural disposition" toward this sort of thing, as though male expectations had nothing to do with it. In a familiar move, the young man gestures toward the "natural" to explain woman's behavior. He goes on to claim that "there's no landscape as beautiful as a woman" ("nessun paesaggio è bello come una donna"), linking the two overtly. Thus the preeminent position of the male spectator is kept intact, and the women become objects, like the rocks and the sea, to be looked at and appreciated by men who are regarded as the rightful owners of the look.[17]

Female faces are, in fact, often juxtaposed with natural formations, especially while they are on the island, and share the screen with them. However, this invocation of the natural leads beyond the exploration of gender, for throughout the search for Anna on the island the natural is presented as the elemental, the background against which all human endeavor seems evanescent and maybe even futile. This effect is enhanced by Antonioni's proclivity for lingering on the landscape after the human departs from the shot; a like effect is achieved in reverse by panning from a landscape shot to suddenly include a human being, as if the human were merely a second thought, an addition to, rather than the center of, creation.[18] Similarly, the frequent panning of the sea and the islands simultaneously works against any sense of human tragedy, because the viewer is forced to regard the latter *sub specie aeternitae*, against the immensity of the natural world.

Curiously, this emphasis on the "natural" is also consistently accompanied by its *aestheticization*. Thus the "scenic," formalized rocks and starkly beautiful vistas, by the very fact of being represented in these aestheticized ways, have the effect of deconstructing the distinction between nature and culture. Can we ever call "natural," the film seems to be asking, that which is being offered in such artistically stylized ways? Is there such a thing as "nature," and does it remain natural when it is in a film?

The same is true of the female body, of course, whose "nature" can only be seen through the cultural terms that (male-dominated) society provides us. In a brief but significant moment near the end of *L'avventura*, Antonioni also implicates himself in this historical dynamic, or dilemma, of representing the female body. As she lies on the hotel bed waiting for the philandering Sandro, Claudia leafs through a magazine that contains an article on Jean Harlow, reminding us through this quintessential sex goddess what the movies are really all about. The fact that we are gazing at Monica Vitti at this (granted, very fleeting) moment in *this* film provides a kind of double framing, a bracing, if fugitive, moment of self-reflexivity that has the potential to call our innocent action into question.

The situation is complicated. On the one hand, the painter-prince's attitude toward women is one that Antonioni seems implicitly to be criticizing, precisely by putting it in the mouth of this adolescent and foppish character. On the other hand, the sensitive male director who looks sympathetically upon woman's plight is always, in fact, simultaneously punishing the woman on camera, precisely in order to demonstrate that she is a victim. Roberto Rossellini and Kenji Mizoguchi come to mind here as powerful examples of this double-edged dynamic. In occupying the consummate seat of (cinematic) male power, the director is of necessity also always *looking* at the woman through the phallic camera, that is, through the supreme technological embodiment and extension of the already powerful male gaze.[19]

But it is important to distinguish Antonioni, whose work is always inflected by varieties of gender ambiguity, from Rossellini and Mizoguchi, who, in most ways, remain "masculine" directors despite their focus on women. Thus I would disagree with Pierre Leprohon's view that, "in spite of the considerable part played by women in it, *L'Avventura* is a masculine film. It deals with human relationships from the man's point of view."[20] It is precisely because of the ways in which he departs from the conventional masculine model that Antonioni's cinema remains interesting. For one thing, Antonioni's camera is almost always less intrusive than Rossellini's or Fellini's. He is thus often content to be a mute, in some ways even passive, witness to that which seems merely to "take place" before the camera, rather than acting the part of the assiduous (and violent) prober of woman's "truth." (Think especially of Mizoguchi's implacable tracking shots.) Rather, as Italian critic Guido Fink has pointed out, Antonioni's signature in this film is normally a withdrawal, a hesitation, rather than an assertion. Though it would be reductive to stress the biographical determination behind all this, one cannot help thinking that the disastrous results that occurred during Antonioni's first documentary outing at the insane asylum, recounted in the introduction, may have forever stifled his need to pursue aggressively (or in a direct, logical, "male" way) the "truth" of any given reality.

Most important, though, Antonioni consistently dismantles the "masculine" authority built into the position he occupies by calling attention to his own presence. This occurs principally through various self-reflexive gestures that have the effect of restraining the all-powerful male gaze by unmasking it, by signaling the fact of its presence and thus stripping it of its most powerful attribute, its invisibility and thus its seeming "naturalness."[21] In *Blow-up*, for example, Antonioni directly correlates his own role as director with the offensive machismo of the David Hemmings character who goes through the world raping women (and others) with his camera. In *L'avventura* such explicit moments are much briefer but remain powerful nonetheless. Recall, for example, the often stunning visual compositions of long hallways (an almost perfect example of what T. S. Eliot called an "objective correlative," that is, a symbolic formal substitution to describe an inner emotional state) and the starkly focused moment on the bench at the end of the film. These have a stylized aesthetic effect that is so self-reflexively powerful that it removes us forcibly (if only momentarily) from the story and reminds us that we are participating in a self-conscious work of art whose relation with reality is heavily conventionalized. After all, powerful visual form, even in the most putatively "realistic" films – think of the stunning, "artistic" compositions of Visconti's *La terra trema* – is often anti-illusionistic in effect. The equivalent aesthetic moments in *L'avventura* make us aware of the director's presence, just as when Sandro points out that the entire town of Noto, seen from above, resembles a stage setting, which from the film's point of view, and ours, it of course (also) is. (Not incidentally, this urban panorama also visually suggests its putative opposite, the barren – and supremely aesthetic – rockiness of the island, implying the staginess of both as sites for the interplay of these figures of textual energy we call characters.)

More subtly, this same self-reflexive dynamic occurs when the camera shows us the island, ostensibly from the point of view of someone on the boat, or more generally simply *from* the boat; the conventional shot would be an uneventful, stationary one that simply reversed camera angle. Here, however, the shot bobs wildly up and down, naturalistically imitating what an actual shot from the point of view of someone on the boat would look like. The effect is to make the point of view radically contingent – the camera is precisely *here*, not effaced, thus keeping before our eyes the very "madeness" of the film. This specific placement works against a sense of an all-powerful, omniscient (precisely because *unlocatable*) camera position that stands in for the all-powerful, unseen (male) director.

Even more noticeable is the moment, later in the film, when Sandro and Claudia pull up in the courtyard of the modernistic church in the completely empty piazza. The camera watches them first in an extreme long shot from above, then from a somewhat closer, same-level shot from an alley. Suddenly the camera begins a pronounced and fairly prolonged tracking movement down the alley, closer to the car (the stairs in the foreground at the lower right of the frame can clearly be seen disappearing as the camera moves forward), though there is no practical or technical need whatsoever for such a camera movement (say, to keep the characters in the frame). The effect is to call attention to the presence of the camera as recording device, or better, as a *maker* of what we see, and by extension, to the presence of the director himself. The fact that this self-reflexive gesture is conveyed explicitly through a tracking movement – a movement that is often correlated with the anonymous "penetrating" power of the investigating male gaze – makes it all the more significant. Here, though, it is a male gesture that is superfluous, irrelevant.

Another scene in the film bears closer examination in this regard. Just before they get to Noto, Claudia and Sandro, at what is perhaps the high point of their romance (or whatever it is), make love on a hillside. The camera dwells on their love-making for the longest time, prolonging it well beyond the normal length of such scenes, which has the uncanny effect of making it more emotional and more sensual even though the sex actually "shown" is not very explicit. The innumerable close-ups of Claudia (and, to a lesser extent, of Sandro) – which are very close, yet which never occupy the entire frame – provoke the same strange, but difficult-to-specify feelings of earlier close-ups that also included some faraway aspect of the landscape in the back of the shot. When the train goes by, we first see it in extreme long shot (ELS) moving across the flat landscape from right to left (disappearing screen left, in the extreme distance), and we motivate the shot by ascribing it, generally, to the point of view of Claudia and Sandro. But then we cut back to the lovers, seen from behind – with no sign of the train for several moments – and suddenly the train roars, through a kind of sunken railway, right past them. The previous shot, in other words, has to be retrospectively deascribed to them for the sequence to make sense, and the viewer is momentarily disoriented. This sequence, along with the slightly strange close-ups, points toward a kind of conscious or unconscious mini-alienation effect of the Brechtian variety, an effect that is enhanced by the unusual length of their kissing.[22] What I am analyzing here in Brechtian terms recurs in various guises throughout Antonioni's films and can be described in a number of theoretical ways.[23]

The sound track, as well as the visual track, functions to remind us of an external presence that is creating, consciously and unconsciously, what is being seen and heard, and thus it, too, functions to demystify the supposed transparency of the cinematic operation. Throughout, there is a welter of significant ambient sounds that go far beyond what Roland Barthes has called the "reality effect" (that is, elements that are included merely to

Figure 4. A moment of joy, with both foreground and background in focus, between Claudia (Monica Vitti) and Sandro

enhance the feeling of realism, the sense of a real world, rather than to add anything thematically meaningful). Seymour Chatman rightly says that these ambient sounds "preserve their integrity against the absorbing pressures of narrative,"[24] but they go further than that, actually calling the centrality of the narrative into question and suggesting an additional, or even alternative, track for cinematic meaning. Sometimes, these sounds are used to supply what would otherwise be supplied visually or through spoken dialogue. Near the end of the film, we can hear the faint sound of bells, as well as a train – two important earlier moments – as if the film were summarizing key events for itself, through the merest aural suggestions.

The use of music is even more important. Thus when the search for the missing Anna begins about halfway through the film, music, largely absent up to this point, suddenly appears. The effect is so jarring that it makes the music – otherwise perfectly acceptable – stand out (which is normally considered a "fault" in classic Hollywood filmmaking) and become a kind of sudden external perspective on matters. We are wrapped up in the characters and their various intersubjective relationships and then suddenly, by means of the film's score, we are forcibly outside them, looking in at them, distanced. More directly than the spoken dialogue, which is necessarily delivered by the characters, the music here acts as extra dialogue spoken by the director or the film itself to comment on what we are seeing and hearing.[25] Again, the effect is to draw attention to the presence of the filmmaker and to the constructedness of the film.

One other phenomenon that needs to be discussed in the light of Antonioni's self-reflexive problematization of gender relations is his insistent conflation, through various visual and narrative means, of the female characters in the film, a phenomenon that has been remarked on by several critics. As the site and embodiment of the male gaze, the film seems at some level to be saying that all the women in the film, despite their individual idiosyncracies – and thus, by extension, *all* women everywhere – are interchangeable with one another. The women in *L'avventura*, in fact, *are* demonstrably different from one another, and do react quite differently to their circumstances, and the film itself, on the level of narrative and dialogue, at least, gives us plenty of evidence of these differences. Yet the men in the film, and their always ambivalent extension and double, Antonioni and his phallic camera, continually seek to reduce them to the level of the same, that is, to an essentialized idea of "woman." Thus essentialized, of course, they do not need to be taken seriously as individuals. It is unclear exactly where the director himself stands on this issue: on the one hand, the film seems to participate fully in this essentializing; on the other, it seems to be pointing out, critically, that this is something men have always done and will probably continue to do.

This equation of women is repeated over and over in the film, often expressed through stunning visual compositions that add their own graphic meaning, as is the case when two women's heads are beautifully balanced in a single shot (one facing the camera, the other turned away), and then suddenly reversed, implying, once again, an interchangeability. The most blatant form of this dynamic occurs at the level of plot and character, for example, when Claudia seems unproblematically to substitute for Anna in Sandro's affections after Anna's disappearance; it is this easy substitution that motivates the entire film. (Later, Sandro even asks her to marry him in the exact manner in which he had asked Anna earlier.) This relation is spelled out and anticipated visually in one of the earliest scenes in the film when Claudia, down below in the courtyard, is juxtaposed with Sandro and Anna (who are about to make love), proleptically implying the future substitution of the women, as well as the fact that it will not really be a substitution of the different, but of the *same*, at least for Sandro. Similarly, when the party guests search for Anna on the island where she has disappeared, the camera several times shows a woman whom we (and the char-

Figure 5. Girl talk (the doubling of women): Claudia and Patrizia (Esmeralda Ruspoli)

acter who is searching) momentarily think is Anna, only to disappoint us. At another moment, a door is closed between Giulia and Claudia, and a strange feeling of simultaneity and repetition results. (This leads once again to the impression that we are watching a *drama of forms* as much as a drama of people.)

Most obviously, this relation is suggested in both the clothes-changing scene (referred to earlier) and the later scene in which the women provocatively exchange wigs, and Claudia is told that she "seems like someone else." (She later appears in Anna's blouse, which she had complimented Anna on.) Appropriately in terms of this doubling motif, we discover that this scene is composed entirely of a mirror shot when the camera pulls back, revealing its frame, oddly derealizing, somehow, what we have just seen. Again, in all of these instances there is a certain unspoken confrontation between, on the one hand, the notion that for the camera and the (male) system that it technologically encapsulates (and for the male characters in the film), all the women *are* the same, and, on the other, a certain playful, self-reflexive tweaking of our expectations by the modernist director who reveals and thus dismantles this male predilection precisely by underlining it so blatantly, and thus thematizing it in turn.

The very opening shot of the film participates in this same complicated gesture. We see Anna coming around the corner of what appears to be a driveway, and the lighting and the camera movement seem consciously to work to flatten her against the background, a common strategy in Antonioni's films. As she turns the corner, the camera seems to struggle to keep her perfectly framed in the center of the image. Then it begins to track backward, forcing her, unnaturally, and in an uncanny way, to remain *stationary* in the center of the visual field, even though in actuality she continues to move forward. The effect is to turn her into an *objet d'art*, something to be looked at, perhaps admired.[26] This situation and placement are repeated a few minutes later with Claudia, her stand-in, when she waits for Anna and is tightly framed in a low-angle shot against the half-timbered ceiling, and later, in a paint store, when Claudia is seen two-dimensionally against a row of cans of paint. (A similar moment occurs much later in the film when Claudia is standing in the waiting room of the small-town train station, in front of a tourist poster that ironically invokes the delights of "summer in Sicily.") In all of these cases, the very gesture of "framing" woman as an aesthetic object to be looked at is undermined by the forced, unnatural quality of the gesture itself. In this, it is similar to the strategy of a painter such as Manet who, while remaining intensely naturalistic in style, also flattens the perspective of his canvas, thus purposely calling attention to the artificiality of the two-dimensional medium. This consistent flattening also reinforces the alternative, formalist way of reading the film that I have been proposing, and, like the opening of *L'eclisse* (in which Monica Vitti deliberately plays with a frame), it authorizes us, once again, to regard the film as an abstract pattern of expressive lines, shapes, and shades of black and white, as well as the site of story and character.

The best example of this kind of framing comes near the beginning, when Sandro and Anna are about to make love and we see Claudia through the window, on the street below. Even after Sandro moves to close the shade, we still see Claudia, in a completely (and purposefully) artificial manner, framed between the curtains, thus defeating the whole point of his action. In fact, most of the characters, both male and female, are seen throughout the film in "framing" terms, through windows, doorways, and so on. (In a similar gesture, when Anna first joins Sandro at the beginning of the film, he clowns about which way she wants him to pose for her.) The necessity of looking at the images as, in a certain manner, animated paintings is underlined by the fact that – and here, Antonioni is clearly instructing us in "proper" interpretive procedures, as he is with the frames that Vitti plays with at the beginning of *L'eclisse* – while Claudia is waiting for the lovers, she enters an art gallery on the square and scrutinizes several abstract canvases hanging on its walls.[27] These images are heavy, weighted, and seemingly full of clues, but clues toward what solution? They are like hieroglyphs in a language whose Rosetta stone has not yet been found.

Neither the specificity of the feminist critique nor the director's visual abstractions, however, should blind us to the fact that much of the film is simultaneously an attempt to portray the wider failures of contemporary Italian society. At the time it was made, Italy had been living through the massive growth and subsequent social dislocation of *il boom*, a phenomenon that reached its height in the 1958–63 period. The great Italian writer Italo Calvino, a lifelong man of the left, recognized this element of critique in *L'avventura* from the very beginning, and his statement deserves to be quoted at length:

> It is a pessimistic picture that does not try to gild or sweeten the pill, that does not want to moralize or to reform the bourgeois way of life and manners as do the radicals or the leftist Catholics. You are in the mire, and there you stay: this is the only serious moral stance. . . . It is a picture of great, unsparing severity, of keen morality, because it is firmly grounded in today's humanity, not in gratuitous or literary abstraction. . . . As a description of society *L'avventura* is just perfect. Its Southern Italian setting, for instance – the inferno of underdevelopment contrasted with the affluent inferno – is the most truthful and most impressive that ever appeared on the screen, without the least indulgence to populism or local color.[28]

This aspect of critique, which was also underlined by the French critic Leprohon, has its formal manifestations as well, as always in Antonioni, and demonstrates that formalism and social critique are not necessarily incompatible. Thus French film theorist Marie-Claire Ropars-Wuilleumier has described Antonioni's particular use of *space* as his way of being historical and critical, since it is space that "reintroduces an involved, real world . . . a fresco comes to life behind the individual portraits, and the more the characters seem to be unaware of the world, the more the world intervenes in their personal adventure in order to comment upon it or contradict it from the exterior."[29]

In any case, with the vague exception of Claudia, the characters in this film are all from the upper middle class or the aristocracy and are greatly affected in direct or indirect ways by their money. They go everywhere by chauffeur-driven car. Anna is not merely a young, modern woman who is unsure whether she really wants to marry Sandro; rather, she is the daughter of a rich and powerful former diplomat, and his arrival on the island after his daughter's disappearance – in a huge helicopter, reminiscent of some rapacious mechanical bird – is an explicitly visual reminder (and aural reminder, given the intensity of the sound of its motor) of this fact. Not surprisingly, this expression of power is manifested in a masculinist way that echoes his not very subtle attempt at the very beginning of the film to maintain his psychological control over his daughter through a mild form of emotional blackmail.

Money seems to have thoroughly corrupted Antonioni's men, especially, and it functions as yet another expression of the ancient competitive drive, reformulated for the modern age. And, as always, it becomes thoroughly enmeshed with sex. In this struggle, the females become trophies by which to measure and announce one's standing in the masculine competition, and Sandro and Anna's father are clearly competing for her loyalty. The fact that at base sex is in some ways merely a function of economics is also seen when the shady journalist, speaking to Sandro, marvels at the fact that to sleep with Gloria Perkins costs 50,000 lire, his entire monthly salary. After having sex with him at the end of the film, Gloria asks Sandro for a "piccolo ricordo," "a little souvenir," and he throws some money at her. The upper-class and aristocratic people seen at various parties and hotels throughout the film are bored, and boring;[30] as in another great film made at nearly the same time, Fellini's *La dolce vita*, Antonioni knows the power of a decadent party to evoke feelings of disgust in the audience and will make it the principal site of his next film, *La notte*.

(Although the critique is perhaps most firmly leveled against the rich middle class, other male characters – such as the lower-middle-class pharmacist, the Sicilian villager who speaks of having chased out French tourists the previous season for wearing bathing suits he found indecent [he mispronounces the trendy new Italian word for bathing suit and Sandro corrects him], and the slimy journalist whom Sandro bribes – indicate that Antonioni's critique goes well beyond that often pilloried group. In any case, class distinctions are always present, even if only by implication, as when the newspaper headline concerning Anna's disappearance refers to a "Ricca Ragazza Romana" [rich Roman girl]. The smugglers who are briefly questioned in connection with the disappearance have strong Southern accents and contrast sharply with Sandro's educated, standard dialect.)

In a frequently quoted sentence from a famous statement Antonioni made at the Cannes festival, the director said that one of the things that the film was trying to show was that "Eros is sick." In the world of these characters, this simple phrase is fleshed out by showing sexuality as mere superficial sensation and exercise of power. The men are voracious and the women are bored; all are vulgar in their dispirited pursuit of pleasure and think nothing of initiating sexual contact or sexual games in front of others. This lack of *pudore* occurs principally in front of Claudia, who, as the product of a poor family (as the audience learns, without much fanfare, near the end of the film), has been figured throughout as the female character with the most integrity and clearest (though dimming) sense of values.

Ensconced in their own precious, selfish selves, these characters are unable to interact or communicate, in any meaningful way. At one point this characteristic is symbolically represented when Claudia calls into a house in the deserted town and is answered only by an empty, lifeless echo, the very figure of solipsism.[31] This lack of communication seems to be reversed when the couple is on the roof of the church in Noto, a living community that is steeped in the Baroque era, at the moment when she accidentally rings the bells and, to her childlike delight, they are "answered," sympathetically, by bells from another church. But the church bells perhaps only *appear* to answer, and in fact, no further communication between the lovers occurs. Similarly, the various bits of languages such as French and English and German heard throughout the film – one of Antonioni's most ubiquitous motifs – seem to mock the idea of communication by presenting its simulacrum rather than its accomplishment.

Another aspect of Antonioni's critique of contemporary society concerns that society's "presentism," its utter forgetting of the past. This is a perennial theme in Italian culture because the past, of course, is always ubiquitous in Italy, as cultural monument or ruin. One of the main problems in the present, Antonioni suggests, is that our nutritive links with a past that might teach us how to live have all been cut. This theme is perhaps exemplified most obviously when an ancient pot is discovered on the island of Lisca Bianca and then dropped by the stupid Raimondo, who seems not to have the slightest relation to it or sense of its worth, monetarily or otherwise. Patrizia's dog is named Cosimo (as in de' Medici), and the hotel in Noto in which they look for Anna is called Hotel Trinacria, the ancient Roman name for Sicily. The Baroque frescoes seen as the camera pans in a quite deliberate fashion over the ancient villa that has been turned into a police station reflect this jarring gap between the past and the present. Sandro, for once, in his role as architect, is the one to notice it, pointing out that if the architect could see what had become of his work, he would be turning over in his grave. When he and Claudia drive into the empty parking lot in front of the equally empty church in the unnamed, probably uninhabited village, the church looks like a copy of the highly artificial EUR architecture that Mussolini fostered in Rome during the 1930s (and that will figure prominently in *L'eclisse*). This architecture is meant to evoke an ersatz "Romanness," similar to the French "Spanish-style" house, with a completely symbolic rather than practical function, that Roland Barthes skewered in *Mythologies* back in the 1950s. In other words, this church represents a kind of proto-postmodern *quotation* of the past, rather than the past itself, as with most churches in Italy. Furthermore, the fact that the church seems hollow and dead testifies eloquently to both the status of the past and the complete absence of traditional religion, for better or worse, in the lives of these modern-day characters.

Contemporary Marxist critic Frederic Jameson has usefully, if somewhat nostalgically, described what has come to be called the "postmodern condition" in terms that seem consistent with Antonioni's critique. He speaks of "the disappearance of history, the way in which our entire contemporary social system has little by little begun to lose its capacity to retain its own past, has begun to live in a perpetual present and in a perpetual change that obliterates traditions."[32] Seen in this light, then, Antonioni seems not so much to be using the broken vase and the empty church to bewail, as a more conservative figure might, the lost values of the classical past, but rather as part of a generalized critique of our complete inability to see, or even represent to ourselves (and thus potentially profit from), *any* part of our collective past.

This division between past and present is also figured formally in the film, in that there are no flashbacks. Like the lives of its characters, *L'avventura* is relentlessly present and, to a lesser extent, future-oriented as well, owing to the forward impetus of the hermeneutic process of the search, though without any of the possibility usually associated with the future. Whenever the past *is* represented in the film, it is always as an absence, a lost presence, traces of which reside in old objects, but it can never be shown "directly." At times, Antonioni consciously plays with the juxtaposition of present and (absent and unavailable) past, as when he told Giovanni Fusco, who wrote the film's music, that he wanted a small orchestra playing a sort of jazz, but "not really jazz. Imagine . . . how they would have written a jazz piece in the Hellenic era if jazz had existed then."[33]

Is there any hope for these sad and empty characters? Perhaps there is a glimmer of it for Sandro in the film's famous ending, which seems to offer the possibility of redemption when Claudia gives in to him and touches the back of his head in that expressly "magical" moment that is highlighted with a haunting musical accent on the sound track. But his crocodile tears of repentance are those of a weakling, a blatant manipulator, a man enslaved by the egotistical expression of his desire. On one level, it may seem a transcendent moment of forgiveness, but on another, it is yet one more failure for Claudia in her quest to live a full, free life. The starkness of the visuals at the end of the film easily supports this reading, though it is only one of the many readings possible. Antonioni has spelled out his intended meaning here:

> On one side of the frame is Mount Etna in all its snowy whiteness, and on the other is a concrete wall. The wall corresponds to the man and Mount Etna corresponds somewhat to the situation of the woman. Thus the frame is divided exactly in half: one half containing the concrete wall which represents the pessimistic side, while the other half showing Mount Etna represents the optimistic. But I really don't know if the relationship between these two halves will endure or not, though it is quite evident the two protagonists will remain together and not separate. The girl will definitely not leave the man; she will stay with him and forgive him. For she realizes that she too, in a certain sense, is somewhat like him.[34]

It is rather strange to hear Antonioni speculate on the fate of his characters "after" the film, since most directors are notoriously reluctant to do this. Elsewhere, he has modified his assessment of the ending somewhat, saying rather that "the conclusion at which my characters arrive is not moral anarchy. They come, at the most, to a kind of shared pity. This, you may say, is nothing new. But without that, what is left to us?"[35]

Despite the "authorization" of directorial intentionality here, it seems best to remain with Giorgio Tinazzi's assessment of Claudia's final gesture as "a sanction for ambiguity."[36] Tinazzi, in fact, sees this sense of ambiguity as so crucial for Antonioni's project that he takes the *lack* of ambiguity elsewhere in the film as an overt indication of the director's displeasure. Thus Antonioni's earlier attempt to give specific reasons for Sandro's behavior, rather than leaving him in ambiguity (as he does with Anna and Claudia), is, according to Tinazzi, a sign that he doesn't care very much for him or any of the other male characters in the film.[37]

I want to close with a brief examination of the statement that the director circulated during the Cannes festival in 1960, in conjunction with the world premiere of the film. I have held off discussing it until now because the vast majority of Antonioni's previous commentators have used it as the basis for their interpretation of the film, but in a way that has robbed it of its innovative power. Although it is true that the director speaks, throughout the statement, in the language of "crisis," the crisis he describes, surprisingly enough, is one between future-oriented science, which he seems to approve of, or at least to accept, and "a rigid and stereotyped morality."[38] What most critics seem unable to digest, in other words, is that Antonioni is *not* condemning the modern world, science, technology, and so on, in favor of a return to traditional humanistic values – clearly the most common posture of "progressive" social commentators during the 1950s and early 1960s – but rather, much more radically, he is criticizing our inability to *adapt* our emotions and our morals to a world that has irrevocably changed.

Just as the fullness of Renaissance man's life was wrecked when the Copernican worldview gained ascendance, says Antonioni, so, too, is modern man fearful and "burdened with a heavy baggage of emotional traits which cannot exactly be called old and outmoded but rather unsuited and inadequate." In this, the director seems to be opposing the classical humanist view that takes man as "the measure of all things," a fixed psychological, spiritual, and emotional entity that will never change, and whose "basic nature" must always be respected by any modern development. Antonioni continues: "He reacts, he loves, he hates, he suffers under the sway of moral forces and myths which today, when we are at the threshold of reaching the moon, should not be the same as those that prevailed at the time of Homer, but nevertheless are."

There is clearly a trace of nostalgia lurking just below the surface here, but one is primarily struck by the unexpected direction of Antonioni's critique. His film, he says, is meant to show "the manner in which attitudes and feelings are misunderstood today. Because, I repeat, the present moral standards we live by, these myths, these conventions are old and obsolete." It is this gap, he continues, that leads to the sexual adventurism and unhappiness that is at the core of the film:

Every day, every emotional encounter gives rise to a new adventure. For even though we know that the ancient codes of morality are decrepit and no longer tenable, we persist, with a sense of perversity that I would only ironically define as pathetic, in remaining loyal to them. Thus moral man who has no fear of the scientific unknown is today afraid of the moral unknown. Starting out from this point of fear and frustration, his adventure can only end in a stalemate.

We cannot understand Antonioni, *L'avventura*, or the films that follow unless we first come to terms with the radicality of this position.

2

La notte (1961)

> Our perspective of life has passed into an ideology which conceals the fact
> that there is life no longer.
>   – Theodor Adorno, *Minima Moralia*

Compared with the relative spaciousness of *L'avventura*, *La notte*, all of which takes place in less than twenty-four hours in and about Milan, promotes an Aristotelian intensity of place, time, and action that gives each tiny gesture of its characters, each minute alteration in its story, immense incremental value. Unlike the earlier film, it has a minimal plot that is easy to follow, as are the motivations of its characters, who are troubled, certainly, but who remain relatively clear-cut and stable. Identities seem less fluid here than in *L'avventura*, and, although curious camera angles continue to be used, the film is somewhat less formally experimental and contains a great deal less in the way of unconventional ellipses and cuts.[1] Yet Antonioni's reliance on striking visual images, spatial juxtapositions, emotional suggestion and nuance, ambient noises, and formal qualities of line, shape, and texture – rather than on the traditional resources of narrative – continues.

Dialogue is also much more significant in this film. In *L'avventura*, dialogue was so sparse as to be merely one more signifying element, on a par with ambient noise, music, and visual imagery, rather than occupying its normally dominant position. In *La notte*, there is a barrage of it, as if, having been so painfully reticent in *L'avventura*, the medium itself has to burst forth, using all of its resources. This investment in dialogue, in language, is of course exactly appropriate to a story set in Milan, Italy's intellectual capital, especially a story about a writer. The problem is that there is *so much dialogue* that we begin to doubt its meaning, its authenticity, its efficacy, even its relevance. One of the themes that *La notte* explores is the nature of a linguistic understanding of the world.

Antonioni has himself described the differences between the two films:

> In *La notte*, the protagonists go somewhat further [than in *L'avventura*]. In *L'avventura* they communicate [at the end of the film] only through this mutual sense of pity; they do not speak to one another. In *La notte*, however, they do converse with each other [at the end], they communicate freely, they are fully aware of what is happening to their relationship. But the result is the same, it doesn't differ. The man becomes hypocritical, he refuses to go on with the conversation because he knows quite well that if he openly expresses his feelings at that moment, everything would be finished. But even this attitude indicates a desire on his part to maintain the relationship, so then the more optimistic side of the situation is brought out.[2]

The very vagueness of this statement indicates, once again, that Antonioni's home ground is uncertainty, dissonance, the secular mystery lying behind the visible: as one Italian critic has put it, "The only certainties in Antonioni are formal and stylistic."[3] Formal elements thus once again predominate over naturalistic dramaturgy, which strives always to make characters "psychologically realistic." As mentioned earlier, the characters, and by a kind of metonymy, the actors, are also the carriers of *formal* meanings, more textual elements than human beings with whom the audience identifies. Yet they remain human beings, creating an innovative and fertile juxtaposition of person and abstract form. As Pascal Bonitzer has pointed out: "*La notte* is not only a film *in* black and white, but a film *about* black and white, a giant chessboard on which the characters move by themselves or are moved by chance, to which they have offered up a desire gone dead. White connotes the absence, the disaffection, the emptiness that paralyzes Antonioni's characters."[4] We might want to disagree with Bonitzer's rather reductive association of white with absence – for surely the same thing could be said about black (about which he says nothing in his essay) – but he is right that in *La notte* Antonioni puts us in a formalized world, yet it is one that still contains recognizable human beings.

This working of the border between the human and the abstract can also be seen in Antonioni's oft-reported penchant for keeping his camera rolling on an actor long after the completion of the "real" scene. The French writer Michel Butor has described the effect of this technique in *La notte*:

Not that Jeanne Moreau was not shot as Jeanne Moreau, but rather she was taken in a suspended moment where she was no longer Mrs. Pontano, but not yet either her own self. Often [Antonioni] preserves these margins, these "ends" as he would say, because the entire sequence then takes on another sense as a new dimension makes its appearance in the disturbance of the natural.[5]

"The disturbance of the natural": a good description of exactly what Antonioni is trying to do in these films.

La notte opens with empty scenes of urban life, and thus it forms a kind of anticipatory loop with the emptiness Antonioni revels in at the end of *L'eclisse*, the film that comes after it. An anonymous bus and tram pass, followed by two shots of empty train tracks, a conjunction that might lead once again all too quickly to the view that the director is here indulging in a ritual denunciation of the "alienation" of modern life. But read in the light of the Cannes statement regarding *L'avventura*, discussed in chapter 1, the opening can just as easily be seen as a neutral, if freighted *description* of a certain condition of modern life, expressing neither approval nor disapproval, merely reminding us of the way things are by drawing attention to what we take for granted, in order that we may judge properly what is to follow. The film is about inhabiting this border, this uncertainty.

The credits play out over a mesmerizing, repetitive descending tilt or tracking shot – it's difficult to know exactly how to label it – that moves down the side of a new skyscraper, the Pirelli building in Milan. Literally and figuratively, the glass building reflects the cityscape that surrounds it, continuing and enhancing the motif of doubling and reflection that was only minimally in place in *L'avventura*, but one that will assume greater importance in this film. Once again our attention is called to the formal question and to what extent meaning in this film is going to depend on visual and aural forms rather than on plot and character.[6]

We cut suddenly to a close-up of Tommaso (Bernhard Wicki), the dying friend of Giovanni (Marcello Mastroanni) and Lidia (Jeanne Moreau), who is being restrained in his hospital bed. Antonioni's special brand of deep focus/close-up (in which a character's in-focus head or upper body is in the foreground of the shot, while objects and people in the background are also in focus) is immediately put into play, with Tommaso's head looming very large in the foreground of the shot, while we simultaneously look beyond and around him, through the open hospital window, onto the "reality" outside. Through this kind of shot (so reminiscent of the films of Orson

Welles, though used toward utterly different ends), Antonioni reveals the complex layering of reality and forcefully reminds us of the placement of the human in both the built and "natural" environments.

For critic Giorgio Tinazzi, this look into the clinic replicates the initial view of the city seen during the credits: "The city gives the feeling of a rationality that has become cold abstraction, like the 'antiseptic' clinic."[7] The published script of the film describes the room as being "rationally furnished" and the clinic as "very modern. . . . In its perfection, it evokes the idea of a perfect and implacable science."[8] This apotheosis of cold rationalism accords nicely with Giovanni's mention of Tommaso's recently published article on German Marxist critic Theodor Adorno. Besides placing Giovanni and Tommaso in a high-powered intellectual/theoretical environment (Giovanni the novelist feels qualified to offer his opinion of Tommaso's essay), the citing of Adorno's name points to his work in such books (written with Max Horkheimer) as *The Dialectic of Enlightenment*, a critique of the "instrumental" hyper-rationality (as opposed to true critical thinking) that has flourished since the eighteenth century. Part of Adorno's criticism is leveled against science, which, instead of fulfilling its promise of greater freedom, has led to the domination of the external natural world and, by extension, man's own internal "naturalness." It is probably not wise to make too much of a one-line mention in the dialogue, but the invocation of Adorno's name does seem to complement the director's stark visual images.

Antonioni's obsessive exploration of sexuality and the status of women continues in the introduction of the "nymphomaniac," a patient in the adjoining room who forces herself on Giovanni when he is on his way in to visit Tommaso. Clearly an extension of Antonioni's sense of a "sick Eros" that taints modern life, first articulated in the Cannes statement concerning *L'avventura*, she demonstrates that the sexual cancer is not restricted to men. Apparently she has become literally sick from desire, and when Giovanni later leaves Tommaso's room alone, she throws herself at him, arousing him to the point that he is ready to have sex with her on her hospital bed until some nurses rush in and slap her around in order to bring her to her senses. (And what about him?) It might be possible to read this episode in a positive light – as a healthy expression of female desire that must be repressed by the authorities – but her sexual desperation hardly seems benign. For his part, Giovanni seems ready to have sex at a moment's notice, like most of Antonioni's male characters, even when it will obviously not have the slightest bit of meaning.[9]

It should be noticed, however, that, in general, women receive even greater attention in this film, and have more power, than in *L'avventura*. The interchangeable-female motif from the earlier film occurs less frequently, and Lidia is rarely in the same sort of overt physical danger that threatened Claudia in Noto. Visually, though, Antonioni's shots of his women characters continue the spatial arrangements and aestheticized, or better, *analytic* compositions that were prevalent in *L'avventura*. Thus, most of our views of Lidia are of her alone, straight on, framed/caught in the center of the image, as the representative, perhaps, of a species to be probed. Similarly, in Giovanni's quasi-sex scene in the hospital with the "young woman" (as she is identified in the screenplay), the woman is pinned against a white wall in a very long take that isolates her visually, and by extension, emotionally and psychologically, and makes her, too, an object to be investigated. Interestingly, the self-reflexive formal gestures that crowd the earlier film are hardly to be seen in *La notte*. This is partly the result of the general lessening of the "experimental" mode in this film and its more straightforward narration, but also the central figure, the novelist Giovanni Pontano, is Antonioni's more obvious stand-in here. In a sense, then, the entire film can be said to exist in an insistently self-referential context.

The traffic jam in which Giovanni and Lidia become caught after their visit to Tommaso is, of course, a facile signifier for the harassment of modern urban life, but it should also be seen in its historical context. In other words, although the depiction of traffic jams may now be trite, in 1960 such congestion was still relatively new in Italy, a direct outcome of the economic boom and the massive consumerism that accompanied it. Antonioni's critique of contemporary life continues in a title for a new story that Lidia sarcastically suggests to Giovanni, after he has confessed his encounter with the woman in the hospital: *I vivi e i morti* (The living and the dead).[10] We wonder, as we are supposed to, if, in the context of this film and this society, it is all that easy to tell the two apart.

What is most interesting about *La notte*, though, is that Antonioni does not content himself with a generalized, abstract critique of modern-day angst and alienation, but rather, beginning with the next scene and moving consistently throughout the film, he focuses his inquiring lens on the role of the alienated intellectual/artist at this specific moment in the history of Italian society.

When they arrive at the book party being thrown in Giovanni's honor, Lidia, overwhelmed by the encounter with the moribund Tommaso, is clearly in a death-mastered frame of mind, that horrible isolating feeling that comes when the world is perceived as happily, unconsciously going about its business while the observer grieves alone. The director is especially good at capturing the vacuity and essential loneliness of social functions such as this. A curious "reality effect" – one that is probably lost on most non-Italian viewers – is also felt here in that the party is being given by Bompiani, the name of a real publishing company. What's more, the real head of the company, Valentino Bompiani, is there, along with a real Nobel prizewinner, Italian poet Salvatore Quasimodo (identified in the screenplay only as "Nobel Prizewinner"). For viewers with specialized knowledge, at least, this represents a powerful intrusion of the "real" into the representation.[11] It is difficult to chart fully the effects of this intrusion, but, clearly, it sharpens the explicit social critique by purposely mixing "documentary" elements into the fiction of the film. These early, relatively short scenes establish motifs and themes that will be developed in the three major scenes to follow: Lidia's long solo walk through the working-class suburbs of Milan, the visit to the nightclub, and the party that gives the film its name and that occupies its longest segment.

Lidia's walk, one of the most famous sequences in movie history, can, like nearly everything else in the film, be interpreted in a number of ways. Tinazzi, for one, sees it as a kind of realistic documentary, which would correlate nicely with the dynamics of the book party just discussed. Calling it *Gente di Milano* (People of Milan, an allusion to Antonioni's early documentary, *Gente del Po*), Tinazzi regards Lidia as Antonioni's surrogate, coolly exploring the modern urban landscape. Like most commentators, though, he sees this experience in completely negative terms: "We feel her coming to understand that her disturbed relationship with her husband is not unrelated to the arid, empty, abstract space in which they live."[12]

Many critics go beyond Tinazzi's negativity and have used this scene to indulge in various forms of energetic *symbolic* readings that have the potential to enrich one's appreciation of the filmic text, certainly, but that can all too easily impoverish it. Thus, although many of the objects that Lidia sees on her small journey do indeed have the potential to be read as sexual symbols, this kind of reading can stupidly lead one to conclude that Lidia simply needs better sex, a "real man." In the context of Lidia's walk, in other words, we need to think about the nature of cinematic meaning itself, and how objects that are visually represented can come to be seen as possessing symbolic meaning.

On the one hand, this film comes at the height of a kind of "literary" cinema, heavily reliant on visual symbols, that is perhaps most clearly exemplified in the films of Ingmar Bergman. The dream sequence of Bergman's *Wild Strawberries* (1957), for example, insists on being read symbolically. (In fact, the clock that Lidia sees on her travels seems to be a quotation of a similar image in Bergman's film.) Inevitably, as already mentioned, this sort of interpretation tends to reveal a great deal more about the critic than about the text he – usually, in 1960, the critic is male – is ostensibly trying to illuminate.

A good example of this sort of symbol-hunting can be found in the following quotation: "Coming upon a row of fireplugs [actually, they're not fireplugs, but rather the heavy, bomb-shaped concrete objects used to prevent cars from parking on sidewalks], Lidia fondles one longingly, in the silliest kind of now-why-can't-my-husband-be-like-that? gesture. And when she phones her husband to tell him how much he'd like the rockets, I thought of a friend's used copy of *The Waste Land* in which someone had circled 'cock' and written 'symbol of fertility' in the margin."[13] Less jejeune critics such as Ian Cameron and Robin Wood are also inevitably drawn to this particular moment: "The most blatant [symbol] of all comes at this point in the film. Lidia threads her way along a row of concrete posts, absently fingering the first few. A tracking shot just above shoulder level behind her leaves us in no doubt of their significance." (Elsewhere, referring to "phallic symbols [that] keep popping up," they even go so far as to include the champagne bottle in Tommaso's hospital room!)[14]

First, it is not exactly clear why this particular shot of Lidia from this particular angle would be a guarantor of any particular symbolic meaning. But beyond that, what's in question here is not very complicated: is the director at fault for "using" such obvious symbols, or the critic for *finding* them and interpreting them in this sophomoric way? In other words, these critics take the presence of symbolic signification itself, beyond the status of the concrete object – as well as intentionality on the director's part – as givens. Thus Cameron and Wood say, speaking of Lidia's walk, that "the symbolism here is pushed a little too hard in a couple of close shots," then cite the shot of the clock and the one of Lidia's hand, replete with wedding band, picking fragments off a wall. They do not, however, say what these images are symbols of. Is it because, once articulated, the supposedly obvious symbolic meanings would appear utterly banal and, more important, utterly insufficient to the rich suggestivity of Antonioni's visual images?

One wonders therefore whether it might be more fruitful to take these images in a more purely *graphic* sense rather than a narrowly symbolic, literary one. In this way, the "meaning" of these human and material forms, beyond their obvious functions in the narrative and as part of the world of the film, would be emotionally expressive rather than intellectually specifiable. It is notoriously difficult to define the precise emotional meaning of visual images, of course, especially abstract ones – what is the "meaning" of Pollock's drips or of Rothko's luminous squares of color? – and this is why so much mistaken emphasis has been placed on reading images in these films in such a consistently literary, and literal, fashion.

Chatman usefully argues that we should look at these films in terms of the rhetorical figure of *metonymy*, which meaningfully relates objects through proximity, rather than that of *metaphor*, in which symbols are taken from another semantic field. In discussing the scene in Tommaso's hospital room, for example, he notes the ways in which the room, Lidia's flowered dress, and the old building seen behind her through the window are interrelated. Chatman prefers metonymy, he says, because it "reinforces the actuality of the world of text" rather than "substitutive figures like metaphor and symbol."[15] This provides a useful corrective to the overly symbolic approach, but it also has the negative effect of redeploying a conventional realist aesthetic – the view that the proper purview of cinema is the depiction of "reality." Given the unspecifiable yet palpable emotional resonance of many of his images, however, it is clear that Antonioni means to work against the restraints of classical realism.

The great Italian novelist Alberto Moravia was thinking along similar lines when he remarked on the image of Lidia's hand picking things off a dark wall. For him, this was the "highest moment in the film" because for the first time in film history, Antonioni was able to translate the means and images appropriate to modern painting and narrative into film images. However, Moravia also inadvertently provides evidence for the dangers inherent in emphasizing the abstract quality of these images; this image of Lidia's hands is so brilliant precisely because in it "Antonioni was able to find the perfect expression of a nameless and history-less anxiety."[16] Of course, an attitude such as this moves us quickly away from historically specific social critique and back toward the familiar themes of general angst and alienation.

However we are to read – or not read – the symbols that lie scattered along Lidia's journey, it is important to remember that in fact a *woman* occupies center stage, and for quite a long time. For one of the first and only times in film history, Antonioni expressly foregrounds female subjectivity, emphasizing that the look is being generated by a specific female, rather than by the usual male protagonist who motivates plot and action or, more generally, by the abstract, invisible (male) apparatus. We saw the beginning of this shift to a female point of view in *L'avventura*, but there it remained tentative. Here the woman looks, and in an uncompromising way.

Nevertheless, we also look at *her* looking. Lidia is, in other words, always *herself* being seen by the apparatus, the covert (male) generator of the images (of her and everything else) that we see. Thus the "autonomy" she displays on her solo walk through the city is in some way always compromised and controlled. Furthermore, our looking, and Antonioni's, is, given the partriarchal history of viewing (and of clothing) in Western society, always sexually inflected, and she inevitably becomes a sexual object for the male viewer. During Lidia's walk, Jeanne Moreau wears a tight-fitting dress that sexually accentuates her every step, precisely at the same moment that she is "freely" wandering, and looking. In this, Moreau's body is similar to the female backs seen in *L'avventura*, which are a function of a woman looking, certainly, but invariably always sexual objects at the same time. Presumably, given the history of Western visual representation, such contradictions in the depiction of the female body are simply impossible to eliminate.[17]

Whatever the gender dynamics at work here, it is difficult to say exactly what Lidia sees. Her journey seems to be one that is psychological and spiritual, as well as literal, but it is also nonspecific, aleatory, postmodern. Despite all the supposedly "blatant" symbols, in other words, we are seldom directed toward a specific, preferred meaning. Rather, once again meaning is made affective, through line, shape, and form.

This is perhaps most famously seen in the modern architecture of the giant cityscapes that overwhelm her tiny, solitary figure. At one moment, we are faced by a gigantic bare wall, with Lidia barely visible as a speck on the lower left (she almost completely disappears on video cassette versions of the film). Paradoxically, the denuded streets end up emphasizing their own facticity, and what develops is a complicated relationship between people and the things that surround them. Giorgio Tinazzi describes this dynamic:

> On one hand, there's still the push that comes from the character, in which things and facts are a function of psychological projection. . . . [O]n the other, these things and facts begin to lose this kind of narrative dependence and acquire the autonomy of simply being present: reality, having lost the subject/object relationship, now constitutes itself through meaning (or non-meaning). Thus, restoring to things their "virginity" and their ambivalence, Antonioni reveals their estranged universe: the relationship between the character and the environment becomes dissonant.[18]

Intercut between scenes of Lidia's wandering are shorter scenes of Giovanni padding about their darkened apartment all alone. Biarese and Tassone helpfully point out that his own wanderings through the apartment, what they call "an anxious, visual poem on absence," in effect double Lidia's wanderings through the city and suburbs. The noises that we hear as he returns to the apartment are powerful and alienating, as are the passing jets that assault our ears during Lidia's walk. This urban aural attack contrasts sharply with the more natural sounds of *L'avventura* and thematically abets the visual track.

The more conventional communication motif briefly discussed in conjunction with the earlier film is further developed in *La notte* when Giovanni begins playing English-language instruction records on his phonograph. The thematic equivalent of the cacophony of languages heard throughout *L'avventura*, it reminds us of the inherent emptiness of language until it is filled with (or surrounded by) a specific, meaningful, human context. Language here, on a language record, is purely functional, infinitely repeatable, and thus empty, for the English sentences clearly do not mean what they would mean if they occurred in a "real" context. This idea of the inherent meaninglessness of language in itself is amplified later in a scene with Giovanni and Valentina (Monica Vitti) when she rewinds an audiotape of her speaking, and it comes out sounding like high-pitched gibberish. These are clues to the way in which we should, to some extent, regard *all* the dialogue in this film, depriviledging it in terms of meaning, despite, or because of, its abundance.

We cut back to Lidia, who continues to be seen, like so many other Antonioni women, against completely solid, neutral backdrops. And, just as we should consider abstract line, shape, and form as contributing to the "meanings" of the film, even if these are not precisely specifiable, so, too, we must consider the physiognomy of Jeanne Moreau herself – especially her famous sad, hangdog look – as a legitimate signifier, rather than as an irrelevant accident. I do not mean to invoke here André Bazin's famous phenomenological description of the neorealist actors in DeSica's films as being so "authentic" that they merely needed to *be* rather than to *act*, nor am I referring to Moreau's *performance* in and of itself, but rather to the meanings of her own particular face, as part of the expressive lines of many different types that each frame contains. The fact that these meanings are difficult to describe in precise terms does not make them any less legitimate or present.

Lidia encounters some young men fighting in a particularly vicious and atavistic way (though the scene is slightly off camera, and not directly represented – a technical choice common to non-Hollywood films of this era because of the difficulties of filming convincing fight scenes). The other young men watching do nothing and seem utterly insensitive to the brutality they are witnessing. But the fighters' performance is also subtly directed toward her, as a kind of sexual display. Interestingly, where there should be words, angry, violent words at least, here, there are none, and the violence is made even nastier by being depicted in silence. This wordless male world is the exact opposite of the world that Giovanni excels in, the wordy world of his books and their parody on the language records, where lots of words still add up to nothing. Finally, Lidia breaks the powerful rhythm of the silence and screams, "Basta!" But once she has intruded with even a single word into this male arena, the men look at her threateningly, the way the men of Noto looked at Claudia in *L'avventura*. This is all of a piece with Giovanni's earlier male behavior in the hospital with the "nymphomaniac."

We cut back to a shot of Giovanni sleeping, as neighbors creepily watch each other from windows in what almost amounts to a parody of urban alienation. When Lidia calls him, asking to be picked up, a woman nearby, overhearing her, offers her a "pensione" if she needs to meet someone on the sly. In the modern age of "sick Eros," this is the form that being a helpful neighbor takes. The director seems almost personally offended by the would-be panderer's offer.

In a moment of conventional romantic nostalgia, Giovanni goes to pick her up in their "old spot" near Breda. The location is described in the screenplay as "squalid and melancholy" once the sun begins to go down, and for the first time during Lidia's walk a specific place begins to assume a personal emotional valence; now, unfortunately, the relevant emotions are dead. We see train tracks that used to function, but that are now all grown over with weeds. (This is not a symbol, but rather an expression, in graphic terms, of their relationship.) The couple's past, the past itself, seems totally to have disappeared; like the characters in *L'avventura*, these two have nothing left but a present that promises very little for the future.

Taking a bath later that evening in their apartment, Lidia tries one last time to arouse some sexual desire in Giovanni but fails. (The situation will be exactly reversed in the final, climactic scene of the film, when she refuses his pathetic, desperate arousal.) The coming amplification of the social/political theme is also announced during this scene when Lidia suggests that the rich Gherardinis have invited them to their party because "every millionaire wants his own intellectual."

The next important scene takes place in a nightclub in which they list-lessly kill time before the party. The black performers suggest a flamboyant exoticism (as the similar motif of Africa and the African tribal dance do in *L'eclisse*, the director's next film) that contrasts strongly with the hum-drum, empty lives of Giovanni and Lidia. The black couple is also clearly coded as sexual, even animalistic, in a manner that is obvious now and probably even racist, but that was a more innocent novelty in the Italy of 1960. As such, their nearly directly expressed sexuality is in sharp contrast to the moribund sexuality of the lifeless, entropic white couple. The female performer's gyrations are so gymnastic (especially her amazing contortions with a glass of wine) that something beyond mere vibrant sexuality is sug-gested, a perfect at-easeness with her entire body that seems remote from the anxious, superficial intellectualism of Giovanni and the frustrations of his wife.

The brilliant centerpiece of *La notte* is the party at the Gherardini's, surprisingly similar to the party in Fellini's contemporaneous *La dolce vita*, which will occupy the remainder of the film.[19] The importance of the long scene for Antonioni is attested to by the fact that he took thirty-two nights, working from five in the evening until seven in the morning, to shoot it. In structure, it resembles the familiar form of the road movie: even though the participants do not really go anywhere, the road movie theme of being adrift from familiar ties and rituals, and thus open to new, life-altering experiences, comes across strongly.

This is also where Antonioni's sociopolitical critique comes to the fore, much more overtly than in *L'avventura*, almost to the point of caricature. The people at the party appear to poke fun at themselves merely by existing and seem unwilling or unable to make genuine human contact; they are all nasty and edgy, especially the women, while the men posture and compete. The social critique develops from a simple, unemphatic positing of details and particularities: the child improbably on horseback at the party, as we learn that Wolfango, the horse, "gets nervous if he doesn't get enough sleep"; the women cattily measuring each other for possible faults; lots of people speaking French (Antonioni's language signifier of empty sophisti-cation, reminiscent of the party scene at the end of *L'avventura*); Signore Gherardini bragging about cutting roses from three thousand rose bushes; the false spontaneity of jumping in the pool with party clothes on; the statue of the satyr that is fondled by the young woman. At one point, a partygoer says, "Leave the past alone," emphasizing the eternal now that these people want to live in.

When Giovanni and Lidia arrive, they find a copy of Hermann Broch's classic, *The Sleepwalkers* (a trilogy that appeared in 1930–2 in Austria, it could be described as a novelistic version of the *The Waste Land*). Amazed, Giovanni wonders aloud who could be reading this heavy tome (they later discover it is Valentina, the Gherardini's twenty-one-year-old daughter whom Giovanni will amorously pursue). Once again, the presence of the book at the party seems an overobvious symbol, similar to the book title Lidia earlier suggested to Giovanni, *The Living and the Dead*, especially since they have just finished saying, before they come upon any other guest, "Is everybody dead here? Let's hope so." However, Biarese and Tassone suggest a better way to look at the book, claiming that it is not meant to be overtly symbolic, but actually "an ironic invention like that – very Buñuelian – of the horse Wolfango,"[20] in other words, part of the social critique.

As the party wears on, shouts are heard, and Lidia wanders through empty rooms in the same way that earlier in the day she had wandered through blighted Milan. She is stalked by a man she has just met – men as sexual predators again – and then hears news of Tommaso's death, reminding us of the most immediate source of her depression. The death of someone close is, of course, an incredibly specific, focused event that can trigger a profound reassessment of one's whole life. In the next shot, the camera tilts up on her, looking devastated; the distance is held, in a kind of pathetic fallacy effect, as we remain as visually distanced from her as she must feel emotionally distanced from the other guests, rather than moving in, as a more conventional director might have done, for the artificial emotional heightening of a close-up.

After she sees Giovanni kiss the young Valentina (in a brilliantly composed shot, with Lidia looking down from above), she seeks revenge, reluctantly, by beginning to flirt with Roberto, the man who has been following her. As the two couples proceed through the remainder of the party, the visuals are superbly choreographed in terms of distance, angle, and elevation. Every shot seems to call attention to itself and its constructedness, foregrounding the fact that what we are seeing has been artfully composed, that there is meaning here that exists beyond narration and character. On a thematic level, much of the scene is reflected through windows and mirrors, indicating the kind of doubling, displacement, and ambiguity of the (modern) self that is Antonioni's constant subject.

One of the film's high points of visual storytelling and signification comes when Lidia goes off in the car with Roberto. There is no dialogue, only laughing conveyed through silhouettes, and heavily expressive chiaro-

Figure 6. Giovanni (Marcello Mastroianni) and Valentina (Monica Vitti) at the party

scuro lighting. This is the moment, as during Lidia's walk through Milan, when graphic line and form come together with character and narrative to give rise to nuanced meanings that could not be achieved in any other way. The shot of the car moving through the rain is held for a long time; the deafening rain obliterates every other sound, becoming expressive and meaningful in its own right. The single line of dialogue comes when Lidia suddenly decides that she cannot go through with it: "Mi scusi, non posso," "I'm sorry, I just can't." The traffic signal blinks, creating further expressionistic lighting effects that merge with the unusual angle of the camera. Sam Rohdie has best expressed the nature of this mini-apotheosis of meaning through form: "And [the place where the narrative seems to die] is there in *La notte* when Lidia drives off in the rain at the party, the camera losing interest in the drama inside the car and the meaning of that escape, for the drama of the form of the car, the rain on the windscreen, the distortions of spaces by light and water and shadow."[21] (Though one might say that rather than "losing interest," the camera is merely showing its interest in the narrative in a different manner, through abstract graphic form.)

The powerful wordlessness of this scene also stands in direct contrast to the verbiage of the scenes involving Giovanni, the wordsmith, and Valentina. He tells her that he is experiencing a crisis affecting his whole life, but as always with him, and with most Antonioni males, one suspects that this may be merely another one of his pickup lines. Whatever seriousness these males may temporarily muster always seems to be betrayed by their obsession with sex.

At another brief but perfect visual moment, the camera suggests a conflation of Lidia and Valentina, a frequent gesture in *L'avventura;* here, however, it is made through a shot/reverse shot sequence. First the camera shoots down the stairs, from Lidia's POV onto Valentina, then from Valentina's POV up the stairs on Lidia. A doubling between the two women is implied, especially since, in his fantasy life at least, Giovanni dreams of substituting the younger for the older woman. At the same time, this sequence clearly has nothing to do with Giovanni. Something else is going on here.

This doubling motif comes up again later in a kind of trick shot, after Lidia's automobile ride with Roberto. We see a woman standing in front of a building, think it is Lidia, and then discover it is really Valentina. These doublings suggest a nascent female solidarity (and consequent disavowal of competition between them) that is stronger than in the earlier film, especially when the two women meet later, as in *L'avventura*, to dry off. But their budding sense of camaraderie is countered by the simple lack of emotional energy that haunts these enervated characters. By way of apologizing for an earlier unkind remark, Lidia says to Valentina, "There was no jealousy in what I said before." And then adds, revealingly, "That's the whole problem." They avoid "girl talk" and speak rather of suicide and death. In a classic exchange worthy of Samuel Beckett, tragedy and pathos are adroitly mixed:

> LIDIA: You don't know what it means to feel all these years weighing you down and not to understand them any longer. (Pause.) Tonight, I only want to die. I swear it. At least this anxiety would be over, and something new would begin.
> VALENTINA: Maybe nothing.
> LIDIA: Yes, maybe nothing.[22]

Figure 7. More female doubling: Valentina and Lidia (Jeanne Moreau)

A few minutes later, when the party is just about over, Valentina – centered, pinned, framed against the wall, in the classic Antonionian manner – will say to Giovanni and Lidia: "You two have really worn me out" (p. 355). Even though she is young, she has been deeply affected by the corrosiveness of their lifeless cynicism.

The most specific aspect of Antonioni's social critique, however, comes in the scenes with Mr. Gherardini, the millionaire industrialist so full of whining nostalgia, who fondly admires a picture of his factory that hangs on the wall. He fatuously tells his assembled guests that he never thinks about money, but rather about "creation": "An artist, when he works, doesn't think about the money he will get from his work of art, but only about the work itself. I have always thought of my businesses as works of art. I almost don't even care about the money I make from them. The important thing is to create something, something that lives after us" (p. 335). Biarese and Tassone usefully identify Gherardini, whom they insist is a completely new character in Italian cinema, as a specific product of the economic boom of this period of Italian history.[23]

The central focus of the critique, of course, is Giovanni, the novelist and intellectual. Clearly, Antonioni is interrogating the place of the artist and intellectual (in Italy these roles coexist in a single figure more easily than in North America) in this new economic order, and, by implication, his own place in it as well. To all appearances, the independent interrogator, which is the classic role of the intellectual, has become a luxury, with no real place in society, except as an employee.[24] Giovanni who, from his first mention in the script, is said to be dressed like "un intellettuale 'inserito' " (an establishment intellectual, p. 302), is jokingly castigated by Valentina: "You're one of those people who worry only about the losers. It's typical of intellectuals: selfish, but full of pity" (p. 340). Biarese and Tassone report that some Italian intellectuals – Alberto Moravia was one – did in fact complain at the time of the film's release that Giovanni's character was too negative and irrational to be believable. While admitting that Giovanni represents only one type of intellectual, perhaps, they also point out that "many guys like Pontano would be seen throughout the 1960's."[25]

What might seem peculiar for a viewer in the late 1990s is the precise nature of Gherardini's proposal to "his" intellectual, for he asks Giovanni to work not on improving his company's image before the public, as one would expect now, but on "communication" between the bosses and the workers. It is this kind of direct sociohistorical commentary referring to the contentious labor realities of Italy in 1960 that can easily be overlooked by an audience watching the film nearly four decades later. (Furthermore, a North American viewer, used to quiescent trade unions, might not understand that in Italy the "political" has in fact frequently taken the form of labor relations.) Giovanni is offered a great deal of money – "Don't you want to live as we do?" he is asked – to become one of the directors of the company, specializing in "internal relations." Instead of, or in addition to telling stories in his novels, they suggest, he will now "tell the story" of the company.[26] The logic of a triumphant capitalism dictates that the intellectual's labor as well will now be available to the highest bidder, while the idea of art seems almost quaint, as does the traditionally leftist, pro-worker stance of the Italian intellectual. One interesting exchange shows what is at stake, as the guests discuss the merits of Ernest Hemingway:

> GUIDO [another guest]: He is really good at his work, he makes as much as he wants. Millions of dollars. Even for an intellectual that's nothing to throw away.
> GIOVANNI: It's hard for an intellectual to know what to keep and what to throw away.
> GUIDO: Money, my dear sir, should never be thrown away. (P. 354).

Earlier, Giovanni himself has made a self-aware, ironic comment to Resy, one of his female admirers he encounters at the party: "I'll tell you the story of a hermit later, an intellectual hermit, naturally, who for years nourished himself with dew. Then one fine day, he went to the city, tasted wine, and became an alcoholic" (p. 346).

Some critics, including Leprohon, have found fault with these scenes, arguing that they rely too heavily on dialogue, whereas Antonioni's speciality is his reticence and his interest in the unsaid.[27] But the very presence of so much dialogue in this film is a significant thematic fact, in and of itself. Giovanni relies on words to earn his living and to express his being; but words are also his strongest weapon, and thus it makes sense that it is precisely here that he will also be at his most inauthentic and superficial. Though we are used to privileging dialogue in art films, words can be meaningless too, no matter how intelligent and sophisticated they sound and no matter with what conviction they are uttered.

After Valentina confesses that Lidia and Giovanni have exhausted her, Antonioni summons his own energies to embark on the brilliant endgame that marks *La notte*, as it marks all his films. The married couple go off together. It is the next morning, the end of the night, the end of *La notte*: a classic scene, with dawn symbolizing, thanks to millennia of literary sources, rebirth of the spirit and a new life. Here, though, as in Fellini's *La dolce vita*, the dawn testifies to something dying rather than being reborn. The modicum of perverse energy left over from the emotional wheeling and dealing of the previous night leads Lidia and Giovanni to look for something new, some new stimulation, but nothing comes.

As though beginning a grand summarizing gesture, the camera moves into a very slow crane shot upward. We watch the burned-out couple from a curiously high angle for a very long time, as if the director were moving to a cosmic perspective on things, before we see what they are watching, a woman crying. We do, of course, *hear* her crying, in a formal gesture that

69

substitutes the aural for the expected visual; here Antonioni again reminds us that we must pay attention to all the meaning tracks of his films.

We follow the couple in long shot as they walk on the grass. The camera seems to be about fifteen feet off the ground, lending an emotional distance to the action. Because the camera remains stationary, as they move further and further away, the shot gradually becomes an extreme long shot. Throughout this final scene, medium shots become extreme long shots, as though there were some kind of leakage, an inability of the camera to hold people and things, to keep them in focus. A kind of global rhythm becomes evident, one that is heavily marked, punctuated, counterpointed, arranged. It is in the images, of course, as it was in *L'avventura* and as it is in virtually all the director's films, but in *La notte*, for once, it is in the words as well.

Lidia talks about their dead friend Tommaso, and then they speak about love. In a tracking movement, the camera follows her as she moves toward a tree, with her back to him. Because her emotions (or the fact of their absence) remain a crucial part of her being, she tells Giovanni: "If I feel like dying tonight, it's because I don't love you any more" (p. 357). This is not an expression of abject female dependency but rather of an emotional authenticity that goes far beyond what Giovanni is now capable of feeling. Finally, she reveals the "pensierino," the little thought, that she had playfully withheld from Giovanni and from us in the nightclub: "That's why I'm desperate. I'd like to be old already, after having dedicated my whole life to you; I'd like to stop existing, because I can't love you any longer" (pp. 357–8). Repeating the word that the director used in an interview to describe what Claudia, that other Antonionian woman, feels for Sandro at the end of *L'avventura*, Lidia tells Giovanni that she only feels "pietà," or pity, for him. The camera moves into an extreme close-up of her face, creating a strong visual contrast to the extreme long shots we have been getting, and vastly complicating the spatial rhythm of this final scene.

She begins to read to him the lovely letter about morning and waking that he has forgotten he had once written to her. This morning they now occupy stands in sharp contrast to that earlier, poetically created one, and, besides making it clear that things are no longer what they once were either between them or within them, the letter raises the suspicion that it was perhaps never more than a "writer" thing for Giovanni, after all, a beautiful creation of words rather than a true expression of his feeling for her. As one of the guests says earlier at the party, in writing, what matters is not the intentions but only the words, suggesting a kind of bankrupt, slick professionalism that Antonioni seems to regard as the trap, or occupational hazard, of all art.

Figure 8. The final desperate moments in the marriage of Giovanni and Lidia

What results is a stunted love scene of sorts, very powerful in its desperation. In a stunning reversal, Lidia now demands *real* language from the
writer, the artist, who has covered himself with inauthentic verbiage from
the beginning. As he tries to kiss her, to reach some preverbal animal level
(perhaps, for Antonioni, the level of the black performers in the nightclub
scene?), she resists him: "Don't. I don't love you any more. You don't love
me. . . . Say it, say it!" When called upon to respond authentically, the man
of words refuses: "I won't say it, I won't say it, shut up." He covers her
with frenetic kisses, but they represent nothing positive, only his negation
of her negation. The camera moves backward, the musical theme comes
up, and finally only the field and trees are visible at the end. As in *L'eclisse*,
a complete evacuation of the human is achieved, however briefly, as we
return to the mute expressiveness of the natural world. But here it's a golf
course, that curious blend of the natural and the artificial, and thus even
the consolation of a return to the (putative) purity and truth of nature is
denied us.

Antonioni's own interpretation of the ending of the film is interesting in
this regard:

That conversation, which is really a soliloquy, a monologue by the wife, is a kind of summing-up of the film to clarify the real meaning of what took place. The woman is still willing to discuss, to analyze, to examine the reasons for the failure of their marriage. But she is prevented from doing so by her husband's refusal to admit its failure, his denial, his inability to remember or unwillingness to remember, his refusal to reason things out, his incapacity to find any basis for a new start through a lucid analysis of the situation as it is. Instead, he tries to take refuge in an irrational and desperate attempt to make physical contact. It is because of this stalemate that we do not know what possible solution they could come to.[28]

Although it is difficult to believe that Antonioni really thinks that the final scene can "sum up" the rich complexity of such a multivalent film, it is significant that once again the woman, far from being the site of nature and animality, of mute gesture and emotion, is in fact the only one, as in *L'avventura*, who is capable of regarding their emotional situation in a rational light. As a summation of this scene, however, if not of the film, I much prefer the concise remark of the late Russian filmmaker Andrei Tarkovsky to Antonioni's cerebral analysis. Tarkovsky said that the final embrace of Giovanni and Lidia is "like the embrace of two people who are about to drown."[29]

3
L'eclisse (1962)

From the very first scene of *L'eclisse*, we know that we are in the presence of something even subtler and more narratively experimental than the films discussed thus far.[1] Antonioni throws the viewer into the story, such as it is, *in medias res*, amid expressive but opaque silences and sighs. It is dawn, that Yeatsian border territory that traditionally gives access to truth, or what's left of it, precisely where Antonioni's previous picture, *La notte*, has ended.

It is clearly the *aftermath* of something; there is a heavy residue of tense feeling that thickens and darkens the atmosphere, but no explanation. This masterful ability to create intimate emotional texture, elicited and described purely through suggestion, and through absence more than presence, is one of Antonioni's great gifts. Here, it signals that this film will be more elliptical, less driven by plot and clear causality than his earlier films, though even there these were already in short supply. In this initial scene, says Sam Rohdie,

> the camera . . . wanders through the room finding images which are variously imponderable, decentred, displaced, upsetting notions of centre, of subject, or object; what fascinates is the movement, the oscillations, the changes, all of which presuppose a refusal to fix anything in the narrative, or in the image, quite against the usual practices and satisfactions of a cinema aimed at fullness and centre.[2]

Dialogue is scare here as well, especially at the beginning, when the viewer's lazier self would perhaps prefer more expository assistance in entering the world of the film. Actually, a primitive sort of dialogue is present, but it's made up of a myriad of apparently ambient noises, now subtle, now insistent, on the sound track. Inside, the fan hums; outside, the wind blows.

These noises function like words, providing alternative sites of meaning, although, like images, they are inevitably much harder to read than words. Again, we are forced to consider the characters we meet as something other, or more, than human beings with a story to tell or live through, as part, in other words, of a multifaceted formal composition.

The music is also handled quite differently in *L'eclisse*, and more complexly. As early as the credits, a sudden and drastic shift of style from popular to more cerebral modernist music signals the importance that music will have as a signifier in the film, especially in the famous last, "visual" sequence, which depends as much on the sound track for its power (though this is seldom discussed) as on the visual track. Antonioni is perhaps not quite as openly experimental in juxtaposing the visual and sound tracks as the French filmmakers Marguérite Duras and Jean-Luc Godard, who often put completely different, apparently incompatible sets of "information" on the two tracks, but neither does he allow the two to blend together and reinforce each other in a traditional, aesthetically unified way. Instead, it's as though he were offering two discrete sets of input that nevertheless lead toward the same end, thus simultaneously incorporating unity and disunity, sameness and difference. In this, he can be said to represent a kind of cinematic high modernism rather than the proto-postmodernism of Duras and Godard.

This expressive use of noise and music is paralleled by a visual abstraction that is even more pronounced in this film than in those already discussed. As early as the opening credits, the frame or context of modern abstract art is strongly suggested with the single vertical line at the left, clearly recalling the "zip" paintings of abstract expressionist Barnett Newman that were being created in America at the same time as the film. Further foregrounding the graphic quality of what we are about to see in the film proper, at the end of the credit sequence the line unzips, as it were, and disappears.

In a more fully developed manner than the earlier films, *L'eclisse* is expressly about humans looking, whether it be at pictures, paintings, photographs, or at one another. (*Blow-up* and *The Passenger* will go all these films one better by being about the creation and nature of visual representation itself.) In the opening scene, Vittoria (played once again by Monica Vitti) is self-consciously looking through an empty picture frame at various objects, some of them art objects themselves, as though Antonioni were demonstrating just how we are to look at the film about to unfold.[3] This represents an almost perfect literalization of the problematic of "framing" that French philosopher Jacques Derrida was to develop some years later.

In Derrida's view, nothing has meaning on its own. Rather, meaning can only be constituted as part of a given *context* or frame – which can always change – and thus any particular given signifier can always have a multitude of possible meanings, depending upon the frame in which it is viewed.[4]

Antonioni's interpretive frame here functions to teach us, through the use of *real* frames and by calling attention to the *film* frame that the characters find themselves in, to consider the images we see and the sounds we hear as modernist abstract forms, as well as conventional forms whose primary purpose is to represent human figures engaged in a recognizably human story. The seemingly aimless cuts – justified *formally* at times, rather than narratively or dramatically – prepare us for the powerful, wordless, and characterless finale of the film. Likewise, the apartment of Vittoria's lover, Riccardo, is full of contemporary abstract art, thus providing another interpretive key for an informed viewing of this film, in the same way that Claudia's visit to the art gallery at the beginning of *L'avventura* prepared the audience to understand that film.

Furthermore, both characters are "placed" throughout this scene in highly artificial, unconventional ways that, owing to their oddity, force the viewer to attend to other things besides realistic narrative. At one point, two strange head-on shots follow one another, in which first Vittoria is perfectly framed for Riccardo (and for us) and then he is perfectly framed for her (and for us). What is striking is the lack of easy transparency of these shots (especially since they are self-consciously symmetrical), a resistance that alerts us to the fact that whatever is going on in this film, it is not realism. This curious series of shots also indicates that formal composition, as well as more traditional loci, will carry its own (always imprecise) thematic burden. The shots are strongly reminiscent of the framing of women in Antonioni's earlier films, but now *both* the man and the woman are thus framed. Here at least, in this opening scene, the director seems to be moving toward a less specifically gendered staging of his formal effects, though thematically there will be little or no change in the sexual dynamic.

Not all critics have approved of the innovative formalism of *L'eclisse*. Tinazzi, for example, says that "sometimes the concern for detail aims at an abstract composition . . . with the risk of preciosity, as when a kind of still life results from certain 'useless' shots: the close-up of a vase of flowers with Vitti's back toward us; or the poster in her appartment which is insisted upon before the character enters."[5] But this objection has force only within the context or frame of a realist aesthetic (the glory and the burden of Italian criticism), something that, on one level at least, Antonioni clearly has little interest in.

Whatever the case, this visual stylization continues throughout the film. The main characters, for example, are often framed within mirrors. Sometimes subsidiary characters are framed like pictures – late in the film, for instance, a woman is precisely placed within the frame of a palazzo window across the way from the apartment of Piero's parents. Again, what is called into question is the relation between real life, especially in its particularly human guise, and representation – and thus the film itself. We come to ask ourselves to what extent, and why, we are to regard these figures – especially the ones that remain anonymous – exclusively as human beings rather than as, at least simultaneously, formal elements (that carry a certain charge of affect) within a composition, or visual signifiers within a field of meaning. A variety of cityscapes, which even more obviously foreground shape and line than does the human form, is also offered to our view, like the architecture of *La notte*, and these are registered at some level as abstract volumes and spaces as well as prosaic, functional objects.

Antonioni chooses also to highlight the necessity of visual interpretation throughout the film. Three or four times – when Vittoria is looking at an objet d'art on Piero's mantle, an old painting in his parent's apartment, or a statue in the park – she thoughtfully moves her head left and right, standing in for us, in the familiar gesture of trying to understand a visual work of art, as though to underline the interpretive effort that must necessarily accompany all visual representation, including the film we are watching.

When Vittoria ascends into the clouds in a small airplane with her friends, she gets a different visual, and, therefore, different psychological perspective on things – one that looks forward to the mysterious, obliterating fog in *Red Desert* – and it gives her an exalted sense of freedom unavailable to her on land. Even once she has landed, the empty expanse of the airfield contrasts brightly with the claustrophobic obsessiveness of the earlier scenes at the stock exchange. The visual gender equality of the first scene, mentioned above, is to some extent undone later, when women again, consistently, come to be visually flattened out in the manner of the earlier films. Here, however, on the airfield, the flattening seems more subtly done or perhaps mitigated by her joyful mood – or is simply less noticeable in a film that relies so heavily on an abstracting, formal line for its meaning – and the effect is, ironically, more "organic" and "natural" (as when the camera tracks smoothly backward, holding Vittoria in place as she walks) and thus less overtly self-reflexive. In addition, Antonioni's general penchant for this Manet-like flattening effect, which usually draws attention, as with Manet as well, to the "facture" or "made quality" of the work, is consistently answered in this film by the density, roundness, and overwhelming "thereness" of, say, the columns of the stock exchange, and many other objects elsewhere, which continue to evoke a certain three-dimensionality. The representational tension created by this juxtaposition of dimensions adds greatly to the visual complexity of *L'eclisse*. The risk for Antonioni, as always, is that all of these subtle, evanescent visual effects may seem only "boring" to a viewer who expects meaning to be advanced chiefly through narrative means or character.

Throughout, as part of Antonioni's exploration of visibility and vision, the characters keep looking outside, through windows, as though some form of escape, or at least some sense of greater understanding, might be possible in that direction. In the film's first scene, Vittoria opens the curtain, and we see the incredible mushroom-shaped water tower that would seem preposterous were it not completely obvious that this is a *real* water tower. (This is the water tower of the famous EUR section of Rome, part of the planned city built by Mussolini for the World's Fair, which Antonioni worked on in the late 1930s. The city was meant to evoke a mélange of ancient Roman and ultracontemporary styles, thus equating the dictator's regime with an earlier era of glory. Much of the film takes place in this area.) As such, it serves as an almost overwhelming symbol of the atomic bomb, a symbol that will come to fruition at the end of the film in an expressive burst of light. It also raises the question, discussed in chapter 2, about the appropriateness of such symbol-making. If the symbol actually exists as an object in the real world, can the director be accused of over-obviousness? Is there not always a built-in nonspecificity to all symbols that will lead the interpreter to "find" more than what the artist has "put" there? For example, Biarese and Tassone choose to interpret the immense, visually striking pillar that comes between Piero and Vittorio at the stock exchange in symbolic terms that are also dismayingly literal: "That column is not there by accident, or for its beauty, like the columns in certain Renaissance Annunciations, for example, that of Piero della Francesca: [rather] it plays a role that we might call symbolic. Between Piero and Vittoria there will always be an obstacle, the stock market."[6] It is true that the director chose to include this particular object within his film frame, and thus in some sense is responsible for it. But he cannot be held responsible – and then, in some cases, castigated – for the specific, often simplistic meanings that others claim to find there.

Another more general and farther-reaching question, one that goes beyond symbol-making, is also raised by these examples. It concerns the very nature and expression of visual meaning in film and, by extension, in any visual medium. Verbal meaning has always been privileged over visual meaning because the former has traditionally been considered more specific, and more specifiable, than the latter. It is always difficult to say *exactly* what any visual image means, and this accounts, in part at least, for much of the "free play" in the criticism of Antonioni's films, which rely so much upon visual suggestion.[7] As much recent theory has demonstrated however, the specificity of verbal language may be more apparent than real. After all, a dictionary never provides unambiguous, base meanings for words, but only more words to look up. The question that is especially relevant to Antonioni's films is this: *Is* there meaning if it cannot be verbalized? How does visual meaning happen, and how can it be described?

Consider the heavily marked traffic "zebra" lines that Vittoria crosses late in the film. (Their presence is also foregrounded in the dialogue.) With the exception of Seymour Chatman, no one, to my knowledge, has ventured a symbolic reading of them, but Antonioni clearly stresses their graphic nature.[8] If we exclude the overtly symbolic reading, then what do they *mean*? Antonioni gives explicit evidence in his screenplays that he thinks visually in this nonspecific, nonsymbolic manner. Describing the crossroads at the EUR, the screenplay says: "A pile of bricks, in the court-yard of the house under construction. The disposition of the bricks makes one think of a view of a big city, with skyscrapers and the houses piled up on top of one another" (p. 420). Elsewhere – though, as noted earlier, it is difficult to know how much one can legitimately credit the screenplay, how much *it* can be taken as a "correct" representation of the film[9] – we read: "Vittoria, who was moving away toward a dark wall, turns around: in her white outfit, she is like a luminous stain" (p. 424). There is, clearly, meaning in both these examples, important meaning, but it cannot be called symbolic. So much the better.

A related question concerns the meaning of visual repetition and rhyming, composition, and balance. How for example, would we go about establishing a meaning for the hands that so often appear as graphic, expressive elements in Antonioni's films? (In *L'eclisse*, the motif is more ambivalent: at one point, the lovers expressively match hands on opposite sides of a glass, but the quasi-erotic charge of the image is dissipated when the same motif is refigured in the hand of the drowned drunk that is sticking out of Piero's sports car as it is hoisted to the surface of the lake.) A more properly speaking "cinematic" rhyming is established in the shot, mentioned earlier, of the camera following Vittoria as she approaches Riccardo in the opening scene. We see her head, but only as a semicircle at the bottom of the frame. A reverse shot then shows his head – now the form is dark instead of blonde – in exactly the same position at the bottom of the frame. Is an equation being made between them? As moral beings? Psychologically? Or is this merely an aesthetic, visual, or emotional link without any specific thematic or narrative meaning beyond that? The same question arises about the many shots that are intricately, self-consciously balanced and composed: is thematic meaning intended, or is the meaning, vague and unspecific as it is, resident in the graphic nature of the composition itself, and thus inexpressible in words?

The same purposeful ambiguity, and the same questions about meaning, exist on the aural level. One example is the continual breeze that moves through the trees in *L'eclisse* and in other Antonioni films. Working on both an aural and a visual level, its haunting effect is clearly foregrounded, and the narrative sometimes completely stops to consider it – but what does it *mean*?[10] On one level, it seems to have a kind of formal meaning, especially insofar as this steady nonhuman noise (like the fan in the first scene) contrasts hauntingly with the silences of the dialogue, serving to point them up even further. On a more specific motivic level, the continual slight breeze that blows through Vittoria's hair, for example, as well as through the trees, reappears again when Piero's papers are being blown around his office by the "same" breeze. Here, the meaning may be slightly more definite: the sense, perhaps, is of the interconnectedness of objects, inanimate forces of nature, and humans in ways that go beyond precise specification.

Another example is the sound that the guywires make as they slap against the flagpole when Vittoria is out looking for Marta's dog. They seem to call to her in some mysterious way that neither she nor we can quite grasp. It is as though both the trees and the guywires, articulated both visually and aurally, represent the facticity and sensual presentness of a world that is addressing her in an unknown, primordial language, a presence (and thus a romantic fantasy on the director's part?) that exists prior to the social and cultural level of human affairs, which is, in these films, so manifestly lacking in force and spirit.

It is difficult to constitute more precise meanings for these moments and, when it is possible, or rather, seems so, the result is almost always reductive. It may simply be better to see these images, both visual and aural, as creating a nonspecific emotional field that accompanies, or enhances, more specifically thematic levels suggested through the conventional means of dialogue, character, and story. The contemporary filmmaker who most resembles Antonioni in this regard is the late Polish director Krzysztof Kieslowski who, like his Italian counterpart, was adored by some for his subtle emotional nuances and derided by others for being "boring." In film after film – such as *The Double Life of Veronique* and the *Three Colors* trilogy based on the French flag (*Blue, White,* and *Red*) – Kieslowski sought to create a generalized expressive texture that seemed to transcend (or to come "before") specific thematic meaning. In fact, as in Antonioni's films, the theme of his films can sometimes precisely be this affectivity itself, articulated simply for its own sake.

Antonioni's social-political critique in *L'eclisse* is equally complex and ambiguous. An important site of this commentary once again is the problematic of love and marriage in bourgeois society and, more generally, the complicated relationships between the sexes. Like Anna in *L'avventura*, Vittoria is *expected* to want to marry, and her only response, an unacceptable (for this society) and frustrating one, just as in the earlier film, is "Non lo so" (I don't know). Typically, in the opening scene Riccardo wants "un motivo," a specific, logical *reason* to explain why she is leaving him, and that is just what she does not have. Piero, wonderfully portrayed by the perhaps too-handsome Alain Delon, is totally devoted to sensation, but, like the men in *L'avventura* and *La notte*, seems to have little talent for real feeling. His constant, deliberate movement (directly thematized in the dialogue) is also contrasted with Vittoria's dreamy wandering, as, for example, when she is at her happiest, at the airfield. He does things boldly, quickly, adroitly (but without thought for consequences, moral or otherwise), much like the photographer in *Blow-up*. This is, apparently, a "male" way of being in the world that is implicitly contrasted with Vittoria's more thoughtful way, and, as always, condemned by the director (though, at least by the time of the later film, increasingly envied as well). Riccardo returns later in the film, only to create some gratuitous violence. Even Riccardo's unnamed *friend* – as soon as Vittoria casually tells him that she has broken up with Riccardo – propositions her on the telephone. Once again, then, Antonioni's men leave something to be desired.

But it is difficult to know exactly how to read Vittoria's (and Anna's) reluctance to marry. Is it a function of the general anomie of the Waste Land that is contemporary Italian society in Antonioni's eyes? (Near the end of *L'eclisse*, the screenplay tells us that even though Vittoria "desires" Piero, she is "incapable of doing anything to communicate this to him" [p. 426].) Piero and Vittoria, in fact, do not really seem all that interested in each other, except in some vague, unconvincing sexual way. Significantly, Vittoria tells him at one point, in language reminiscent of Lidia's in *La notte*, "Vorrei non amarti o amarti molto meglio" (I'd like to love you not at all or love you much better). On the other hand, it may be that Vittoria is reluctant to marry for very specific, if unspoken proto-feminist

Figure 9. The Milan stock exchange: Piero (Alain Delon) in his element

reasons. Does she regard the marital institution, at some level, as a trap for women, even if this objection must remain unarticulated in 1961?

It should also be noted that Vittoria is perhaps much more specifically neurotic than the two earlier heroines (thus looking forward to the full-blown, crippling neurosis of Giuliana in *Red Desert*, Antonioni's next film). The film in fact offers tentative explanations for a presumed neurosis in her mother's neglect and the fact of her father's early death, but, despite the textual evidence, Antonioni has disagreed strongly with this view of Vittoria. When Jean-Luc Godard expressed it to him in an early interview, Antonioni abruptly replied: "Vittoria, the character in *The Eclipse*, is the opposite of Giuliana. She's a calm, well-balanced girl who thinks about what she is doing. There is absolutely no symptom of neurosis in her. In *The Eclipse*, the crisis has to do with emotions."[11]

The sexual and emotional aridity of the highly stylized scene in Riccardo's apartment that opens the film leads naturally to the shouting and brutality of the stock exchange, a conscious rhythmic shift that also implies an equivalency (through total opposition), or perhaps even a cause–effect relationship. Sex (in its sublimated form) is at the Borsa as well. At the

81

beginning of this scene, for example, one broker shows another a photograph of a woman in a bikini and makes sexual puns that equate buying and selling on the stock market with buying and selling the woman (p. 369).[12] Later, when the stock market collapses, the frenetic intensity of the moment has unmistakable overtones of (displaced) sexual intercourse.

The target of Antonioni's social criticism is obvious here, especially during the sequence that includes the moment of silence for a deceased colleague – after which the intense hubbub starts again as if nothing has happened – a sequence that would be laughable if it were not so depressing.[13] After making the general social point, the director proceeds to demonstrate the extent to which such greed and such misplaced values affect personal relations. Vittoria's mother, like so many other good middle-class Italians at the peak of the economic boom of the early 1960s, is out to make a fortune through the stock market, the classic bourgeois instrument of wealth, and she pays little attention to her confused daughter. When the stock market does fall, Vittoria's mother blames "the socialists, who ruin everything" (p. 397), and later the "center-left" government (p. 400). Tinazzi regards the precariousness of "il boom" at this moment of the integration of the petty bourgeoisie into the Italian "economic mechanism" as the precise historical locus of the film.[14]

There is another more pointed sociopolitical commentary that is perhaps more clearly expressed in the screenplay than in the actual film. When Piero and Vittoria enter her mother's apartment, they see a series of photographs of a young married couple on her nightstand. The screenplay states: "There is in these photographs the love story of poor people. A sordid village can be seen. And, in front of the door of a shack, Vittoria's mother when she was young" (p. 404). The mother is so emotionally wrapped up in the stock market, obviously, because her present good fortune is a slippery product of the economic boom. Picking up the photograph, Vittoria tells Piero, "This is what scares my mother, poverty" (p. 405).

The audience's relationship with Piero is emotionally complicated and seems purposely full of contradictions: he is handsome and inevitably, in the code of cinema, to some extent the focus of the film simply by virtue of his maleness. But his utterly mercenary values and his lack of interest in his fellow human beings make him unpalatable at the same time. For one thing, he worries more about the loss of his car than he does about the drunk who was killed while stealing it. Piero is also nasty, in a particularly arbitrary way, to the girlfriend that he is no longer interested in now that he is thinking about Vittoria. Later, Piero (and the camera) are vulgarly fascinated with Vittoria's breasts, continuing Antonioni's critique of the small-minded, obsessive lust of his male characters. At another moment, Vittoria finds a childish pen of Piero's that shows a naked woman when tipped upside down. Antonioni is playing an interesting, risky game here with the viewer's attraction/repulsion to this central character, so obviously a product of the times.

On a completely different level, the one other moment of obvious social commentary concerns what might be called the "atomic bomb" motif, which is clearly suggested by the mushroom-shaped water tower that appears throughout the film, as well as by the newspaper headlines ("The Atomic Arms Race" and "The Peace Is Weak") and flash of light at the end (which is actually from a streetlight, but which seems meant to visually suggest an atomic blast). But one cannot imagine the director seriously offering the bomb as either an explanation or a result of the characters' anomie and superficial values. Rather, in line with the earlier films of the trilogy, it seems to represent one more scientific, modern assault on all-too-ancient, unreconstructed human sensibilities. In any case, seen in its proper historical light, this motif reminds us just how powerfully the threat of nuclear holocaust weighed upon the 1950's and 1960's psyche, and to what extent the bomb became a general signifier for the nameless dread that had been so vividly described by existentialists of the postwar period, as well as by their numerous popularizers.

Modern life has also become increasingly abstract, and the stock market, which reflects perceptions rather than realities, is a perfect symbol for the abstraction that money has always represented. Significantly, Vittoria asks Piero, after the stock market crash, just where all the money *goes* when something like this happens, and he is unable to answer. As in the earlier films, the historical past is held up as a hopelessly remote or irrelevant alternative. An old church, for example, is glimpsed through a window of the stock exchange, a common enough device in Antonioni, which can be seen in the complex layering of Tommaso's hospital room at the beginning of *La notte*. In another scene, an old church that Vittoria catches sight of through a window in the apartment of Piero's parents seems utterly beside the point in the modern world (at least as described in the screenplay):

In front of the house, the street widens to give place to a huge church. All around, houses piled up on one another, with so many empty windows. All of it a world that is still and tired, as if waiting to die. Also the baroqueness of the church, also the group of people who are exiting the afternoon mass. Also the soldier who is eating an ice cream cone while leaning against the wall. (p. 426)

Throughout the film, Vittoria passes various statues and acknowledges their presence, as well as their pastness, but when Piero is asked who painted the picture in his parents' apartment, he does not have the slightest idea, nor does he seem to have any connection with or interest in the photographs of his ancestors. At another point, Vittoria decides to hang up a fossil that is made much of in the screenplay,[15] and still later, after Piero has torn her dress, its whiteness and simplicity make it resemble the drapery found on Greek statuary, especially after she throws her necklace on the bed. In all these ways, the past is continually quoted but remains always inaccessible.

A more ambiguous alternative to the emptiness of modern urban life is a motif that continues from *La notte*, that of Africanness or blackness in general. Whatever is "African" is exotic, as it was in the earlier film's nightclub scene, and seems to offer the promise of escape into a true sensuality, if only in the imagination. When the three girlfriends get together in Marta's apartment to bang drums, dress up in native costumes, and dance wildly, Vittoria seems more genuinely alive than at any other moment in the film. (In the screenplay, the photograph of an African landscape that Vittoria looks at attentively is described as giving "a sense of grandness, liberty, and nobility" [p. 378].)[16] In the next scene, Vittoria reflects: "Maybe over there [in Africa] they think less about happiness, and things just move forward on their own. . . . Here, instead, everything seems like a lot of work. Love too" (p. 381). Later, when she stops in a cafe at the airfield, during one of her happiest moments, we see some young black Africans sitting out in front of the cafe, a gentle reminder of the African motif. "Si sta così bene qui," she says simply, "it's so nice here." Again, the Africans in this scene do not have a specific *symbolic* meaning but are related metonymically to her happiness and thus provide a subtle, visual rhyme to the earlier joyous scene in Marta's apartment.

But there is also another side to the exoticism of Africa, as Antonioni knows too well, even though the subject was rarely broached in the early 1960s. Thus the grotesque elephant feet on the living room table provide a jarring note in this vision of Africa as paradisal Other and seem to indicate that, at least in the context of colonialism (of which the viewer is subtly reminded through Marta's English accent in Italian and frequent use of English words), Africa is not a possible solution to the problem of their lives, either. For reasons that are not entirely clear, Marta is suddenly angered by their foolery and says that that's enough of "playing the black." A bit later, another of her outbursts gives evidence of the fear of the reality that lies behind the exotic alternative:

Figure 10. Vittoria (Monica Vitti) and the exoticism of Africa

MARTA: There are 60,000 whites, do you understand? And 6 million
blacks who want to throw them out. Luckily, the blacks are still up
in trees and have only recently lost their tails, otherwise they would
have already thrown us out. (p. 379)

She continues: "All I'm saying is that if there are ten chiefs who've studied
at Oxford, all the others are apes. Six million apes. . . . Look at the Congo!
After finishing primary school, they all think they're ready to be ministers"
(p. 380). By putting such racist logic in Marta's mouth, Antonioni's condemnation of colonialism seems clear here, and his distinction between
Africa as fantasy symbol for bored first-worlders and Africa as political
reality is surprisingly prescient for 1961. (Thirteen years later, Africa will
reemerge in a political light in *The Passenger*.)

Many of the foregoing visual and sociopolitical motifs reappear during the
justly famous ending of the film, though with a great deal less specificity.
Vittoria and Piero frolic on his sofa, their inscrutable moods quickly changing yet once again. As in crucial moments of earlier scenes in the trilogy,

85

Figure 11. The last gasp of love: Piero and Vittoria

their heads are shown in strange foreground shots, followed by nearly startling reverse cuts from the front of a head to the back, a rhetorical visual
figure that foreshadows the larger emotional reversal to come. Smiling,
Vittoria hugs Piero at the door in a way that seems calculated to convince
herself perhaps more than him, as they repeat the banality of their promise
to "see each other day after day." "We'll see each other tonight at eight at
the usual spot," they say, though they seem strangely nervous and fearful
at the same time.[17]

  She telephones him later, but does not reveal her identity. We then cut
to the building site that will reappear several more times in the final se-

quence, as the covering straw mats on the building under construction are moved by a breeze, thus echoing the wind through the trees, to the accompaniment of slight piano accents, as at the end of *L'avventura*. In a matched cut of Vittoria and the evocative trees, she is quietly but devastatingly erased from the narrative.

What then begins is the magnificent series of shots (which Chatman has described as a kind of "disestablishing shot")[18] motivated presumably by the lovers' unkept promise to meet each other in the "usual place" that evening. These shots bring the film to a brilliant emotional and aesthetic close that is accomplished almost solely by formal and abstract means. The main characters have been completely removed, the dialogue is spent, and explicit narrative has disappeared. Evocative traces of the narrative do remain, however, especially many of the aleatory characters who were in the background or in minor "events" that occurred when the main characters were present; for example, the man passing in the horse and cart, the bus arriving, the nurse with the baby carriage. It is as though what we are now seeing was constituted by the "remainder" or inherent excess of the previously coded narrative. Most important, the light fades throughout the sequence, implying that most basic narrative of all, the movement of time, as the music builds to a grand, almost traumatic climax. In other words, there remains, as always, temporality and duration.

What might be called the "human track" is completely evacuated in the final minutes, to be replaced by nondiegetic music, the mark of the filmmaker's presence (because nothing in the story proper motivates its existence). Here, at the end, the music also signals a complete abandonment of the "natural" and the triumph of the "made." What follows represents the zenith of the graphic insistence traced throughout this book. In the earlier films, the characters are expressive graphic integers as well as representations of human beings. Now they are completely gone. But the moral and ethical realm that attends human relations does not disappear as a result, and it feels curiously stronger in the absence of the human characters. It is as though Antonioni needs character and incident to involve us on an emotional level, but his artistic and moral resolution, in this film at least, can ultimately come only in formal and abstract terms.

Obviously, these are not merely random shots and must not be thought of in that way. Antonioni achieves formal unity of the visuals and the sound here, but once again, the precise meaning, of necessity, remains vague. Some critics find the end of the film "arid," but Tinazzi is closer to the truth when he suggests that the finale can be read as a display of the intense mystery of reality. "It shows the loss of the sign, its crisis in terms of its reference to something other. For this reason I would be very careful about attributing symbolic meanings – which might seem very obvious – to such perceptible fragments."[19]

Things refuse to represent or to point to an elsewhere, to a something, or a meaning, beyond themselves. This now apparently humanless terrain also attests to the power of the sheer facticity of objects in the world – which we saw earlier in the wind in the trees and the singing guywires on the flagpole – a truth that reminds one of the phenomenological insistence that Being is always being *in the world*. Antonioni has himself said: "I love objects, I love them like I love women; I believe that we have feelings toward objects; it's yet one more way of grabbing onto life."[20]

The water sprinkler and the construction materials are down lying about in shot after shot, as the camera revisits all the places in which Vittoria has appeared throughout the film. Nearly every cut is accompanied by a light musical accent, and a piano is heard throughout. As we subconsciously (and fruitlessly) wait for the characters to reappear in order to focus things for us, we are also inevitably confronted with the complex relation of character to narrative. Meaning and emotion, nevertheless, continue to cling to place in the absence of their human agents; the human has somehow leached into the nonhuman, thereby giving it human meaning as well. This meaning comes about both through formal relations of metonymy (the fact that we remember Vittoria and Piero near this or that object, in this or that place) and through the abstract, graphic nature of the shapes and forms of what we see. According to Chatman, however, Antonioni has completely foreclosed the reading of the ending as "abstract":

> Some talked . . . about Antonioni's excursion into "abstract art." However, he denied that intention point-blank: "The seven minutes have been called abstract, but this is not really so. All of the objects that I show have significance. These are seven minutes where only the objects remain of the adventure; the town, material life, has devoured the living beings."[21]

When the director says that the objects have "significance," he means this, presumably, in narrative terms. Yet narrative significance seems in no way to preclude other, more abstract emotional and intellectual meaning.

The question raised earlier in regard to the nature of what one might call literary symbolism arises here again, especially in conjunction with matters such as the apparent atomic bomb explosion at the very end or the seemingly obvious motif of water, particularly after the water is suddenly turned off. Is this simply to be condemned as heavy-handed symbolism, or is there a way to recuperate this area of meaning that makes it correspond with the purposeful imprecision of so much of the rest of the film? Geoffrey Nowell-Smith has pointed to this very image as an example of Antonioni's "horror of obvious symbolic correspondences":

> Speculating here, I should also say that if it had been pointed out to him that the shots of the emptying water butt and the water running to drain in the final sequence of the same film would be taken conceptually as a straightforward symbol of Vittoria and Piero's affair running out, then he would probably have cut them out or altered them so as to minimise, if not eliminate, the association.[22]

Such associations, by diminishing or even eliminating the powerful facticity of these objects in favor of a secondary role as merely signs or symbols of something else, would massively reduce the power of this formidable final sequence.

This question of facticity versus representation (of something that is by definition not there) is related to an ongoing interplay of absence and presence that characterizes many of Antonioni's films, one that we will continue to consider. Pascal Bonitzer's suggestive description of this relationship, seems particularly appropriate in the context of *L'eclisse*:

> Since cinema, like the unconscious, does not know negation, emptiness in Antonioni exists positively; it is haunted by presence. There is no more beautiful moment in an Antonioni film (and each seems structured to reach this end) than that in which his characters, his human beings, are cancelled, only so as to leave behind, it seems, a space without attributes, a pure space. . . . Empty space is not a void: full of mists, of fleeting faces, of evanescent presences or of random movements, this space represents that final point of being finally freed from the negativity of intentions, of passions, of human existence.[23]

4

Red Desert (1964)

JEAN-LUC GODARD (apropos of *Red Desert*): So the drama is not just
  psychological, but also plastic.
ANTONIONI: Well, it's the same thing.
  – "The Night, the Eclipse, the Dawn"

Red Desert, though it is often appended to the "trilogy" that preceded it
(perhaps because it once again stars Monica Vitti and seems to deal with
alienation), in fact represents an important turning point in Antonioni's
work, one that the director himself clearly recognized. Speaking to Godard
in a celebrated interview conducted in 1964, Antonioni said: "This time, I
haven't made a film about feelings. The results that I had obtained from
my previous films – good or bad as they may be – have by now become
obsolete. The focus is on something completely different" (p. 287; translation modified). He continued: "At one time, I was interested in the relationships of characters to one another. Now, instead, the main character must
confront her social environment, and that's why I treat the story in a completely different way" (p. 287).

Red Desert was to be the last film in which a woman appears as the
central protagonist, and it was to be Antonioni's last Italian film, strictly
speaking, as well. Many critics have in addition detected in this film a major
shift in the director's approach to central epistemological and moral questions such as the nature of vision and our relation to reality. Even its quality
has been hotly contested; Mario Soldati, a well-known Italian director of
the time who was a member of the Venice festival jury that awarded *Red
Desert* the Golden Lion in 1965, summed up the ambivalence: "It's Antonioni's best film, but also his most defective."[1]

What is obviously different about this film is its most immediate, most obvious form: the glorious, inescapable fact of *Red Desert* is color. It announces itself everywhere, from the title to the end of the film; it engulfs the frame and the characters, restricting, commenting, blocking, enhancing. In the formulation of French critic and theorist Marie-Claire Ropars-Wuilleumier, the shot of the street lamp, the final shot of Antonioni's previous film, *L'eclisse*, "invaded the screen and returned it to being a white surface. The only thing that was missing to complete this canvas was color: it's a painter's space that appears in *Red Desert*."[2]

Antonioni's space has always been that of a painter, a graphic artist "painting" in black and white; now, however, to the formal austerity of composition, shape, and line Antonioni adds the fulfillment of color. And though the abstract linear beauty and signification of the monochromatic shapes and forms are still there – as, for example, when Giuliana wanders diagonally down an empty, expressive street (a shot that strongly recalls the long hallway Claudia slowly traverses near the end of *L'avventura*) – such forms are even more emphatic when embodied in vibrant blues, reds, and yellows.[3] But color is not a fulfillment in the sense that it leads inevitably, in a necessary, natural progression, toward greater *realism*, as some realist theorists, such as André Bazin and V. F. Perkins, have suggested. Rather, color here becomes a kind of apotheosis of formalist *abstraction*, part of Antonioni's antirealist campaign – despite the fact that color supposedly makes a film look more like the world does – thus ironically enhancing the expressivity of line, shape, and form, and thus inevitably diminishing the importance of narrative and character-driven drama. This is especially the case since Antonioni has stressed the artificiality of his use of color. He told an interviewer:

> In *Red Desert*, I had to change the very face of reality, the color of the water, the roads, the landscapes, I had to paint them, literally. It wasn't easy. As long as you're in the studio, it's easy, but when you're shooting outdoors, violating reality becomes a serious problem. All it takes is a white frost to ruin everything. I painted an entire woods gray to make it look the color of cement, and it rained and all the color got washed away. Three days and three nights of work down the drain.

Looking forward to later experiments with television in *The Mystery of Oberwald*, the director continued: "With television, you can do all that electronically, and so it becomes like painting a film, there's a great deal of freedom."[4]

It is true that Antonioni distinguishes between "cool colors" and "warm colors" and later expatiates on the intense fact of *red*, which seems to transcend all other colors in this film in its meaning-bearing capacity.[5] (Thus, in the interview with Godard, he says that he would not have included the scene in the shack in which Corrado, Giuliana, and her husband disport with their friends if he had been shooting in black and white because the color red was necessary for the spectator to be able to "accept the dialogue" in that scene [p. 295; translation modified].) In general, though, it seems useless to attribute *specific* symbolic meanings to specific colors as they appear throughout the film, as many critics of Antonioni have been unable to keep themselves from doing.[6] It seems much more profitable to think of these colors in a suggestive, vaguely emotional way, as an enhancement of the graphic element, rather than as deliberately schematic, preordained to suggest detailed concepts or themes.[7]

Accompanying and enriching this new emphasis on color is a new emphasis (new both to Antonioni and to cinema history) on camera focus as a signifying element. Even in the credits, the industrial scenes that form the background are completely out of focus, as the words that make up the credits pop up on the screen in sharp outline, suggesting from the first few seconds of the film the profound crisis in vision that Antonioni is here exploring. (The director was to employ out-of-focus images under the credits once again in *Zabriskie Point* [1969].) Another early shot shows the workers passing by like automatons, out of focus. It is almost as though Antonioni were playing with us here, because when the visual relief for our impatience with the out-of-focusness does come, in the person of Giuliana (a rhythm of unfocus/focus that has already been clearly established by the credits), she ironically has her back toward us.[8]

Throughout the film, a scene will begin out of focus – then a head, upper body, or even, in one case, a foot – will suddenly move into the frame in focus, organizing the space, making sudden visual sense of things for the viewer. In the scene in Giuliana's shop, the out-of-focus colors give the image a Rothko-like intensity that puts Antonioni's abstract signifying on another level entirely, where blocks and fields of color have their own expressive signification that escapes mere words. But the main effect of this creative use of focus is to foreground the viewer's powerful hermeneutic desire to make coherent meaning out of a confused visual field.

The emphasis on color and focus is also abetted by stylization in the cinematography and the editing and a new foregrounding of the object. In the early part of the film, in particular, Antonioni does not hesitate to violate the standards of conventional "good" filmmaking by cutting suddenly from a fairly tight two-shot of people talking to an extreme long shot

Figure 12. Giuliana (Monica Vitti) lost among the accouterments of the modern, technological world of *Red Desert*

of some brightly colored industrial forms, themselves expressive, which dwarf the human inhabitants.[9] One effect of this technique is that the ontological reality of objects (or, viewed another way, the epistemological relationship we have with them) becomes even more important in this film than in the earlier ones. As Antonioni told an interviewer: "Up until *L'Eclisse*, I was only interested in the clash of individuals. . . . With *Red Desert*, I wanted to move to a new stage. The object now enters the field, not as an accessory, but as a character."[10]

Similarly, the huge blast of steam that engulfs the characters when Corrado is being taken on a tour of the facility (and that looks forward to the famous fog scene later in the film) occupies the screen for an abnormally long time and through a whole series of cuts in which merely the angle is changed, again in "violation" of conventional cinematic form. The effect is both expressive and self-reflexive, as the audience is overwhelmingly made aware of the director's presence when the rules are thus broken. Likewise, when the camera neglects the human characters in order to linger on mechanical and structural surroundings for their own sake, we are being told that these are the true frame (aesthetic, psychological, narrative, sociopolitical, as well as physical) for what we will see – in the same manner as the interpretive clues provided at the beginning of *L'avventura* and *L'eclisse*. Lest we miss the point, in *Red Desert* the big black shapes of various abstract paintings are most improbably placed right in the turbine room of the factory. Giuliana's Rothko-like patterns in her shop continue this effort of teaching us how to look.

Even an ostensibly nonexpressive, nonmeaningful "real" object comes to signify abstractly when, fairly early in the film, the camera focuses on what at first appears to be another abstract painting but that is seen to be a wall, when the camera pulls back to reveal Corrado getting out of his car in front of Giuliana's shop. Sam Rohdie has described the dynamic component of the abstract meaning produced here: "The white patch of the roof of the car changes the compositional structure of the image and alters the tonal relations in the wall colours. The 'appearance' of a narrative figure, Corrado and his car, does not erase the plastic 'subject' of the wall, its colour, the shift in composition; indeed, it helps to form it."[11]

Rohdie's further remarks illuminate a crucial aspect of Antonioni's art:

The representational codes of the cinema tend to privilege volume over surface, the figure over the image. Narrative devices are important in this balance [if, for example, the wall had had *narrative* significance it would have been recognized sooner by the audience as a wall] . . . , [but in this sequence] figuration is itself suspended, the entire volume and depth in which things take place in narratives seems momentarily absent and in its place appears the "emptiness" of a surface image, unmoored, unidentifiable, narratively blank, a kind of eclipse of narrative into abstraction.

The wall materialises out of nothing both narratively and visually, but when it does its other status as image remains: while one part of the pressure of the scene is towards the construction of "facts," of "incidents," of lending support to character and action, and sustaining these (a chain of events: Corrado parks his Alfa on a street outside Giuliana's shop, they meet, they talk), another part of the scene moves toward dissolution, nothingness, an abandonment of character, a dead time without action: a discoloured surface; movement along the wall which changes its light intensity, alters volume and density; character becomes only an object figured in a landscape, like the momentarily immobile Corrado and Giuliana beside the fruitseller. Here the narrative is suspended not by the removal of character or figure, but by freeing them from any narrative function and equalising them with the landscape.[12]

94

Even the length of the shots seems to be involved in the process of abstraction. Antonioni explained that in his earlier films he had relied on long takes but only understood why much later. "For *Red Desert*, on the other hand, I chose very short takes. Perhaps it was the fact that I was using color that suggested this technique to me, this deep-seated need to deal with it in large blotches, as if they were pulsations that penetrate chaotically inside the characters."[13]

This movement toward abstraction carries with it, perhaps inevitably, a corresponding antirealist impulse. When Godard questioned Antonioni about his use of unfocused shots for abstract purposes, the latter replied: "I feel the need to express reality in terms that are not completely realistic. The white abstract line that breaks into the shot of the little gray road interests me much more than the car which is coming toward us" (p. 293). This strategy affects even the choice of lens: "I often used a telephoto lens to avoid depth-of-field, which is of course an essential element in realism. What interests me now is to put the characters in contact with things, because today what counts are things, objects, matter" (p. 294; translation modified).

But the film's expressive use of color and out-of-focus shots carries with it a deeper problematic and leads one to ask what might be called the "Caligari question": Whose point of view is being expressed here? As with the masterful silent German film, *The Cabinet of Dr. Caligari* (1919), whose wildly expressionistic sets could be attributed to the mind of the insane protagonist or to the film itself, so, too, in *Red Desert*, one wonders if the out-of-focusness and the (often clashing) colors are to be read as a projection of the neurotic, even suicidal mind of Giuliana, or whether they spring from a third-person point of view (the director's or the "film's") on the industrial wasteland? Or something in between?

Most critics have regarded the fable of the mysterious, sundrenched natural island as a direct expression of Giuliana's point of view, since it is a fantasy that she narrates herself and one that she deliberately contrasts with the actual life she is currently living. According to the director, this was, in fact, the only location that was not manipulated, but rather was left in its "natural colors." "In that sequence," Antonioni claims, "the plot is suspended, as if the eye and the consciousness of the narrator [presumably, the narrator of the film] had been distracted elsewhere. In fact, that sequence, in which each element – and first of all, color – tells a fragment of human experience, shows reality as Giuliana wishes it were – that is, different from the world that appears to her as transformed, alienated, obsessive to the point of being monstrously deformed."[14]

One wonders, though, if it is possible for the consciousness of the film's unseen narrator to be completely "absent," or whether a film can ever pass along a character's viewpoint in an unmediated fashion. This question is important, for in some sense it is merely a variant of a similar question that we have been asking throughout this study: Where is Antonioni in these films? In other words, to what extent is it legitimate, or productive, to interpret the film in terms of authorial intentionality? The situation is particularly acute for *Red Desert*, because the placement of the author is even less clear than usual. On the one hand, much of his harsh, alienating imagery (both visual and aural) leads inescapably to the conclusion that Antonioni is denouncing the contemporary industrial wasteland, or at least, this particular manifestation of it. On the other hand, as already mentioned, the director has repeatedly said that he is not *condemning* anything, but merely describing the huge, perhaps tragic gap between the modern industrialized world and atavistic human emotion so out of place within it. As he pointed out to Godard in a crucial statement,

> It's too simplistic to say – as many people have done – that I am condemning the inhuman industrialized world which oppresses the individuals and leads them to neurosis. My intention . . . was to translate the poetry of that world, in which even factories can be beautiful. The lines and the curves of factories and their chimneys can be more beautiful than the outline of trees, which we are already too accustomed to seeing. It is a rich world, alive and serviceable. (pp. 287–8)

The director went on to say that it is largely a question of adaptation to this new world – some do it quickly, whereas others are still too linked to the "structures, or the rhythms of life that are now old-fashioned. . . . I think that if we learn how to adapt ourselves to the new techniques of life, perhaps then we will find new solutions to our problems" (pp. 288, 290; translation modified).

Talking to another interviewer, Antonioni expanded on these notions in even stronger terms that move sharply away from standard interpretations of the film:

> I'm not saying that we have to return to nature, that industrialization is harmful. Actually, I even find it very beautiful that man masters matter. For me, these pipes and girders are as moving as trees. Of course, it's maddening to think that the birds that pass through this smoke die on the spot, and that the gas prevents anything from growing for kilometers, but each era has demanded sacrifices upon which

other things were built. There's no evolution without crisis. . . . When I saw this landscape, I wanted to find out how the people who resided there lived. It was so violent that it had to have changed their morals, their feelings, their psychology. These people are without doubt the most advanced human beings in these areas. Their reactions will perhaps be ours if no accommodation occurs.[15]

This entire oppositional dynamic is perhaps most tightly encapsulated in the film's title, which, Antonioni suggested, might be read in the following manner: " 'Desert' maybe because there aren't very many oases left, 'red' because of blood. The bleeding, living desert, full of the flesh of men."[16]

But the violence of such imagery also clearly casts doubt on Antonioni's claim to refuse to judge. Likewise, his talk elsewhere of the old Ravenna (which was the site of the Byzantine empire on the Italian peninsula and which remains full of precious sixth-century mosaics) is imbued with nostalgia, and the present-day landscape that surrounds the characters is clearly horrific, in a more direct and uncompromising – one might even say, unsubtle – way than in any of his previous films. As he explained to Godard, "I wanted the grass around the hut to be colored in order to accentuate the sense of desolation, of death. I also wanted to capture a certain truth of the landscape: dead trees really are that color" (p. 296; translation modified). The sickly hues of the ubiquitous garbage, in turn, clash with the bright primary colors found in the factory, which themselves remain ambiguous: Are they vibrant or ghastly? Elsewhere, Antonioni links color, industrialization, and his ongoing engagement with *objects* in a complicated way:

In *Red Desert*, we are in an industrial world which every day produces millions of objects of all types, all in color. Just one of these objects is sufficient – and who can do without them? – to introduce into the house an echo of industrial living. Thus, our houses are full of color, and our streets and public places are full of colorful posters.[17]

It is unclear whether this invasion of color suggests the promise of a bright future, enhanced by technology, as color does, say, in the paintings of Roy Lichtenstein, or whether it demonstrates just how far from a nurturing, organic nature we have come. Is it a sign of life or a sign of death? Abstractly beautiful and humanly alienating at the same time, it seems to be both.[18]

This ambiguity is also found on the aural level, for the sound track's strange electronic music – both hauntingly lovely and gratingly inhuman – seems to go beyond merely signifying the technological, toward signifying neurosis itself. As such, it seems located, like the visual imagery, somewhere between the consciousness of the character and that of the director or film. The early scenes are accompanied by a constant pounding noise that is intrusive and threatening; the noise is so loud that often the audience can scarcely hear the spoken dialogue. When a powerful blast of steam is emitted, Corrado holds his ears momentarily in a vain self-protective measure, and Giuliana cringes. The noise is in fact incredibly brutalizing throughout the film and massively exceeds even the jangling telephones and stock market hubhub of *L'eclisse*. Antonioni explained that "the electronic music, a sort of transfiguration of real noises – especially in the first part of the film, the part about the factories – finds a counterpart in the sounds that Giuliana hears. It was the only musical score that seemed suited to those images."[19] This comment preserves the ambiguity of point of view, of the emotional *source*, as it were (Giuliana the character or Antonioni the director), of the music.

Another ambiguous element in the film concerns the problem of symbolic force or obviousness already present in the earlier films. Early on, when Giuliana goes into her son's bedroom to check on him, we see his toy robot, automaton-like, repeatedly smashing into the wall, an apparently obvious symbol for the mechanistic and industrial alienation that Antonioni is exploring here. Appropriately, neither Giuliana's head nor upper body can be seen throughout this entire sequence – an alienating gesture in its own right – and, at the end, when the door has been closed and the room is returned to darkness, the only thing that can be seen is the glow of the robot's electric eyes. Again, if looked at solely from the perspective of today, this symbol seems painfully obvious; historicized, though, back to the original audience watching the film in 1964, the robot may have been considered a strikingly innovative and appropriate symbol to express the fears of human standardization that filled the discourse of popular culture at the time, both in Italy and elsewhere. (But if the robot *is* a symbol, can we be so sure what it is a symbol of? Once again, Antonioni turns the tables on normal expectations, claiming in the Godard interview that the presence of the robot in the boy's room is actually quite beneficial, "because if he gets used to that sort of toy, he will prepare himself for the type of life that is awaiting him. . . . [S]uch a child would have no problem going into space on a rocket, if he wanted to" [pp. 209, 291].)

More frequently, something that might be read as "symbolic" – as when

Figure 13. The scene in the shack: Max (Aldo Grotti) and Giuliana

a newspaper drifts down on Giuliana and Corrado early in the film – is perhaps better read as an example of visual, graphic expressiveness. Giuliana points out that it is today's paper, but one would be hard pressed to find specific thematic meaning here; the "meaning," such as it is, seems to reside in the way that the paper floats down to the ground, from its completely unknown source, and skitters along the street. Similarly, the film abounds in prisonlike imagery, with characters frequently peering through bars, grillwork, and the like, but pat symbolic interpretations from Film Appreciation 101 seem useless here.

Aside from the formal developments that this film represents, new departures have been made in the person of the central female character. These changes point, among other things, to the coming exhaustion of interest in this figure, as Antonioni shifts definitively to male protagonists in subsequent films. *Red Desert* is unique because its putative "hero," Corrado, is a transitional figure, a feminized male, who occupies a space somewhere between the female protagonists embodied by Monica Vitti and others in previous films and the central male figures of *Blow-up, The Passenger, Identification of a Woman,* and *Beyond the Clouds.*

For the first time, Antonioni is dealing with a decidedly unbalanced female lead, one that makes the idiosyncracies of Vittoria in *L'eclisse* seem positively benign in comparison. But given the fact that another female character – the wife of the worker whom Corrado tries to lure to his new enterprise in South America – is also highly nervous, the film seems to suggest a universal model of "hysterical" woman that all women are or have the potential of becoming. What remains unclear is Giuliana's relation to the female protagonists of the trilogy, especially in light of her suicidal tendencies. Is she a woman of a completely different order, or does she differ from Antonioni's earlier female characters merely in degree of personal alienation?

Certainly, the men of *Red Desert* are just as brutishly portrayed as those in the earlier films. At two key moments of Giuliana's greatest psychological distress, both her husband and Corrado think that what she really needs is sex. These encounters are painful to watch, as intergender understanding seems here to be at a nadir.[20] There is also the unpleasant, decadent sexuality of the scene in the shack, in which several couples, plus Corrado, engage in overt sexual play. In this elaborate but discordant symphony of not-so-subtle looks, touches, and hints, the characters discuss the aphrodisiac power of eggs (a discussion that takes on an extra shade of double entendre in Italian – not reflected in the subtitles – since "eggs" is one equivalent of the English slang word "balls"), and the proper cream to maintain an erection. Later, a slatternly lower-class woman, brought to the shack by a worker obviously for sexual purposes, is introduced into the scene. Yet no one seems in the least embarrassed by her presence or about the open sexual innuendo directed toward other people's spouses, indicating an utter lack of *pudore* that harkens back to similar (though milder) scenes in *L'avventura.* Max, the host of the party, an older, balder version of Piero from *L'eclisse,* is touted equally for being a skirtchaser and an aggressive businessman (we learn that he specializes in raping bankrupt companies): in this group, the two powers are clearly related, and one of the female characters makes the connection overt in the dialogue.

There is other, more explicit political commentary in the film, but its status is ambiguous. In the very first shots, for example, we can see that the workers are on strike – the signs stuck in the car windows read "sciopero" (strike), a word that is not translated in the subtitles – but the camera is at such a great distance that the audience is barely aware of the fact. There is also a bit of business with a strikebreaker whom the strikers make fun of, but the entire episode – which goes unexplained, uncontextualized, and unresolved – seems little more than a gesture on Antonioni's part, a kind of a quotation or "reality effect" to serve as a background for Giuliana's problems.[21] Though the initial encounter in the film between Corrado and Giuliana's husband Ugo begins with the assumption of a no-holds-barred struggle among the capitalists for the available skilled laborers, by and large Antonioni seems in *Red Desert* to be letting specific political commentary go out of focus as well.

Where a subtle critique does arise is in the lightly posed but significant contrast between the principal characters' middle-class angst and the earthier *Weltanschauung* of the more robust workers.[22] This occurs at two key moments. The first is when Corrado holds an open meeting in an attempt to recruit workers to go to work in Patagonia, at the extreme southern tip of South America. The workers' concerns are the exact opposite, and almost a parody of, the kinds of stresses that the middle-class characters, especially Giuliana, have been experiencing. Instead of worrying about their hold on reality, they wonder whether they will have access to television and sports newspapers, and how often they will be able to telephone their wives. Their concerns seem almost silly in light of the existential and psychological crisis that Giuliana is undergoing, but they have a specificity and substantiality for which Antonioni seems to be nostalgic. The second moment comes when Max's worker brings his sexual prize to the shack, obviously intent on doing more than just talking about sex, unlike the shack's bourgeois inhabitants, whom the woman mocks.

In this same scene in the shack, the survival gesture of Giuliana's early in the film (when she hungrily devours a sandwich like an animal) is echoed when the inhabitants of the shack literally tear it apart in order to warm themselves with a fire. Giuliana's gesture springs from real anxiety, whereas they seem to be merely looking for an unconventional, but still socially acceptable *frisson*.) Later, the women think that they have heard a cry, but they are unsure (restating an epistemological thematic about the subject–object relation that harkens back to the uncertainties of *L'avventura*) and, under the pressure of her husband's sharp, mocking questioning, the wife gives in and says that maybe she did not hear it after all. (Giuliana asks her why she replied "può darsi" [maybe] to her husband, implying a hint of a mild, proto-feminist upbraiding of her friend.) Here the possibility of a fixed intersubjective reality is questioned again, and it is given a gendered nuance.

Like Antonioni's previous heroines, Giuliana is literally pushed up against the wall in shot after shot, but now the director goes one step further, often jamming this neurotic woman, cowering, into a corner as well. At various key moments, her body writhes, as in the space in her shop and in the elaborate dance she and Corrado do when she comes to his hotel room. Her body language here becomes a more blatant, more highly charged version of the signifying graphic line discussed earlier.

While not denying the female specificity of her malady, and the presence, however attenuated, of Antonioni's ongoing critique of the male way of being in the world, Giuliana's psychological difficulties also seem to point, ambiguously, but perhaps more than in the previous films, to a *general* crisis in selfhood, or subjectivity. When the film opens, she seems already to have been reduced to a kind of lowest common denominator, and through the animal-like way she devours her sandwich while neglecting her child, Antonioni seems to be calling into question such platitudinous certainties as "mother love." Throughout, she makes various animal noises, as she does near the end, when she is in the lobby of Corrado's hotel. And when she tells the story of the girl in the clinic who asked "Who am I?" (a character who, we discover later, is actually herself), the same problematic of identity comes up.

Males, too, in this film that begins to concentrate on the male figure almost as much as on the female, are involved in the same questioning of identity. The director has spoken of Corrado as a figure halfway between Giuliana's neurosis and her husband's rough good health. As such, he is one of the first "sensitive males" in an Antonioni film, but he, too, will fail to minister properly to the woman's deep need. Visually, Corrado's feminized self-questioning, so similar to that of Antonioni's women, can be seen in the way he looks out upon a landscape, with the camera shooting him from behind, a motif and composition reminiscent of the work of nineteenth-century German painter Caspar David Friedrich, whose characters always seem to be questioning the epistemological relation of the self to the external world.

Many of the characters, both male and female, are often centered in shots in an unusual and alienating (in both the conventionally psychological and Brechtian senses of the word), straight-on fashion. This open acknowledgment of the presence of the camera points also to the way in which the camera constitutes them as characters and thus seems to deprive these attenuated figures of agency even further. One particularly striking shot/reverse shot sequence, which occurs during the hotel room scene and is reminiscent of a shot in the first scene of *L'eclisse*, shows Corrado neatly blocking our view of Giuliana; then, after a cut, Giuliana blocks our view of Corrado in exactly the same, extremely artificial, head-on fashion. Momentarily, at least, the shots turn these "people" into shapes and forms with almost solely formal and graphic expressivity.

But from the vantage point of the late 1990s, the questioning goes beyond that of simple identity, a common theme during the 1960s, when the mechanizing, leveling effects of rampant technology were first becoming apparent. For to put the matter simply in terms of *identity* is to assume that there is or *can* be such a thing as a more or less fixed self, something that can be lost or recovered, a core being around which temporary mood or attitudinal changes can come and go. More recent psychoanalytic and poststructuralist theory, however, has indicated that each of us – at least, in terms of our core sense of self – can just as easily be regarded as an *effect* of language and cultural meaning, that various "subject positions" that we occupy are preconstituted for us, as it were, by the culture of which we are a part. In this light, Giuliana could be said to lack a centering device, like her son's gyroscope, that would help her find a place in society and keep her balanced there.

Thus Giuliana's greatest difficulty – and, according to this model, the greatest difficulty of all those deemed "mentally ill" in Western society – is her inability to understand the exact nature and demands of her "appropriate" subject position, a position that is not at all natural or given. If all subjectivity is always a kind of unconscious "performance" (which is especially true, perhaps, of gender and sexual roles), then she has forgotten her "lines," she has lost the script provided by the culture. And a woman's role in this culture is clear: Giuliana is a wife and mother in early 1960s Italian society, and thus certain sexual and social behaviors, certain goals and hopes and dreams, are appropriate and expected for this particular subject position. But these are roles and expectations that the confused Giuliana can no longer feel comfortable with, can no longer accept as natural.

Her "mental illness," then, rather than representing a profound change in the Antonioni heroine, as it is usually seen, is perhaps only a more serious version of that reluctance to accept a predetermined female subjectivity (in terms of marriage, especially) that we saw in such earlier female protagonists as Claudia, Lidia, and Vittoria. Since her hospitalization, Giuliana tells Corrado with ironic bitterness, she has learned her proper social role quite quickly: "I've succeeded so well at reinserting myself into reality that I've even become an unfaithful wife." She does not seem to be very successful in her socially mandated role as mother, however, and when she realizes that her son has been faking his inability to walk, a crisis erupts. When describing his wife's problems to Corrado, Ugo says, "non riesce a ingranare," she can't manage to get herself in gear. As Biarese and Tassone point out, Ugo "unconsciously uses exactly the right term: Giuliana, in fact, refuses to become a cog in the machinery of a dehumanized world in which she cannot recognize herself."[23] Trying to achieve the fixed and untroubled selfhood that everyone else around her seems to enjoy, she instructs herself, like a child, "I must remember that everything that happens to me is my life."

And because of this crisis in her subjectivity, she cannot be sure of the external world, either. When she enters Corrado's hotel room and touches all the objects as if trying to verify their existence, she is, by extension, attempting to verify her own, as the subject who is experiencing them. Earlier on the ferry, Giuliana has told Corrado that for her the central question has become "What should I look at?" which is an epistemological question, of course, and he replies that he wants to know rather "How must I live?" which is an ethical question. Ultimately Corrado says that they are in fact the same question, implying, perhaps, that ethics can only be based on a prior and functional sense of self and its relation to others and the external world.

Corrado, ever the rationalist (like some, but not all of Antonioni's male characters) says that her problem is only a "malattia," some disease, some illness. In what might be described as the male manner, he wants to know *precisely* what she is afraid of, and of course she cannot tell him. I want to hit people, too, he says, and admits that "we all need treatment." "Why do I always need others?" she responds plaintively. She tells Corrado that she wants everyone who has ever loved her to form a wall around her, and in the stylized matched-within shot described earlier, he sits directly in front of her, between her and the camera. Forming much more than the wall of loved ones she has asked for, he seems to obliterate her completely.

Appropriately for this scene in which Giuliana's fragile sense of self seems to unravel even further, the visuals are much more stylized and expressive than in any other scene in the film. The red bar that forms part of the bed and that keeps intruding into the visual field resembles the line of tape that police put up at the scene of a crime and, in fact, looks much wider from behind than it does from the front, further suggesting an instability of vision. Even more interestingly, the director underlines his presence here – and thus the problematics of cinematic vision – by allowing these front and back shots of the bar to call each other into question. (The front shot shows that the wall is directly behind the bar of the bed, yet the shot of the same bar from behind the bed seems to have no trouble accommodating the camera; it is an impossible space.) Strange camera shots from

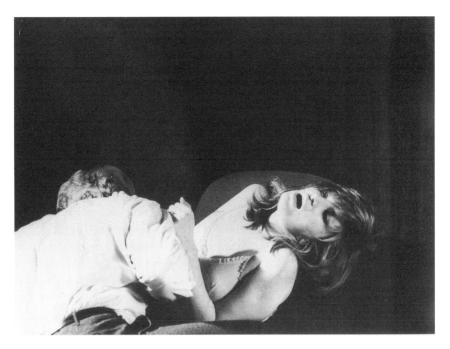

Figure 14. Corrado (Richard Harris) sexually "consoles" Giuliana in his hotel room

behind Giuliana's head alternate with shots that show her making animal-like gestures with her hands and arms and with other shots that focus solely on her restless legs, which become the signifier of her emotional state and yet are also sexual. The sexuality implied in the shots of her legs seems to be dispersed – is it Giuliana's, the director's, or, by implication, the specta-tor's? – and thus a delicate ambiguity as to whether she actually wants to make love with Corrado is maintained visually. This ambiguity also raises the question of what it would mean for someone as disturbed as Giuliana is to "want" anything. In her state, is it possible for her to be responsible for her acts? The elliptical cutting signifying the passage of time also ex-tends the ambiguity to the point that it is not clear exactly what has taken place here.

This problematizing of subjectivity is seen most dramatically during the famous fog sequence, when the various characters come and go like insub-stantial wraithes. There is no sense of spirituality here, no redeeming tran-scendence. The fog accentuates the separateness of the individual characters and thus articulates the common, even banal existential theme of the ultimate isolation of all human beings. When the others "disappear" in this fashion, Giuliana feels even more anxious, and this leads directly to her apparent suicide attempt – actually more like a signal of intention than a real attempt – when she impetuously drives right to the edge of the pier.[24]

But the scene goes beyond the question of existential aloneness, because the figures are posed in such a highly stylized fashion. This foregrounds the director's presence once again and accentuates the status of these figures as expressive forms. All human difference and distinction between them is wiped out, including, for a moment at least, even that of gender, as dramatic close-ups focus on each head as it slowly disappears. The figures are posed symmetrically in the fog, with varying, precisely determined degrees of visibility, in a way that reengages and deepens Antonioni's ongoing investigation into visibility and, by extension, the nature of being itself.

Giuliana's fantasies are also part of this attempt to find a viable self from which to negotiate the world, even though this "self" can never, for any of us, be anything more than a necessary fallacy. Thus, when she tells the story of the girl on the lovely island, we easily infer that she is talking about herself (as she was, in fact, when, in another key, she told Corrado the story of the suicidal girl in the clinic). Lacking a clear subject position, a fixed "I" – a structural necessity for narrating or even merely representing to herself her own life story – she must displace it onto another.

In the fantasy tale, all the colors are natural (recall that Antonioni said that these are the only "natural" colors in the entire film), somewhat pastel earth and sea tones, rather than brightly acidic, like the colors in the industrial landscape, and there are no alienating, intrusive noises, only the most soothing aural manifestations of nature. The expressive female voice that is heard – an apparent fantasy signifier for the simple purity of "nature" – refers back to the opening credit sequence, where it was heard in explicit binary opposition to the electronic music and jarring sounds of technology. The thematic and expressive importance of the visual and aural tracks here accounts for the fact that this fantasy story is actually *dramatized* rather than merely recounted orally, as would be more conventional. Everything in the story is exceptionally clean and perfect (a common fantasy among the gravely neurotic, apparently), and the story's shapes are all very human or humanly accommodating. As the lovely voice is heard singing, we see rocks that are reminiscent of *L'avventura*, but here they seem to be more organic and welcoming; the director has in fact pointed out in interviews that they are meant to look like flesh and body parts. Giuliana's personal fantasy, not surprisingly, is that everything in her life should be made to come together, to harmonize, to center itself, as happens in the fairy tale she tells. Her desire for stable meaning, for a happy ending to the story that is her life, can also be seen in the short fantasy tale at the end of the film, this time told rather than dramatized, about the little bird that successfully avoids the dangerous pollution emanating from the factory's smokestack. Given the environment in which the film is set, this fantasy seems equally unrealistic.

In Giuliana's island fantasy a mysterious boat carries the weight of the other, the not-here; similarly, the larger tale of *Red Desert* itself is replete with strange ships that are often shown in visually incongruous positions that provoke a sense of mystery and wonder. One example is the ship that appears magically to be proceeding through the woods, obviously by means of a body of water that we cannot see. The psychological and thematic charge of exoticism carried by "Africa" in some of the other films is also found in these ships that appear and reappear, especially perhaps in the sailor speaking Turkish to Giuliana near the end of the film (but which to our unaccustomed ears functions more as a signifier for the seemingly impenetrable babbling of the completely other), and, most specifically, in the Patagonia that Corrado is recruiting workers for (the map he uses figures as the visualization of this "other" in the midst of this Italian scene).

Self and Other, character and graphic formalism, come together in the kinetic dynamic of the film that goes a long way toward organizing it, both formally and thematically. This dynamic lies in the contrasting binary between movement and stasis, and it is returned to time and again in both the formal graphics of the film (which, as we saw in Rohdie's description, are always moving, rarely stationary) and in much of Corrado's dialogue, in which he speaks continually of his rootlessness and need for movement. Giuliana herself comments that she cannot look at the sea because "Non sta mai fermo, il mare," the sea is never still, and she fears losing interest in the static things of the land – in other words, all that we normally take to be real life.

By the end of the film, Giuliana seems to have a somewhat surer grasp on this "real life" that she seeks connection to. The final scene offers a slight hope for a traditional, positive, if not actually "happy," resolution, as Giuliana is now actively taking care of her child. This contrasts with her actions at the beginning and signifies perhaps that she has begun to overcome her neurosis, that she, like the bird in the fable she recounts to her son, has learned how to fly around the noxious fumes.

But what would it mean for her to become better adjusted to a world that looks like this and in which people act as they did in the shack? In this world that Antonioni has so brilliantly portrayed for us, any victory at adapting, at fitting in, will inevitably also be a defeat.

5
Blow-up (1966)

It is difficult to say anything new about Antonioni's next film, *Blow-up*, made in 1966. Literary critics, philosophers, anthropologists, and a host of others, slumming from time to time in the movies, seem invariably to have felt the need to talk about this particular film. One reason is that it was an international art-house success, even beyond that of the trilogy (in no small part because of its steamy – for the time – sex and drug scenes), with a relatively well-known cast that had wider drawing power than less familiar Italian actors.[1] Even more important, the film was made in English and placed in a more easily recognizable setting, and, for those reasons, it seems to be more immediately accessible than his earlier films. Above all, the film seems to have been tempting to commentators precisely because its meanings end up being so *ambiguous* and apparently multiple; in fact, the variety of interpretations inspired by this film is nothing short of astonishing.

By the time *Blow-up* appears, it has become clear that Antonioni prefers to put meanings *in play*, rather than to follow a prearranged, clearly worked-out plan – as he himself has always insisted in interviews – and it is this factor, more than any other, that accounts for the wide disparity in critical interpretations. (This free play also strongly marks the rather tenuous relation between the film and the short story by Argentinian writer Julio Cortàzar, "Las babas del diablo" [The devil's drool] on which it is ostensibly based.)[2] Paradoxically, despite the film's many ambiguities, things initially appear much less complicated in *Blow-up*, and the surface more welcoming. Antonioni himself also seems to have felt that this film marked a new departure for him, as he told an interviewer for *Playboy* magazine that it was completely different from his earlier films, because now he was examining the relationship between an individual and reality, rather than interpersonal relations (p. 48). (As noted in chapter 4, he said much the same thing to another interviewer about *Red Desert*.)

Some elements do not change, however. For example, Antonioni continues the pattern established in the earlier films of indicating, even in the first few minutes, potentially enlightening ways of watching the film. Thus the intercuts between the merrymakers and the homeless men emerging from the "doss house" (shelter) with which the film opens are heavily, almost didactically, oppositional and seem meant to nudge us in the direction of seeing the film as a set of binary oppositions. Modestly, and ambiguously, Antonioni's earlier penchant for specific social critique survives in this almost too obvious contrast between the revelers of the "swinging sixties" (the mimes here are an explicit figural symbolization of the irresponsible and drug-besotted mod London seen throughout the film)[3] – a historically specific phenomenon that the film seems, on one level, to want to document – and the oppressed and despairing men of the homeless shelter. Alternatively, in the context of the 1960s, the anarchic revelers who refuse to play by the rules may very well represent that rebellion against authoritarian structures for which the decade is chiefly known, especially since many of the people that the merrymakers pass (for example, the nuns and the palace guard) are wearing their own sorts of uniforms, which connote repression. Thus the binary structure of the film is established from the beginning, but the exact terms of the opposition remain unclear.

What might be called the "epistemological" theme of the film – most evident, famously, in the photographer's attempt to reconstruct the murder in the park by enlarging his photographs – is also stated in the beginning when the photographer, played by David Hemmings, appears to be simply one of the men filing out of the shelter early in the morning.[4] Since he was hardly a recognizable star at the time the film was made, no one thinks that he is any different until he suddenly jumps into his Rolls-Royce. Thus the interrelationship among truth, reality, appearance, and art that will become increasingly important in the film is also posited from the beginning.

Politically speaking, the film's stance is less than obvious, since any overt reference to local politics is, as in the opening workers' strike of *Red Desert*, reduced to a nearly empty signifier. Here, the Hemmings character comes briefly into contact with a "Ban the Bomb" parade and just as easily passes through it, when one of the protestors' signs, significantly, flies out of his open car. But as the astute Italian critic Lino Miccichè has pointed out, the film is political in its own way, in its demonstration of the dissatisfaction that led to the political and social explosions of 1968.[5] Miccichè also believes, as mentioned in the introduction, that Antonioni more than fulfills the primary political responsibility of the filmmaker, that of being responsible for his means of expression rather than simply relying on regressive formal models.

A more consistent and perhaps more important way in which Antonioni expresses his politics, as was the case in the earlier films, is in his exploration of gender issues, though now, for the first time, the director's focus is resolutely, even claustrophobically, on his principal male character rather than the female one.[6] Critic Sam Rohdie believes that "the change from female to male protagonists . . . is accompanied by a change from a subjective camera and narration to a rigorously objective camera and objective narrative position" (p. 184).[7] By "a rigorously objective camera and objective narrative position" Rohdie probably means that the film is shot from a perspective that is outside the characters, in contrast to the perspective of the earlier films, but this claim is not borne out by a close analysis of individual shots. The easy equation of male with objective and female with subjective may also show evidence of gender stereotyping that has more to do with the critic than with the filmmaker.[8]

The Hemmings character is in any case the complete narcissist, and one "socioethical" reading of the film might focus on his trajectory, throughout the film and culminating at its end, toward a more social sense of shared, participatory meaning. Since we see everything – with one or two tiny but significant exceptions – from Hemmings's point of view (pace Rohdie's claim that the perspective in this film is "rigorously objective"), *Blow-up* is also about perception, specifically, artistic perception, and even more specifically, male artistic perception. Consequently, the director's self-placement here (especially since Hemmings is a photographer), as well as his own emotional identification with the central character (who is now, like him, male), is more complicated than in the films discussed thus far. (Or actually, in the case of identification – male with male – it is presumably *less* complicated, at least in gender terms, than in the earlier female-centered films.) In fact, Antonioni himself has referred to this connection: "I came to know reality by photographing it, when I began taking it with the movie camera, a little like in *Blow-up*; in this sense, I think that it's my most autobiographical film."[9]

Hemmings's still camera and the movie camera used to make the film that the audience is watching are directly linked, visually and physically, as well as thematically. Thus, when Hemmings begins his erotic photo shoot of supermodel Verushka, Antonioni's camera performs a minicrane shot (the camera head, alone, seems at first to be tilting upward, but actually the whole camera is moving) directly alongside Hemmings's still camera, which

Figure 15. The photographer (David Hemmings) indulges in some pretend sex with his model Verushka

is sitting on a tripod. Admittedly, this is a brief moment in the film, but the effect is to make Hemmings's still camera itself appear to be moving down in tandem (it ends up approximately in the same place as the movie camera), thus further linking the two apparatuses in this shot. More conventionally, the still shots of Verushka taken by Hemmings are signified by various frozen jumpcuts in the film we are seeing, in other words, through the movie camera. Later, in the initial scene in the park, the movie camera pans back and forth, replicating both the movement of Hemmings's gaze and the movement of his still camera. Much later, when the photographer begins to put together the crucial blow-ups in order to reconstruct the

Figure 16. The woman (Vanessa Redgrave) pays a call on the photographer

murder in the park, Antonioni's movie camera abruptly zooms in on the still pictures as though forcefully to remind the audience both of its presence as mediating agent and its connection to the photographer's camera.

It is difficult to fix Antonioni's intentions here, but virtually all of his films, as we have seen, can be interpreted as questioning, ambivalently, perhaps, the phallic, penetrating power of his own camera. His decision in this film to move to a male protagonist who is a photographer seems, among other things, to have been made to more directly foreground this problematic. Hemmings is an obnoxious human being, a predatory male who says he is sick of all the "birds" and "bitches" he comes in contact with. The models he lives off of are grotesquely anorexic beings, horribly made up, who have been turned into near-monsters. The screaming artificiality of their clothes, hairdos, and poses (underlined by the presence of artificial props such as clothespins, carefully placed out of sight of Hemmings's camera) strip them of any residual humanity. These women have been completely made into objects for the dominating male gaze, a literalization of a conventional power dynamic that, if contested by more recent feminist film theory, seems in full operation here.[10]

Furthermore, Vanessa Redgrave walks through nearly their entire scene together in his apartment naked from the waist up, in a supremely vulnerable position. The director seems to implicate himself as well in the creation of this vulnerability, since the camera performs an elaborate choreography to keep from showing her breasts (thus paradoxically foregrounding them even more, while still avoiding the threat of censorship). Hemmings's biggest compliment to her is that she would make a good model, and earlier in the scene in the park, several shots were aimed down on the Redgrave character, putting her in an extremely servile position visually.

Hemmings treats the cockney "birds" with disgust (asking one of them her name and then quickly saying, "What's the use of a name?" and "Just tell me what they call you in bed") and pulls their clothes off, making them, like Redgrave, embarrassed and vulnerable as well. (Note also that their offer of sex – like Redgrave's – is part of an economic exchange, conditioned on getting something nonsexual from him in return, and that the "orgy" takes place on and through the blue background of the models' photo shoot, further equating the two groups of women.) They are "appropriately" servile when putting his shoes back on him after the orgy, before he ruthlessly dismisses them.

Though on one level he may be critiquing "typical" male behavior in the person of Hemmings, the director seems also to be enjoying vicariously, as it were, the parade of women who show up to abase themselves at the photographer's feet. In fact, the director told interviewer Aldo Tassone: "I like the protagonist, I love the life he leads. When I was preparing the film I also led this kind of life and I had a lot of fun. It was an agreeable life, but one that I was leading in order to follow the character, and not because it was my own."[11]

It is important to point out that many male critics tend to see the film, and all its attendant self-reflexivity, as a benign exploration of the nature of artistic creativity and not in any way as a critique of the male figure. Seymour Chatman, for example, takes Hemmings as nothing more than an unproblematic stand-in for Antonioni and his own artistic problems and sees Hemmings as a creative artist, in completely positive terms. The most negative thing Chatman can think of to charge the rapacious Hemmings with is "childlike amorality."[12]

The orgy scene, especially, has elicited from these critics vastly different readings from the one offered here. William Arrowsmith, anxious to defend the film against the moralists, thinks that the whole sequence of sexual rough-and-tumble on the violet paper is meant to convey the sense of animal high spirits and childish gaiety. Nothing is salacious or offensive about it; the dominant note is childish play, animal hilarity. . . . The whole scene is intentionally amoral, not immoral: there is no moral consequence to a tumble in the waves between two teenage Nereids and a would-be frogman.[13]

Nowhere does Arrowsmith consider the imbalance of power and vulnerability that now, at least, seems so painfully evident in this "innocent" scene.

A continual blur of movement, the photographer is a crasser, nastier version of Piero in *L'eclisse*, never content, never able to stay still for even a moment. Hemmings tells his editor that he is "fed up with those bloody bitches!" as though it is all *their* fault, and, most naively and unconvincingly of all, "I wish I had tons of money, then I'd be free." (At the moment he says this, the camera shows a photograph that he has taken of a homeless man: the jarring juxtaposition of visual and aural tracks here seems implicitly to call into question the nature of freedom, as least as it is defined for someone like Hemmings.) The polar opposite of Giuliana in *Red Desert*, so ill at ease in her reality, the Hemmings character is, in Penelope Houston's description, "a man who accepts, exploits and enjoys the contradictions of his society."[14]

Related to the exploration of gender relations is the reprise of Antonioni's long-standing depiction of marriage as a trap, especially for the female partner, and the character played by Sarah Miles is shown briefly in two scenes as apparently caught in an unfulfilling relationship with the painter, Bill, while helplessly in love with Hemmings. The photographer asks her at one point, "Did you ever think of leaving him?" "No," is the simple, undeveloped response. Appropriately for the swinging ambience of *Blow-up*, this couple does not actually appear to be formally married, but the relationship is in any case constricting. Hemmings is himself divorced and in speaking to Redgrave about his former wife can only brandish riddles.

On a more formal level, aspects of the graphic and visual dynamic that we have been tracing reappear as well, as with the identical binary color scheme structure of *Red Desert*, which, in *Blow-up*, shows the buses and many of the houses in bright, sharply contrasting primary colors that alternate with ugly, gray cityscapes.[15] Even the sickly looking grass with which *Blow-up* opens and closes is reminiscent of the picture of an unhealthy and corrupted Nature that was developed in Antonioni's film made two years earlier, and the opening binary opposition between the doss house and the revelers places the former in depressed urban surroundings (note the single, skinny tree Hemmings passes) and the latter amid a sparkling new down-town filled with modern skyscrapers reminiscent of *L'eclisse*. Similarly, the striking, long-held extreme long shots and the visual and aural beauty of the wind in the trees, so much a staple of films such as *L'eclisse* and *La notte*, reappear in the scenes set in the park, investing them with a similar foreboding and existential resonance.

But rhythmically and in other, more important ways, the film feels com-pletely different from those that preceded it. The long-take, expressive lon-gueurs of the previous films have now been replaced, for the most part, by quick cuts and sudden, popping perceptions. A cynic might argue that An-tonioni has speeded things up primarily for the benefit of his new, interna-tional audience with its presumably shorter attention span – we are, after all, a long way from the brooding, nearly wordless seventeen-minute mon-tage that ends *L'eclisse* – but it is clear that these changes have important thematic implications.

For Lino Miccichè, it is as though the director is purposely avoiding all focusing of interest in order to call into question the idea that reality can have any "meaning" beyond that of its sheer presence. Antonioni does concentrate occasionally on minor, nonnarrative details, as when we briefly watch Hemmings, in a close-up of his hand, do a neat cowboy trick with a coin. But this seems more like a detail meant to build up "character traits" in the traditional way – like his double-take on the "queers" walking their dogs near the antique shop, or the various self-consciously insouciant things he does while driving around in his Rolls-Royce, or the ebullient kicking up of his heels when he first goes to the park – than an "object" or nonnar-rative event focused on in order to gauge and savor its philosophical or symbolic resonance, the kind of thing that was often foregrounded in the earlier films.[16] The only apparent exception to this purposeful lack of focus on real objects – and it is a major one – is the park, which is obviously central to the project of the film. According to Miccichè, however, the park is foregrounded precisely to drive home the original point even more fully: "The profound truth that [the park] seems to offer ultimately reveals itself as absolutely unknowable, precarious, provisional."[17]

William Arrowsmith and Andrew Sarris, among others, have focused on the park in order to support their view that Antonioni's themes operate through fixed binary oppositions. Not surprisingly, therefore, the park be-comes an important site of a traditional Nature/culture division that these critics find throughout the director's work. What they forget, though, is that every bit of Nature seen in *Blow-up, especially* the park, is in some way also a product of culture. As anthropologist Clifford Geertz once pointed out, Nature is in fact a cultural concept. We must go beyond these rigid, finally untenable binaries to find out what is going on here.

If we move to the ending of the film, which, like all of Antonioni's work, revels in its open-endedness, we can see that Miccichè's distinctions, though provocative, are perhaps not quite subtle enough. For it is not that reality has no meaning, it is that it does not have any *inherent*, immutable, fixed meaning; rather, its meaning is always socially (and therefore historically) determined. Thus, by participating in the celebrated ball-less game of tennis with the mimes at the end, Hemmings can be seen as shaking off his narcissism (which actually amounts, in the epistemological context of the film, to a kind of solipsism), by implicitly admitting that reality is always unconsciously *constructed*, and constructed *socially*, that is, along with other human beings. Anything can mean anything, anything can stand for or represent anything else, anything can *be* anything, but only to a group, never to an individual (at least not for long).[18] Once Hemmings accepts the authority of this group to name meaning and thus configure reality, he can "find" and return the ball to them.[19] The director himself seems to have favored this more positive view of the ending, since he told the *Playboy* interviewer that the Hemmings character learns many things by the end of the film, "including how to play with an imaginary ball."[20]

Another way of saying this is that all reality and all meaning are achieved *contextually*, by means of the frame around a given bit of reality, since someone watching from afar, not participating in the group's meaning-giving operation, would think that they were all insane. The importance of context and framing in the establishment of meaning is demonstrated earlier in the film when Hemmings fights wildly for the broken piece of guitar that one of the members of the Yardbirds rock group has thrown to the audience. Once Hemmings is out of the club, out of the meaning-giving context, he realizes that the broken piece has absolutely no value whatsoever, and tosses it away. Emphasizing the point, another man comes along, picks it up, examines it quizzically, and then throws it away again. (The film itself is "framed" by the mimes at beginning and end, and they themselves are doubled by the same patch of grass that is below the opening credits and that fills the film's final shot.)

During the mimed tennis match at the end of the film, for a while we watch the photographer watching the invisible ball, but then he and we even begin to *hear the sound* of the ball. Here the inherent (but usually disguised) split between the visual and aural track that marks all films is used expressively, in this case, perhaps, to imply that membership in the meaning-giving group is always open to us as well. We are part of the way there, in other words, if not the whole way; an act of will, like Hemmings's, can presumably complete the loop of communication. It is also suggested that membership in this group is only a logical extension of film spectatorship itself, through the film apparatus, which, after all, is already dependent on a group understanding of its cinematic codes. The camera ostentatiously participates in this construction of meaning from the beginning of this scene, when it "follows" the arc of the invisible ball through the air, over the fence. The camera then comes to rest at a specific point in the grass, implying that even if we cannot see anything there, the camera does, or better, it *puts* it there, through its very act of attention.

The crucial presence of the cinematic codes (and the fact that meaning is never natural but always a product of an unconscious, group construction) is further, and wittily, underlined when the photographer suddenly disappears in a jump cut worthy of the early silent films of director Georges Méliès, just before we read "The End."[21] This technique reminds us that the photographer is not a real person, but a fictional character, a graphic mark, a made-up "sign" for the purposes of the film, which the director can now decide playfully to delete if he so chooses. We are also forcefully made aware of the presence of the director, of a controlling hand, an Other, outside the confines of the story and the film itself. According to Seymour Chatman, Antonioni has said that Hemmings's disappearance at the end is the director's "autograph" (p. 145).[22]

Closely related to the questions that we have been exploring is what might be called the film's aesthetic theme, which is pronounced by another visual artist, the photographer's painter friend, Bill. Bill represents a curious doubling, on Antonioni's part, of the artist figure and suggests that one character was not sufficient to explore the ambivalences and nuances of this thematic area. This time around, Antonioni seems to want to make explicit the linking of abstract painting and filmmaking/photography that has been present in his films from the first. (This specific attention to abstract art, thematized even in the dialogue, may also explain why the cinematography of *Blow-up* is, paradoxically, itself much less abstract in design.) The first painting that Bill shows Hemmings looks cubist in inspiration. He tells Hemmings that "they don't mean anything when I do them, it's just a mess. Afterwards I find something to hang on to. Like that leg [he points]. Then it sorts itself out and adds up." In the plainest link to the unfolding film he is a part of, Bill goes on to say that "it's like finding a clue in a detective story."[23]

The second painting he shows Hemmings more closely resembles a drip painting by the abstract expressionist painter Jackson Pollock, which Bill

Figure 17. The blow-up in *Blow-up*

claims has not yet come together for him and thus remains unfinished. Characteristically, Hemmings spontaneously offers to buy it. Later, after he has purchased a huge, unwieldy airplane propellor in an antique shop, the photographer himself indulges in a bit of aesthetic commentary when he borrows from Kant (without attribution!) to explain that he bought it because it is beautiful and that it is beautiful precisely because it is useless. Later, a direct link is made between Bill's paintings, Hemmings's photographs, and, by implication, the aesthetic project of the film, when the character played by Sarah Miles says pointedly that the photographs that Hemmings is enlarging have begun to resemble Bill's abstract paintings.

Joining the question of the nature of reality with the aesthetic question is the heavily foregrounded relation of the photographs to the "reality" that they have purportedly captured. In an important and often-discussed scene, Hemmings blows up his negatives to a larger and larger scale in order to seek a visual truth, that is, a correspondence between representation and reality. In so doing, he constructs a *narrative*, just as a director does in a film, by juxtaposing the individual shots and organizing them through the same system of looks that we know, from film theory, is what holds a movie together. In other words, Hemmings the photographer tries to construct a narrative logic through what is essentially a *cinematic* montage, and again Antonioni's camera (and eye) pans back and forth between the images, linking itself with Hemmings's eye and *his* camera. In fact, Antonioni keeps following (and underlining) the trajectory of an eyeline match with Hemmings's gaze, a standard visual suturing device in film, the device that makes space psychologically consistent for the viewer. By the time Hemmings's blow-ups reach the third degree, the camera is cutting back and forth between the photographer and the still photos, as though constructing a normal shot/reverse shot – the character looks, then we cut to what is being seen. Here the process is, in semiotic terms, paradigmatic or synchronic, as he goes "deeper" into the image. But it is also syntagmatic and diachronic, that is, through time, as when the montage is contructed by using *several* different still photos. The effect is to lay bare and thus demystify the filmmaking activity itself, because it is precisely by means of these two axes, the paradigmatic and the syntagmatic, that the cause and effect dynamic of meaning is accomplished in the cinematic editing process.

Most critics (and the director) have agreed that what this process demonstrates, paradoxically, is that the more the picture is blown up, to the point of abstraction, the less that is actually visible. This has never made complete sense to me, however, for Hemmings *does* in fact discover a gun and a body by means of the enlargements, and, when he goes back to the park, the presence of the body, at least, is verified by Antonioni's camera. It is as though the film were saying that "truth" *can* be arrived at even, or especially, through abstract representation. But what no critic to my knowledge has ever focused on is the fact that Hemmings takes a *new* photograph of a blown-up detail in order to blow it up even further. Yet this process cannot produce more bits of visual information that were not already there, and thus enlarging a photograph of an enlargement would be fruitless. This gesture of the photographer, fruitless or not, seems in any case to harken back to something that Antonioni said years earlier, but that is especially appropriate for a discussion of *Blow-up*:

> We know that under the revealed image there is another one which is more faithful to reality, and under this one there is yet another, and again another under this last one, down to the true image of that

absolute, mysterious reality that nobody will ever see. Or perhaps, not until the decomposition of every image, every reality.

Therefore, abstract cinema would have its reason for existing.[24]

Here we can see the way that the varying projects of Hemmings the photographer, Bill the abstract painter, and Antonioni the filmmaker neatly mesh.

When Hemmings returns again to the park and there is no body, another question arises: if there is no body and no evidence of the crime (except for a photo with a bunch of dots, which only has meaning in the context of the narrative that is already gone and is no longer available for scrutiny, and in the context of the larger photos that have all been stolen), has there been a crime? Again, it is a question of shared social reality, as with the mimes' tennis game at the end of the film. Thus Hemmings's desire to have his friend come and look at the body in the park is understandable; since reality is constructed intersubjectively, this external verification is crucial for the photographer, and when it does not take place, he cannot ever really "know" whether the murder occurred or not. When Hemmings realizes that his friend is completely stoned, and thus not a good candidate for the intersubjective verification he seeks, he replies, out of frustration, but significantly, that he saw "nothing." (The complicating, asymmetrical factor here is that the camera [and thus the audience] *did* actually see something, even though it is no longer there.) Interestingly, the director told *Playboy* that the photographer, through his photographs, shows an element of reality that seems real, and it is. "But reality has a quality of freedom about it that is hard to explain."[25] This very "quality of freedom" seems to represent the free play, the bad fit, between any "reality" and its representation, and this is perhaps figured, in the film, in the asymmetry just mentioned. In a similarly ambiguous vein, Antonioni told Aldo Tassone: "I wouldn't say that the appearance of reality equals reality, because there can be more than one appearance. There can also be more than one reality, but I don't know it, and I don't believe it. Maybe reality is a relation [rapport]."[26]

French critic Marie-Claire Ropars-Wuilleumier has developed a complicated but fascinating reading of this obviously crucial segment of the film. In an early essay entitled "L'espace et le temps dans la narration des années 60: 'Blow up' ou le négatif du récit," Ropars discusses the Antonioni film in the context of avant-garde film and fiction of the 1960s. Her project is to outline the response of *cinematic* language to the deconstruction of classical narrative brought about by the French New Novel during this period, and more specifically, to chart exactly how *Blow-up* "intervenes in the conceptual displacement precipitated by this crisis."[27]

For Ropars, what is interesting about the montage of enlargements at the center of the film is that it has to proceed differentially, each image canceling the previous one. The pictures are pure fragments of space, but the enlargements cause the detail to erase the whole, thus allowing multiple, contradictory lines of narrative to be posited. Filling in some holes invariably opens others. For example, although it is true that the photographer "finds" a revolver through this process, it is impossible to determine whether the revolver, at this point, is merely threatening or has already been used to murder someone. This montage, which she calls a "negative mise-en-abime," a negative mirror within a mirror, will be opposed by another at the end of the film, when the mimes play tennis. The earlier montage contradicts the finale by showing the *lack* of connection between *looking* at the object and the object itself, which results from trying to find the exact connection between them (unlike Hemmings's concentration on the invisible ball, which almost seems to produce it). For Ropars, this realization is tied up with the ontology of photography itself, a medium and form of representation that is based on a negative that reverses light, stops time, freezes gesture, and so on.

The "blow-up" section differs not only from the ending but also from the rest of the film. All of the shots the photographer has taken in the park seem slightly different from what we ourselves have seen through Antonioni's camera. And besides, how can one of the photographs show the corpse if they are all represented in the film as being taken while the older man was still living? Ropars points out that "the body will be successively confirmed (at night), then erased (during the day)," but death itself can only be there as a kind of trace, an absent presence, a ghost that is both there and not there. It is this problematic, contradictory space or interval that interests her: "The instant of death can only be seized under the form of a trace (that single photo that remains hanging on the wall and which actually resembles a painting); it comes always either before or after, in the interval between the photograph and the filmic image: death can't take place, can't have a place, in the Writing of Blowup."[28]

There is thus always *another* story beneath the surface that "doubles" the temporal thrust of the primary narrative, just as Hemmings's photos double Antonioni's cinematic image while calling it into question. "The center of the film thus defines itself as a decentering exercised on the film," Ropars explains. This process also results in a kind of a *counter-meaning*, a "subtle discontinuity" that runs throughout the narrative embodied in the cinematic images and that disturbs it.[29]

Ropars gives two examples of what she means here. The first is "the doubling of the look," which derails the look of the character, Hemmings, from one shot to the next. The way this works is that the film constantly shows the look of the photographer, doubled by the look of the camera lens, but rarely gives the spectator the chance to look with the very same look as the photographer, and thus to identify with him. And it is within this difference that the look of the filmmaker, the camera, the film intervenes: "Between the aim of the [photographer's] eye and the represented vision what inserts itself is the interval of another look, which is absent yet active, a look of a camera that is distinct from the subject, which it doubles" (p. 215). The best examples of this particular doubling, Ropars says, are the pictures taken in the park, where there are gaps – for instance, when, after a cut from the photographer looking, the film shows a new, different shot of the photographer, when we expected a shot of what he *saw*, or when a succeeding shot shows him looking in the opposite direction from the one that we expected. Another good example of this gap between the two "looks," not mentioned by Ropars, is the bit of self-reflexive play near the end of the film when Hemmings returns to the park the morning after the party to find that the body is no longer there. The camera, shooting down on him, shows him suddenly looking up at something. We cut to the familiar Antonioni shot of the tops of the moving trees, ostensibly from the photographer's POV. But then, the camera pans back down, in the same shot, back on *him*, now standing up, indicating that he was *not* the source of the look (since he cannot be looking at himself), not the motive of this particular shot, as we had thought. One could also add that this doubling of the look is the only real resemblance between the film and the Cortàzar short story on which it is based, where a similar result is accomplished by an explicit and regular alternation between first- and third-person narration.

This impossibility of a unified vision is reinforced, Ropars points out, by temporal ellipses that are vague and uncertain (unlike the ellipses in classic narrative, which are always present but are usually clear and well marked). An example occurs when we cut from Redgrave with her naked back to us, to a shot of her laughing on the sofa. In this manner, according to Ropars, both the logical and the chronological, which Roland Barthes identified as the foundation of all narrative, are undone (p. 215).

Lorenzo Cuccu, the Italian critic who has probably written most trenchantly about the philosophical aspects of Antonioni's films, makes a point that is closely related to that of Ropars, though expressed somewhat differently. For him, in the last shot of *Blow-up*, in which the "subject," Hemmings, suddenly disappears, *"the look that is making the film* puts itself directly into question by means of its very exercise and its dynamic."[30]

Cuccu's view of the mimed game of tennis at the end of the film, as an expression of the communal aspect of meaning-giving, accords to some extent with my own interpretation offered earlier, but Cuccu tends to regard it in a negative, nostalgic light. He translates the mimes' actions as saying to the photographer: "Reality isn't necessary for your images either." "The game is played without a ball, mimetic fiction doesn't represent but rather *substitutes itself* for life, behind the image there's no mystery that is capturable as meaning, the search for meaning is only a fiction that serves to 'justify the image' " (p. 29). Like some other critics, Cuccu sees the final scene with the mimes as an undoing of the meaning that had ostensibly been found through the photographs.

But Cuccu's reflections on the film's ending go far beyond this and are closely related to the scene in the park. Thus he provides a useful shot-by-shot comparison between the photographs that Hemmings takes in the park (as registered by Antonioni's movie camera, at any rate) and the photos that the photographer later blows up, showing in the process just how many of the latter are not included in the former. This offers specific, material evidence for Ropars's view concerning the gap between the look of the photographer and the "look" of the film itself.

Specific moments emphasized by Cuccu include, for example, the shot in the original park scene (identified by him as shot number 6 of this scene), which is a shot from the *side* of the man and woman (rather than from the front, from Hemmings's POV), as they realize the presence of the photographer. What Cuccu calls the "Other Look" is present in other places besides the park, as well, for example, when the camera is following Hemmings in the car. First the camera accompanies the car, then slows down and stops, and then speeds up again to turn and follow it. "The look of the narrative seems to enter into the concrete contingency of the diegetic space," says Cuccu; "it seems to make itself an autonomous diegetic presence" (p. 42). And though neither Ropars nor Cuccu mention it, the filmmaker's Other can suddenly manifest himself and his "look" *aurally* as well as visually, as when we faintly hear the wind moving through the trees in the park (a long-established Antonioni motif), even though we are now inside the apartment, watching Hemmings reconstruct the scene through his photographs.

As for the sudden disappearance of the photographer in the last shot of the film, Cuccu sees this as a powerful statement of presence on behalf of the Other (especially since the shot itself is a jump cut from the previous shot):

> The final shot is a gesture by means of which the narrative accomplishes a step beyond the discourse, reopening its disquieting, problematic tension: with this act, the subject of the look [the originator of the film's look, that is, the filmmaker, the camera], cut off from every false pretext, presents itself in a "pure state" and remains alone before the enigma of the green lawn, which now reveals itself to be none other than the specular image of the Look itself. The classic symmetry of the "framed" story/discourse thus transforms itself into an unexhausted circularity, in the reopening *en abyme* of the enigma, and the reflexion on the image finally achieves its own true target. (P. 43)

For Cuccu, in other words, this final shot of the grass, after the photographer has been cinematically whisked away, represents a "pure look" on the part of the filmmaking apparatus and, by extension, the director. It reveals that the "true target" of Antonioni's work is a reflection on precisely what he is doing when he looks, that is, when he makes a film: "From the lucid, compact surface of conventional cinema [cinema della trasparenza] has emerged, at the end, in a purer form the 'cinema of subjectivity,' of 'pure self-reflexivity.' The final act of *Blow-up* has gone beyond the image/reality problem, toward the discovery of the *subject of the look* as true object of reflexion, as true enigma" (p. 43). But there need not be any contradiction between Cuccu's emphasis on Antonioni's self-reflexivity and the director's critical exploration of the "image/reality problem." Clearly the one implies the other, and neither makes sense alone. The last, most eloquent word belongs to the filmmaker himself:

> I don't know what reality is like. Reality escapes us, it changes continually. When we think we've reached it, the situation is already something else. I always doubt what I see, what an image shows me, because I "imagine" what's beyond that; and what's behind an image is unknown. The photographer of *Blow-up*, who is not a philosopher, wants to see more more closely. But what happens is that because he enlarges too much, the object itself decomposes and disappears. Therefore, there is a moment in which one seizes reality, but the moment immediately after, it escapes. That is, to some extent, the meaning of *Blow-up*. It might seem strange for me to say this, but *Blow-up*

was in some ways my neo-realist film on the relation between the individual and reality, even if it has a metaphysical component precisely because of this abstraction of appearances.

After this film, I wanted to see what there was behind, what was my own appearance in the inside of myself, a little bit like I had done in my earliest films. And what resulted was *The Passenger*, another step forward in the study of contemporary man. In *Blow-up* the relationship between the individual and reality is perhaps the principal theme, while in *The Passenger*, the relation is the one of the individual with himself.[31]

6

The Passenger (1975)

The opening shot of *The Passenger* is full of whites and grays and muted earth tones, and it provides a clear indication of what is visually to come. The bright primary colors of *Red Desert* and *Blow-up* have now been evacuated, and the ebony bodies of the African men contrast sharply with their shining white clothes, reducing the world to a visual Manicheanism. This whiteness spreads in all directions, like spilled paint, combining with the dull, unemphatic earth colors to produce an insistent blankness that pervades the film and is echoed in the desert, the various washed-out Spanish towns the principal characters travel through, and the sea. The film is a blank canvas on which identities will be projected, explored, and refashioned. Thus much of the landscape, for once, is there only negatively; an unmarked sheet of paper, it is a palimpsest on which to write the self. The implacable silences of the sound track contribute hugely to this sense of blankness, silences that are paradoxically heightened throughout by scraps of unknown languages, the faint cries of children playing, and faraway musical instruments that we will never see.

This blankness goes beyond the merely visual and aural. Antonioni has said that what attracted him to Africa was something else: "More than the desert in and of itself, I always felt the need to live in a different historical context, in a nonhistorical world, or in a historical context that is not conscious of its own historicity."[1] In another interview, he said:

> Now, from *Zabriskie Point* through *The Passenger*, by way of "Tecnicamente dolce" ["Technically Sweet," a film, never shot, that was to be set in the jungle], I noticed a sort of obscure dissatisfaction, the need to escape, by means of the characters, from the historical context in which I and they lived – that is, the urban, civil, and civilized

Figure 18. David Locke (Jack Nicholson) attempts some cross-cultural communication

context – to enter into a different context such as the desert or the jungle, where one could at least imagine a life freer or more personal and where this freedom could be put to work. The adventurous nature [of the story] and the character of the journalist who changes identity in order to liberate himself from himself were born out of this need.[2]

This escape from history into the blankness on which a new identity might be written is embodied in David Locke, played by Jack Nicholson, a television journalist who has come to Africa to interview a guerrilla leader. He looks utterly out of place in the desert, unlike the photographer in *Blow-up*, so thoroughly at home in swinging London. Torn from everything familiar, Locke is the perfect specimen for that exploration of the interior self that Antonioni said he wanted to accomplish in this film, which, though it was based on a script written by someone else – for the

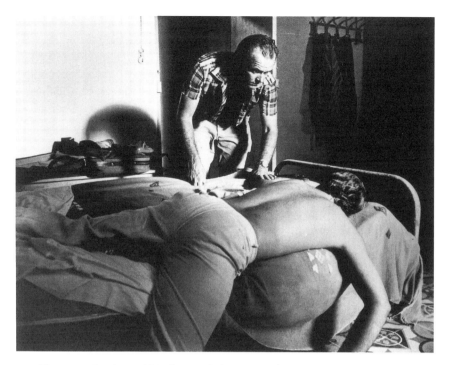

Figure 19. Locke and his deceased alter ego Robertson (Chuck Mulvehill)

first time in the director's career – accorded perfectly with his own interests.[3]

Most of the film's techniques and themes are established early on. When Locke returns exhausted to his hotel room after failing to get the interview, he finds that the only other white occupant, Robertson, with whom he had become friendly, has died, apparently of natural causes. Death is a strange presence throughout this scene because the corpse – the exact opposite of the almost evanescent one in *Blow-up*, since it is more present, more viscerally real – occupies an unconventionally large amount of screen time. (This effect is enhanced by Robertson's dead eyes, wide open, staring straight up.) Locke comes uncomfortably close to Robertson's lifeless face, as though death itself were somehow erotically charged. It is at this moment, apparently, that Locke gets the idea of exchanging identities with Robertson, for reasons that Antonioni, not surprisingly, never fully spells out. The proximity of their heads makes the exchange feel more curiously physical – as well as more figural – rather than remaining merely intellectual. This effect of physical presence is heightened by the fact that slight wisps of hair – significantly, of both men – are being softly blown by the fan.

Obviously crucial to Locke's assumption of Robertson's identity is a switch of passports, and Locke begins assiduously to exchange photographs. Appropriately for a film about identity and subjectivity, much emphasis is placed on these documents; the passport is the largely artificial, if bureaucratically efficient way in which governments unsuccessfully attempt to name and fix human identity. The very title of the film, in Italian, "Professione: Reporter," is reminiscent of a space on a passport that is meant to assist this effort to say *just who we are.* (Its curious linguistic hybridity adds to the sense of the complex artificiality of the resulting construct.) It also connects the idea of work or profession to one's identity or one's self, something that defines and gives shape and expression to a subject's status. (Early on in their only conversation, Locke tells Robertson, "I'm a reporter," as a way of identifying himself.) This nuance is lost in translating the title of the film into English as "The Passenger," though other thematic resonances are obviously gained in the process.[4]

The intricate play between the two characters and their identities is enacted in formal as well as dramatic and narrative ways. A crucial early scene in the film, the one in which Robertson and Locke meet and talk in what is apparently Locke's hotel room, is actually the product of an elaborate and brilliant technique that Seymour Chatman has usefully dubbed a "glideback" (thus distinguishing it from a simple flashback). While Locke works on the passports, we begin hearing their previous conversation in voiceover, with no indication of when or where it occurred. Locke tells Robertson that he is putting together a documentary on Africa; "I'm finished here, thank god, or almost finished," he says.[5] Then the camera pans from him, working on the passports in the present, to a tape recorder, revealing for the first time that the source of the conversation is not merely Locke's subjective memory, nor the "memory," that is, voiceover, of the film itself. The camera pans back to Locke, and then slowly across the room to the window. Through the window we see the back of a man, looking out at the landscape in the manner of a Friedrich painting, as have so many other Antonioni heroes and heroines, but we do not know who he is: it could be Locke, and we perhaps assume it is him, but then we realize that this is not possible given the visual logic of the shot (especially since the man is wearing a shirt, whereas at the beginning of the shot Locke was bare-chested). The ambiguity is resolved (momentarily, at least) when Locke joins the man from the right, and we suddenly realize that the unknown figure must be Robertson, and that this must be a flashback to their first meeting. In effect, the sound and the visual tracks of this earlier event have been neatly separated and just as neatly rejoined, without the slightest sign of temporal disjunction appearing on the surface. In addition to suggesting the fluidity of identity, the film here raises for the first time the question of subjectivity versus objectivity that will preoccupy it, for although the scene on the balcony is perhaps a product of Locke's subjective memory, the conversation captured on the tape, which has apparently given rise to this memory (though the balcony scene is in no way attributed directly to Locke's consciousness), is clearly an *objective* trace of that earlier event.

Other unconventional flashbacks in the film continue to produce purposeful temporal and spatial dislocations. One, which involves Locke's wife Rachel (played by Jenny Runacre), occurs while Locke is wandering around a baroque church in Munich, waiting for his first appointment as Robertson. A sudden cut shows him burning leaves in a backyard and for once the director gives us some help in orienting ourselves, as the character is referred to by other characters as "Mr. Locke" or "David," thus confirming that this must be a flashback to something that has occurred in the past, before he assumed Robertson's identity. But we are not at all sure about the precise mental "location" of this flashback. His wife comes out into the yard, and they seem to be having an argument; she reenters the house, and he looks up after her. We then cut to the back of an unidentified woman in an unidentified bedroom looking out through a window; when we see that she is looking down on a yard, we logically conclude that it is Rachel, without actually having seen her face. The camera moves forward in a fast track and then looks out and over the edge of the window to show that there is nothing and no one in the yard. Clearly the scene that began with Locke burning leaves has been a flashback, but whose? The location of the camera and the fact that the sequence ends with Rachel looking out into the empty backyard suggest that the flashback is hers; on the other hand, the sequence is preceded and followed by the scene of Locke in the Munich church; hence it could just as easily be his flashback. (The return cut to Locke in the church begins, significantly, on his feet – a more anonymous place than his head, obviously, and thus a factor in the ambiguity of attaching the flashback to his consciousness.)

What these flashbacks are concerned with is *memory*, specifically memory as a function of subjectivity and identity. In this regard, Locke's name appropriately recalls that of the English empiricist philosopher John Locke (1632–1704) who made a decisive contribution to epistemology with his theory that humans are born with no innate ideas, that the mind is essentially a blank slate that experience writes upon. According to Locke, "Personal identity is consciousness of being the same thinking self at different times and places," and therefore memory is the "single necessary and sufficient criterion of personal identity."[6]

These ideas seem to be explicitly foregrounded in a bit of dialogue, tantalizingly brief, between Locke and the Woman (the nameless character played by Maria Schneider), when they meet in Barcelona. The first words he says to her are, "Excuse me, I was trying to remember something." She responds, "I can't recognize you. Who are you?" And he answers, "I used to be somebody else but I traded him in." A bit later, she says, "I hope you make it. People disappear every day." He answers, after a pause, "Every time they leave the room."

Spatial and temporal discontinuities also occur in other scenes that are not specifically marked as flashbacks. Thus, after the discovery of Robertson's body, the camera is on Locke, who is wearing a red-checked shirt; the camera then tilts up on the ceiling fan, and then back down on Locke, whom we now see in Robertson's shirt, even though there has not really been time enough for him to change. (A few moments later, when he leaves the room, we can see that he has the red-checked shirt balled up in his hand.)

In fact, the editing throughout the film is decidedly unconventional. Locke's discovery of Robertson's body, for example, is conveyed in the following sequence: first, we see Locke looking at something, and then instead of cutting to what he sees, as we would in a "normal" sequence, we see his expression slowly change, and only then do we cut to the dead body. Here Antonioni continues to problematize the nature of vision in a way similar to that in *Blow-up*. Much later, when Locke is in a restaurant with the Woman, Antonioni twice chooses to pan back and forth to follow passing cars on the street in front of the restaurant, for absolutely no narrative reason and without attributing this "look" to either of the characters. Another moment comes when the passage of time during their trip is shown with a simple, unmarked cut, a purposeful error in continuity that suddenly and inexplicably shows the Woman in the back seat of the car, though she has been sitting in the front up until then. In all these cases, the look of the director, or of what Lorenzo Cuccu calls, "the Other," is clearly being foregrounded and distinguished from the looks of the characters.

There are many other moments in which information seems to be withheld from the audience purposely in order to replicate in it, perhaps, the sense of uncertainty and rootlessness that the characters are experiencing. Even once the basic cross-cutting pattern between Locke and his wife Rachel has been established in the second, "chase" half of the film, the director will often, in a given scene, first show us a nondescript, perfectly unimportant employee, say, before he shows us the character that we already know and are looking for. And in the important flashback scene between Locke and Robertson, many of the shots are extreme close-ups (which contrast strongly with the vast long shots and wide pans of the desert) that are not used in the conventional manner, to heighten emotion – in fact, they block it by objectifying the humans and hiding facial expression – but rather make it difficult for the audience to get information or fully sort out who, what, and where things are. This difficulty adds to what we have been calling the "epistemological" theme in Antonioni's films; here, to a basic sense of the impossibility of sure and fixed knowledge about anything has been added a specific focus on the constructedness of all subjectivity.

In fact, the expository connections of *The Passenger* are, with the possible exception of *L'avventura*, less clear than those of any film Antonioni ever made, but the resultant state of uncertainty seems perfectly in keeping with the film's themes. Equally foregrounded is the notion of how much we must always interpret even to understand the basic *narrative* line of the film, let alone its meanings, however that word is construed.[7] In fact, the familiar self-conscious longueurs and the aimless wandering that mark this film make us more certain that the jazzy, jumpy narrative of *Blow-up* really was there for artistic reasons, not mercenary ones, for in this third film of his putative "commercial" series, the director seems to have fully returned to his "normal" mode.[8]

Related to this purposely disjunctive narrative style is the director's refusal to abide by the conventional genre of the suspense film. In his interview with Alberto Ongaro, Antonioni said:

> The only certain thing was my need to reduce the suspense to a minimum, even though there had to be some left – and I do think some has been left, even it is an indirect, mediated element. It would have been very easy to make a thriller. I had the pursuers and the pursued; nothing was missing, but it would have been banal. That wasn't what interested me.[9]

All of these purposeful narrative, generic, spatial, and temporal dislocations, many of which we saw in *Blow-up*, along with the visual doubling that goes back at least as far as *L'avventura*, augment the film's depiction of subjectivity or identity as something fluid and contradictory. Curiously, this is further accomplished in this film, by the introduction of a certain "objectivity" in viewpoint that several critics (as well as the director) have pointed out. It is clear from interviews, however, that Antonioni did not intend this word to carry its usual meaning, but wanted rather to convey a negative sense, to signify an avoidance of the individual, subjective viewpoint of his characters.[10] Locke is, in fact, more looked at than looking in this film; in Chatman's words, he "is often picked up accidentally and contingently, as if diegesis (or at least this diegesis) were not the camera's real responsibility. . . . [T]he camera seems to be conducting its own inquiry, one not quite at the service of the character."[11] But, paradoxically, the effect of this "objectivity," especially given the unconventionality of the film's narrative and cinematic technique, is to insist even more strongly on the presence of a new subjectivity, that of the *director*. The splitting of perspective between these two subjectivities thus makes us aware of the contingency of subjectivity itself, calling it into question.

The Passenger also makes use of other techniques and motifs that have been a part of Antonioni's armada since the earliest films, such as the graphic or figurative element of his images.[12] For example, the bright red of the little boy's shirt at the end has been predominant from the beginning, clashing continually with the film's dominant blankness, especially in the immense expressionistic splashes found in the Avis car rental offices in Barcelona and elsewhere. In one scene in an Avis office, the first thing we see is some broad, intense red and white stripes on the wall – as usual, not contextualized for us – which strongly suggest the stripes of the American flag. (This association is entirely appropriate, given that Avis is a U.S. company.) We are so close to the giant red letters that it takes some time to recognize that they spell out "Avis." Again, it is a question of scale, as it was with the enlargements in *Blow-up*; in both cases, it is another clear reference to the necessity and difficulty of interpreting even the most obvious signs that surround us.

At another point early in the film, a strongly expressionistic moment, with no apparent narrative function, occurs when the camera lovingly focuses on the white cord against the white wall in Locke's hotel room, with accompanying black bugs. Much later in the film, in his frustration at not being able to outrun the authorities, Locke places a bug on a similar white wall and crushes it, and the camera lingers a few moments on the abstract pattern created by the plaster. Still later, near the end, Antonioni's camera self-consciously tilts up to the artwork decorating Locke's last hotel room (with no narrative or dramatic justification), almost seeming to enter into this insipid picture of a church near a lake, as if to foreground the difference between this merely decorative, mass-produced art and his own idiosyncratic visual artistry.

Architecture, much less important to the director's mise-en-scène in *Blow-up*, also makes a strong comeback in *The Passenger*. Playing off against the white, blank spaces that we call natural (the desert, the sea) and the white spaces of "primitive" architecture that predominate in the second half of the film is the architecture of advanced Western urban society. This is primarily seen in the wonderfully surrealistic creations of the Catalan architect Antoni Gaudí (who is described by the Woman, an architecture student, as a man who "was hit by a bus") that are foregrounded in the film, especially when Locke and the Woman meet on the roof of the Casa Mila apartments, one of Gaudí's dizziest creations.[13] Characteristically, Antonioni chose this setting to make a specific point, as he explained in an interview: "The Gaudí towers reveal, perhaps, the oddity of an encounter between a man who has the name of a dead man and a girl who doesn't have any name."[14] (The director also chose to stage Locke's meeting with the guerrillas in a baroque church in Munich precisely to show that this quintessentially rootless, identity-less modern man is just as out of place there, in the church, as he was in the desert.) In contrast to the refreshing flamboyance of Gaudí's creations, many of the places toward which Locke and the Woman run contain a dull similarity that recalls Robertson's earlier remark to the effect that "everything has become the same." It is precisely the implacable external sameness of modern mass culture that has caused us to rely more upon internal markers for our sense of self, markers that themselves have begun to atrophy through lack of use.

Appropriately, it is never made clear exactly why Locke wants to assume Robertson's identity. Nor do we really know what is wrong with his life as Locke. This correlates perfectly with the themes discussed in the preceding chapters, but to some extent the lack of information may also be due to the cuts that Antonioni was forced to make during the editing process. In an interview with Luigi Vaccari, the director complained that even the European version was drastically altered, from which he said he felt like removing his signature. According to the director, the European version, much less the American, does not tell the story very well as a result of what he called a "grave mistake" on the part of the producers. He had to omit a scene that more clearly explained the failure of Locke's marriage and showed to what extent it weighed on his mind and subsequent decisions.[15] Furthermore, he had to shoot much more footage on this film than was his normal practice, because he had less time to prepare; since Nicholson was busy with other engagements, the director was forced to shoot as quickly as possible.[16] And since he was not able to cut the script as needed (and thus presumably clarify necessary plot aspects), the first filmed version ran four hours, the second two hours and twenty minutes, and the third two hours.[17]

As mentioned earlier, I was recently able to see, for the first time, the "European" version, in English. This print, which is owned by Jack Nicholson's company, Proteus, carries the title "Profession: Reporter" and contains two important scenes that are not in the American version of the film available on videocassette. The first occurs when Locke returns to London, immediately after exchanging identities with Robertson. (Other scenes set in London remain in the American cassette version as well, but without this initial London scene, Locke's location is unclear.) He goes to his own house, lets himself in, and finds a note to his wife from her lover (or vice versa). He gets some papers out of a box, and next to it we can see the English translation of Alberto Moravia's *Which Tribe Do You Belong To?*[18] In the second scene missing from the American cassette version, Locke and the Woman, after they have been to the Plaza de Iglesia near the end of the film, find themselves in a serene lemon grove. She picks lemons while he rests in the grass. Locke says that he wants to give up trying to meet Robertson's appointments and then says: "Let's go and eat, the old me is hungry." The Woman refuses, saying, "I'm not interested in giving up." She takes her things out of the car and ends up in a desertlike gulch while Locke remains in the lemon grove, a division that seems heavily, if once again ambiguously, symbolic. The Woman hitches a ride with a local man; Locke catches up with her, makes her get out, and they continue their journey together.

Even with these scenes restored, Locke's behavior is far from transparently explicable. We have to probe more deeply. Antonioni suggested that Locke's profession was part of the problem: "He can't get involved in everything he reports because he's a filter. His job is always to talk about and show something or someone else, but he himself is not involved. He's a witness not a protagonist. And that's the problem."[19] Presumably, then, taking on Robertson's "activist" life will make him feel more fully alive. Further clarifying Locke's relation to Robertson, Antonioni told Alberto Ongaro that when Locke

finds out that the man whose identity he has assumed is a man of action – a man who takes an active part in life, and isn't just a passive witness – he tries to take on not only his identity, but also his role, his political role. But this other man's history, which is so concrete, so built on action, becomes too much of a burden to him. Action itself becomes problematic.[20]

But the problem seems to go beyond Locke's profession and his envy of Robertson's active stance toward the world. He does accept the money from the Liberation Front for the weapons that Robertson was to have delivered, but financial gain seems not to be the principal motivation for his assumption of Robertson's identity and is not mentioned again. More important is the sense he conveys, in the flashback scene with Robertson early in the film, of tired and hopeless *Weltschmerz*, a disgust with life in general that afflicts many Antonioni characters. Later Locke meets an old Spanish man in the Parque in Barcelona who bemoans the fact that each succeeding generation of children perpetuates the mistakes of adults: "It's a tragedy, they can't get away from us," he says, and Locke appears to agree. Even when he is told that Robertson is "in danger," he replies, "in danger of what?" putting the matter in cosmic terms, and continues blithely to assume the other man's life. Toward the end of the film, Locke seems to insist on tenaciously sticking to Robertson's appointments – though his resolve weakens occasionally – merely because these appointments seem to provide a purpose or focus that is missing in his own life.

Maintaining his new identity seems also to become important to the Woman, and it is even harder to fathom her motivation. It is as though Locke's assumption of an externally provided meaningfulness to his life grants her one as well. Toward the end, it is in fact her insistence that he remain Robertson that gets him killed, but she seems to be motivated by the knowledge that without Robertson's identity, Locke would have none at all.

In a curious way, Locke blends his identity with the woman's as well. For one thing, once they meet they are rarely separated, even though they know hardly anything about each other; this lack of knowledge seems to be precisely the source of attraction between them. But they are also visually linked in two powerful rhymed moments. In the first, Locke pretends to "fly," hanging dangerously out of a gondola window when he first gets to Barcelona, while we see nothing but the field of sea beneath him. This moment is visually duplicated when, in the car, the Woman is kneeling in the back seat of the convertible, looking backward, and she is framed against the quickly moving field of trees.[21] Both moments seem to express an intense, rare sense of utter freedom; significantly, though, each character performs the gesture alone.

Gender relations somehow seem to be taken for granted in *The Passenger*, rather than problematized as in earlier films. This is perhaps due to the intensity of Antonioni's focus on the male character, but a similar focus did not keep the director from examining gender issues in *Blow-up*. Locke and the Woman meet, have sex, and travel together, but they seem to have little impact on each other's profound loneliness. Rachel says that she did not care at all for her husband before, and now that he is dead, or so she thinks, she does care for him. Her new lover (who is never introduced to us) has the best line, though the thought is not pursued: "Perhaps if you try hard enough," he taunts her, "you can reinvent him." Another facet of the question of identity is thus articulated, from the other direction – who is this person that I love, or think I love?

Locke once again presents us with a wandering figure, a figure that goes back to Lidia in *La notte*, and even further back to Aldo in *Il grido*, though he is now, for the most part, wandering in a car, like the photographer in *Blow-up*. And, like the photographer, Locke seems to be one of those male figures the director half rejects and half envies. (The rejection disappears with *Identification of a Woman* [1984] and with Antonioni's most recent film, *Beyond the Clouds*, and it is precisely this lack of tension, this direct identification of the director with the characters, that makes these films less interesting.) As Antonioni told Gideon Bachmann, Locke desires freedom, and as such, is a direct stand-in for the director: "I can direct [the camera] any way I want: as the director I am God. I can allow myself any kind of liberty. Actually, the liberty I have achieved in the making of this film is the liberty the character in the film tried to achieve by changing identity."[22]

But Antonioni is related to Locke in even more complicated ways, centering especially on the latter's role as a journalist. Antonioni told Bachmann that "a journalist sees reality with a certain consistency: the ambiguous consistency of his viewpoint, which to him, and only to him, seems objective. Jack in the film sees things in his way and I, as the director, play the role of the journalist behind the journalist: I again add other dimensions to reproduced reality."[23]

This critique of traditional journalistic practice has both a specifically historical and a more generally political aspect. When viewing the film now, some twenty-five years after it was made, it is important to remember that the historical context for Locke's narcissistic flight from the self and his assumption of Robertson's identity is the many liberation movements that flourished in the 1970s in Africa immediately following the first wave of decolonialization. It is easy to regard this aspect of the film as an unimportant backdrop to the plot and to Locke's private drama, but it is precisely this kind of commitment, Antonioni shows us, that Locke desperately lacks in his own life. The guerrilla leader makes a point of thanking Locke for being sympathetic to his cause, but the real Locke, in his role as "neutral" journalist, has not been sympathetic at all. In fact, in accordance with Western journalistic protocol, he is very easy on the corrupt black president in his filmed interview, which upsets his wife Rachel, who is present. When she castigates him, he replies that these are "the rules" and that he could not just tell the president to his face that he thought he was a liar.[24]

Beyond this rather conventional critique of journalism's illusory "objectivity," Antonioni is mounting a broader investigation of the nature of the image and its relation to reality. This relation was closely questioned in *Blow-up* in an epistemological or more generally philosophical way, and the same kind of probing occurs in *The Passenger*. Lorenzo Cuccu, for example, describes Antonioni's self-reflexive presence in the film

> not as a stripping down to the bare structure, or as an open exhibition of the apparatus and its articulations, but in a less striking, less "direct" manner, which is, however, perhaps deeper. What's in play here, I mean, isn't the mechanism of the look [as in *Blow-up*], but its "value," its "meaning," its capacity for having a relation with something that the "mind" of the author synthesizes in the term "reality."[25]

Cuccu is right here, for it is clear that Antonioni's exploration of the image in this film is the most profound it has ever been. Even more important, this investigation is also more explicitly, and more broadly, politicized in *The Passenger*, as Antonioni seems to begin to understand how much is at stake in the context of the 1970s. Antonioni himself has said that he had made Peploe and Wollen's script even more political than it had been originally.[26] Asserting that the politics in the film was more implicit than explicit, Antonioni specifically addressed this question in an interview with Alberto Ongaro, which goes counter to the usual view of Antonioni as apolitical artist of angst and alienation:

> I do take an active interest in politics, I follow it closely. Today, especially, it's a moral duty for all of us to find out how we are governed, check what the people who guide our lives are doing, because there is no alternative. We only have one life each, and so we must try to live it in the best and most just way possible, for ourselves and for others. Naturally, I am interested in politics in my own way, not as a professional politician, but as a filmmaker. I try to make my own little revolutions with my films; I try to highlight certain prob-

lems and contradictions, to bring out certain emotions in the audience, to have them experience certain things rather than others. Sometimes it happens that the films are interpreted differently from the way the director intended, but perhaps this isn't important. Perhaps it doesn't matter whether films are understood and rationalized; it's enough that they are lived as a direct personal experience.[27]

His stance here recalls the view of Lino Miccichè, quoted earlier, that perhaps the truest way to judge a filmmaker's politics is on the basis of his exploration of the crucial questions that ground his métier, rather than on whatever public stand he takes on specific political issues.

At its most basic level, the film concerns the ongoing question of the interpretation of signs, the fact that the world is not simply given, but must be interpreted. This is in itself a political position, an acknowledgment that all interpretation proceeds inevitably from the position of the interpreter.[28] From the beginning, Locke is reading signs, as he does when the African men signal that they want a cigarette; the negative version of this communication comes when the man on the camel passes Locke without the slightest recognition, even though Locke has made a gesture to him. Most important here are the remarks about signs that Locke makes to Robertson, which seem to have come from the pen of semiotician Peter Wollen. (Wollen claims that he no longer remembers who wrote this bit of dialogue.) When Robertson says that airports and taxis are the same all over the world, Locke replies, "I don't agree; it's us who remain the same, we translate every situation, every experience into the same old codes, we just condition ourselves." "We're creatures of habit, that's what you mean," Robertson helpfully rephrases. "Something like that," replies Locke. Locke goes on to say that they talk to "these people" all wrong and never get their confidence. Robertson responds: "You come at them with words and images, fragile things, and I come with merchandise, concrete things, and they understand me right away." We do not yet know that the "concrete things" Robertson speaks of are the armaments he supplies to the liberation front, but in any case this exchange registers as a variety of the discourse about objects, the debate about the relation between reality and its representation, that came fully to the fore in *Blow-up*.

Related to this point is the way that various pieces of apparently actual documentary footage, especially that of the black man shot by the firing squad, keep turning up throughout the film. (Antonioni has always refused to indicate a source for this footage.) It is clear that by using it, the director is problematizing the internal borders of his own film, the question of the frame, of the outside and the inside. Where, exactly, does "his" film stop and start? This documentary footage is extraneous to *The Passenger* in that it exists prior to Antonioni's film, but is also *within* the film – where its meaning changes because of the change in frame. While insisting that he did not alter reality in this film as he had in *Red Desert*, the director said that he looked at reality "with the same eye with which the hero, a reporter, looks at the events he is reporting on. Objectivity is one of the themes of the film. If you look closely, there are two documentaries in the film, Locke's documentary on Africa and mine on him."[29]

These topoi, once again, are clearly related to those being explored in *Blow-up*. One of the most important moments in *The Passenger* comes when, along with Rachel and Martin Knight (played by Ian Henry), we watch the footage of Locke's interview with the unnamed African opposition leader. Locke, off-camera, asks a series of questions. The leader responds that there are perfectly good answers to all these questions, but that they reveal more about the questioner than the answers would reveal about him, the interviewee. "We can have a conversation, but not only about what you think is sincere, but also about what I believe to be honest," he tells Locke. He insists on turning the camera around, on Locke, making the reporter very uncomfortable by equalizing things, unmasking the transparency, revealing the madeness of the documentary, and thus of all documentaries, of all visual records, of all representation. In this way, Antonioni is also implicitly questioning the status of his own "documentary" on Locke.

The various themes and visual motifs swirling through *The Passenger* come to a climax in the film's deservedly famous final scene. The whole last part of the film – as though self-consciously moving toward a grand yet understated artistic resolution, if not the resolution of Locke's troubled identity – is more formally composed. Visual arrangements are more stately and self-consciously aestheticized, especially the shots connected with the Hotel de la Gloria at the end: the Woman framed in the mirror, the hotel proprietor in the window to the side of the door, and so on. Here, for the first time, architecture seems to become almost completely benign. Locke's glasses lie prominently on the bed, and twice during their time together in the hotel room, Locke asks the Woman what she sees out the window, as if to foreground once again the act of seeing, and the very nature of visuality itself. To show what an ambiguous gift vision is, Antonioni has Locke tell her the story of the blind man who suddenly regained his sight. After a while, the man became afraid, lived in darkness, and never left his room. Three years later, he killed himself, having become disillusioned by all the unsuspected ugliness in the world.

This apotheosis of the visual culminates in the film's penultimate shot, the final, famous long take, lasting seven minutes, an extremely slow tracking shot through Locke's hotel room and out the barred window onto the plaza outside. This brilliant and powerful long take is roughly equivalent in thematic and formal weight to the final shots of *L'eclisse*, though there it was montage that reigned. Much of what is shown is apparently random: two old men on a bench talking; a dog; a car used for driver training, with a sign attached to its roof; a child in a red shirt playing with a ball; the Woman after she leaves the room. Then come the hired killers who have been chasing Robertson/Locke, but the viewer needs to be watching carefully to register their arrival and to understand who they are, because Antonioni characteristically refuses to underline their presence in any way. One of the agents enters the hotel and the other briefly restrains the Woman.

At this heightened visual moment, the audio track, in complementary fashion, takes on a supremely important role, principally because of the evacuation of any clearly "meaningful" sound. We hear bits of a foreign language, presumably Spanish, some trumpet music associated with bullfighting, and aleatory fragments of noise, some of which is extremely significant (yet never underlined), as, for example, when the killers discretely open and close the door of Locke's hotel room. For Antonioni, everything that we see and hear throughout this long take represents, in a phenomenological sense, "the world." Explaining its philosophical and psychological significance, the director told an interviewer: "Being, says Heidegger, is being-in-the-world. When David senses the end (although probably not even he himself is sure of it), he is no longer in the world. The world is outside the window."[30] (The interviewer also suggested that it is almost as though David is behind the camera here, reporting on his own death, and though this seems to be completely foreign to the mood created, the director concurred. Maybe he was just being agreeable.)[31]

The camera moves incrementally but relentlessly through space, through the bars, out into the dusty plaza. An odd sensation results, a curious mélange of dark portentousness and promise of liberation. Ultimately coming to focus on a police car that includes Rachel, immediately after the killers' car has left, the camera pans right, back toward the room, and then moves back *in through* the window from the plaza.[32]

Antonioni explained the genesis of this shot by saying that he wanted

Locke to die, but did not like the idea of showing his death. Then an idea from Hemingway flashed through his mind: *Death in the Afternoon*, Hemingway's book on bullfighting, with its dusty arena, the corrida music, and so on, all of which is suggested by what occurs outside Locke's window. In addition, "You see the girl outside and you see her movements and you understand very well without going closer to her what she's doing, maybe what her thoughts are. You see, I am using this very long [take] *like* close-ups, the shot actually takes the place of close-ups."[33]

The most intriguing description of the philosophical thrust of this shot is undoubtedly that of Sam Rohdie. For him, the shot is "objective" because it shows something that no character sees. Perhaps romanticizing a bit the exigencies of on-location shooting, he claims that "the camera watches the fiction as it unfolds, but independently as a separate presence. . . . As the events take place the camera becomes aware of them." He concludes that one purpose of "this autonomous but non-dominant narration is to seek out meanings, not to proclaim them."[34]

What is most important for Rohdie is that the long take, in a sense, includes the camera itself in the external reality it films; in other words, "it also watches itself watching them. . . . It is not, as Antonioni commented, a thought illustrated by a sight, but a thought in the process of formation which includes a reflection on its own thinking" (p. 150). Because the camera stands outside both any character's POV and a dominant narrational POV, the spectator does not identify with any character or with any narrator and hence comes to participate in the same freedom as the camera. Like Locke, who has become both subject and object, the camera is double:

> It moves, it looks, as a subject, but at the same time it is an object of its own regard; it turns around the square and looks at itself turning. And just as the camera ends by registering its own movement, and the duration of its look, so too the audience finds itself in a similar position, looking at that movement of the camera, but catching, as it does so, its own reflection. (P. 151)

With the help of Rohdie's analysis, we can see this camera movement as the apotheosis of Antonioni's experimentation with narrative and consistent questioning of the status of the visual image and his own part in creating it.

Locke's dualities end in his drive toward death. When Biarese and Tassone asked the director if Locke knew what he was heading toward, he replied:

Figure 20. The Woman (Maria Schneider), Rachel (Jenny Runacre), the police inspector (Angel del Pozo), and the hotelkeeper (Jose Maria Cafarel) surround the dead Locke

The whole film lies behind this question. I could say that the desire to die has simply become nestled in his unconscious, unknown to him. Or that Locke begins absorbing death from the moment he leans over Robertson's corpse. But I could also say that he keeps the appointment for the opposite reasons: in fact, it's Daisy he's going to meet, and Daisy is a character from his new life. But Locke can't really believe very strongly in this new opening. At the point he's at, he no longer identifies with anything.[35]

At the end the police ask Rachel if she recognizes the body, and she replies, with appropriate and pregnant ambiguity, "I never knew him." We watch as the driver of the driver training car, a white Seat, starts his engine and moves off. The camera pans to a long shot of the hotel, now gorgeous in the glow of the evening, its electric lights contrasting impotently but magically with the fading sky. The proprietor of the hotel lights a cigarette and walks around with a contented air. The happy sounds of a guitar are heard. Despite Locke's death, a strange sense of fullness and completion, even rightness, engulfs the scene. The credits begin to roll, and it is the end.

Filmography

Gente del Po (People of the Po Valley)
Documentary short
Production: Artisti Associati, ICET – Carpi (Milan)
Script: Antonioni
Photography: Piero Portalupi
Editing: C. A. Chiesa
Music: Mario Labroca
Cast: Nonprofessionals

N. U. – Nettezza urbana (Sanitation department)
Documentary short
Production: ICET (Lux Film)
Photography: Giovanni Ventimiglia
Music: Giovanni Fusco, with J. S. Bach
Cast: Nonprofessionals

L'amorosa menzogna (Lies of love)
Fictional short
Production: Edizioni Fortuna Film Roma (Filmus)
Script: Antonioni
Photography: Renato del Frate
Music: Giovanni Fusco
Cast: Anna Vita, Sergio Raimondi, Annie O'Hara, Sandro Roberti

Superstizione (Superstition)
Documentary short
Production: ICET – Carpi (Giorgio Venturini)
Script: Antonioni
Photography: Giovanni Ventimiglia
Music: Giovanni Fusco
Cast: Nonprofessionals

Sette canne, un vestito (Seven tubes, one suit)
Documentary short
Production: ICET (Milan)
Script: Antonioni
Photography: Giovanni Ventimiglia

La funivia del Faloria (The Faloria tram)
Documentary short
Production: Theo Usuelli
Script: Antonioni
Music: Theo Usuelli
Photography: Goffredo Bellisario and Ghedina

La villa dei mostri (The villa of the monsters)
Documentary short
Production: Filmus
Script: Antonioni
Photography: Giovanni de Paoli
Music: Giovanni Fusco
Cast: None

Cronaca di un amore (Story of a love affair)
Fictional feature
Production: Villani Films
Story: Antonioni
Script: Antonioni, Daniele d'Anza, Silvio Giovaninetti, Francesco Maselli, Piero Tellini
Photography: Enzo Serafin
Music: Giovanni Fusco
Cast: Lucia Bosè, Massimo Girotti, Ferdinando Sarmi, Gino Rossi, Marika Rowsky

La signora senza camelie (The lady without camelias)
Fictional feature

Production: Domenico Forges Davanzati for ENIC
Story: Antonioni
Script: Antonioni, Suso Cecchi D'Amico, Francesco Maselli, P. M. Pasinetti
Photography: Enzo Serafin
Music: Giovanni Fusco
Cast: Lucia Bosè, Andrea Cecchi, Gino Cervi, Ivan Desny, Alain Cuny, Monica Clay, Anna Carena, Enrico Glori

I vinti (The vanquished)
Fictional feature
Production: Film Constellazione
Story: Antonioni, Suso Cecchi D'Amico, Diego Fabbri, Turi Vasile, Giorgio Bassini
Script: Antonioni, Suso Cecchi D'Amico, with Diego Fabbri, Turi Vasile, Giorgio Bassini and, for the French episode, Roger Nimier
Photography: Enzo Serafin
Music: Giovanni Fusco
Editing: Eraldo da Roma
Cast: Italian episode – Franco Interlenghi, Anna-Maria Ferrero, Evi Maltagliati, Eduardo Cianelli; French episode – Jean-Pierre Mocky, Etchika Choureau; English episode – Peter Reynolds, Fay Compton, Patrick Barr

"Tentato suicidio," episode of *Amore in città* ("Suicide attempt," episode of Love in the city)
Episode of fictional feature
Production: Faro Film
Script: Antonioni, Cesare Zavattini, Aldo Buzzi, Luigi Chiarini, Luigi Malerba, Tullio Pinelli, Vittorio Veltroni
Photography: Gianni di Venanzo
Music: Mario Nascimbene
Editing: Eraldo da Roma
Cast: Nonprofessionals (playing themselves)

1955

Le amiche (The girlfriends)
Fictional feature
Production: Giovanni Addessi for Trionfalcine-Titanus
Story: Adapted from Cesare Pavese's story "Tra donne sole," originally published in *La bella estate*
Script: Antonioni and Suso Cecchi D'Amico, with Alba de Céspedes
Photography: Gianni di Venanzo
Music: Giovanni Fusco
Editing: Eraldo da Roma
Cast: Eleanora Rossi, Valentina Cortese, Yvonne Furneaux, Gabriele Ferzetti, Franco Fabrizi, Ettore Manni, Madeleine Fischer, Annamaria Pancani, Maria Gambarelli

Il grido (The cry)
Fictional feature
Production: Franco Cancellieri for SPA Cinematografica
Story: Antonioni
Script: Antonioni, Elio Bartolini, Ennio de Concini
Photography: Gianni di Venanzo
Music: Giovanni Fusco
Editing: Eraldo da Roma
Cast: Steve Cochran, Alida Valli, Betsy Blair, Dorian Gray, Gabriella Pallotta, Lynn Shaw

L'avventura (The adventure)
Fictional feature
Production: A Cino del Duca Co-Production: Produzioni Cinematografiche Europee (Rome) and Société Cinématographique Lyre (Paris)
Story: Antonioni
Script: Antonioni, Elio Bartolini, Tonino Guerra
Photography: Aldo Scavarda
Music: Giovanni Fusco
Editing: Eraldo da Roma
Cast: Gabriele Ferzetti, Monica Vitti, Lea Massari, Dominique Blanchard, Renzo Ricci, James Addams, Dorothy De Poliolo, Giovanni Petrucci

La notte (The night)
Fictional feature
Production: Emanuele Cassuto for Nepi-Film (Rome), Silva-Film (Rome), and Sofitedip (Paris)
Story: Antonioni
Script: Antonioni, Ennio Flaiano, Tonino Guerra
Photography: Gianni di Venanzo
Music: Giorgio Gaslini
Editing: Eraldo da Roma
Cast: Marcello Mastroanni, Jeanne Moreau, Monica Vitti, Bernhard Wicki, Maria Pia Luzi, Gitt Magrini, Vincenzo Corbella

L'eclisse (The eclipse)
Fictional feature
Production: Robert and Raymond Hakim for Interopa Film, Cineriz (Rome), and

Paris Film Production (Paris)
Story: Antonioni and Tonino Guerra
Script: Antonioni, Tonino Guerra, Elio Bartolini, Ottiero Ottieri
Photography: Gianni di Venanzo
Music: Giovanni Fusco
Editing: Eraldo da Roma
Cast: Monica Vitti, Alain Delon, Lilla Brignone, Francisco Rabal

1964

Il deserto rosso (Red Desert)
Fictional feature
Production: Antonio Cervi for Film Duemila, Cinematografica Federiz (Rome) and Francoriz (Paris)
Story: Antonioni and Tonino Guerra
Script: Antonioni and Tonino Guerra
Photography: Carlo di Palma
Music: Giovanni Fusco, electronic music by Vittorio Gelmetti
Editing: Eraldo da Roma
Cast: Monica Vitti, Richard Harris, Carlo de Pra, Aldo Grotti, Valerio Bartoleschi

1965

"Prefazione: Il provino," episode of *I tre volti* ("Preface: The screen test" episode of The three faces)
Episode of fictional feature
Production: Dino DeLaurentiis
Story: Antonioni
Script: Antonioni
Photography: Carlo di Palma
Music: Piero Piccioni
Editing: Eraldo da Roma
Cast: Soraya

1966

Blow-up
Fictional feature
Production: Bridge Films (Carlo Ponti) for MGM
Story: Based on "Las bavas del diablo," a short story by Julio Cortàzar
Script: Antonioni and Tonino Guerra
Photography: Carlo di Palma
Music: Performed by the Yardbirds and The Lovin' Spoonful
Editing: Frank Clarke
Cast: David Hemmings, Vanessa Redgrave, Sarah Miles, Peter Bowles, Verushka

Zabriskie Point
Fictional feature
Production: Carlo Ponti for MGM
Script: Antonioni, Fred Gardner, Sam Shepard, Tonino Guerra, and Clare Peploe
Photography: Alfio Conti
Music: Pink Floyd, Kaleidoscope, the Rolling Stones, the Youngbloods, the Grateful Dead
Editing: Franco Arcalli
Cast: Mark Frechette, Daria Halprin, Rod Taylor

1972

Chung-Kuo China
Documentary feature (shot on super-16 mm)
Production: RAI (Radiotelevisione italiana)
Photography: Luciano Tovoli
Sound: Giorgio Pallotta
Editing: Franco Arcalli
Cast: Nonprofessionals

1975

Professione: Reporter (*The Passenger*)
Fictional feature
Production: Carlo Ponti for MGM; Co-production by Compagnia Cinematografica Champion (Rome), Les films Concordia (Paris), and CIPI Cinematográfica (Madrid)
Story: Mark Peploe
Script: Mark Peploe, Peter Wollen, and Antonioni
Photography: Luciano Tovoli
Editing: Franco Arcalli and Antonioni
Cast: Jack Nicholson, Maria Schneider, Jenny Runacre, Ian Hendry

1980

Il mistero di Oberwald (The mystery of Oberwald)
Fictional feature (originally shot on video)
Production: Sergio Benvenuti, Alessandro von Norman, and Giancarlo Bernardoni for the RAI
Script: Antonioni and Tonino Guerra, based on Jean Cocteau's play *L'aigle à deux têtes* (The eagle with two heads)
Photography: Luciano Tovoli
Editing: Antonioni and Francesco Grandoni
Music: Brahms, Schoenberg, Strauss
Cast: Monica Vitti, Paolo Bonacelli, Franco Branciaroli, Luigi Diberti, Elisabetta Pozzi

Identificazione di una donna (*Identification of a Woman*)
Fictional feature
Production: Giorgio Nocella and Antonio Macri for Iter Film (Rome) and Gaumont (Paris)
Script: Antonioni and Gérard Brach, with Tonino Guerra, based on a story by Antonioni
Photography: Carlo di Palma
Editing: Antonioni
Music: John Foxx
Cast: Tomás Milián, Christine Boisson, Daniela Silverio, Marcel Bozzuffi

Par-delà des nuages (*Beyond the Clouds*)
Fictional feature
Production: Sunshine, Cine B, France 3 Cinéma, Cecchi Gori Group Tiger Cinematografica, Road Movies Zweite Produktionen
Direction: Antonioni, Wim Wenders
Script: Antonioni, Tonino Guerra, Wim Wenders
Photography: Alfio Contini, Robby Müller
Music: Lucio Dalla, Laurent Petitgand, Van Morrison, U2
Editing: Claudio di Mauro, Antonioni, Peter Przygodda, Lucien Segura
Cast: John Malkovich, Fanny Ardant, Irène Jacob, Sophie Marceau, Jeanne Moreau, Marcello Mastroianni, Jean Reno

Notes

Note: Unless otherwise indicated, all translations are mine.

Introduction

1 To many critics in the 1960s, these films seemed especially, and perhaps illegiti-
mately, "novelistic." French critic Pierre Leprohon worried about this, particularly in regard to *La notte* (1961):

> Does it not present a real danger, that of once again drawing the cinema
> out of its proper domain? Is it not possible that this new approach, making
> use of all the techniques of the novel [whatever that might mean, since,
> after all, these *are* films], may create a literary cinema which will soon
> prove as vain as the theatrical cinema it is meant to replace? (Pierre Lepro-
> hon, *Michelangelo Antonioni: An Introduction*, trans. Scott Sullivan [New
> York: Simon and Schuster, 1963], p. 76)

2 Leprohon, *Michelangelo Antonioni*, p. 59.
3 For a fuller discussion of the question of the frame, in all the senses of the word,
see Peter Brunette and David Wills, *Screen/Play: Derrida and Film Theory*
(Princeton, N.J.: Princeton University Press, 1989), esp. chap. 4.
4 See Gianni Vattimo, *The End of Modernity: Nihilism and Hermeneutics in Postmodern Culture* (Baltimore, Md.: Johns Hopkins University Press, 1988).
5 Gian Piero Brunetta, *Storia del cinema italiano*, vol. 2, (Rome: Editori Riuniti,
1982), p. 739.
6 One example among hundreds: a male critic describes the *colors* of the love scene
in Corrado's hotel room in *Red Desert* as well as those of the scene of Thomas's
frolicking with the young girls in *Blow-up* as "alive and playful," thus implicitly
regarding these scenes themselves in the same light. From a feminist perspective,
they can just as legitimately be seen as obnoxious.
7 Pierre Leprohon, *The Italian Cinema*, trans. Roger Greaves and Oliver Stallybrass (New York: Praeger, 1972), p. 168. Interestingly, though, and somewhat
bafflingly, Leprohon asserts elsewhere that it is not "useful to enter into a discus-

sion of Antonioni's atheism or his interest in Marxism. While it can be argued that they explain his moral position, they certainly do not determine it" (Leprohon, *Michelangelo Antonioni*, p. 68). It should also be noted in passing that during the 1950s Antonioni was a frequent contributor to the communist film journal *Cinema nuovo* (which, unfortunately for the director, did not keep that journal from attacking his "bourgeois" films later on).

8 Armando Borrelli, *Neorealismo e marxismo* (Avellino: Edizioni di Cinemasud, 1966), p. 148.

9 Borrelli, *Neorealismo e marxismo*, p. 171.

10 "A Talk with Michelangelo Antonioni on His Work," in Michelangelo Antonioni, *The Architecture of Vision: Writings and Interviews on Cinema*, ed. Carlo di Carlo and Giorgio Tinazzi, American ed. Marga Cottino-Jones (New York: Marsilio, 1996), p. 40. (Originally published in *Film Culture*, no. 24 [Spring, 1962], this interview was translated from "La malattia dei sentimenti: Colloquio con Michelangelo Antonioni," in *Bianco e nero*, vol. 22, nos. 2–3 [February – March 1961].)

11 Lino Miccichè, *Il cinema italiano degli anni '60* (Venice: Marsilio Editore, 1975), p. 27.

12 Richard Roud, "Five Films," *Sight & Sound*, no. 30 (Winter 1960–1), p. 9.

13 Yvonne Baby, *Le Monde*, September 16, 1960, and in several other interviews.

14 In talking about *Il grido*, Antonioni said: "The workers go to the heart of the questions, to the source of the feelings. Everything is more true (with them)" (quoted in Vittorio Spinazzola, *Cinema e pubblico: Lo spettacolo filmico in Italia 1945–1965* [Milan: Bompiani, 1974], p. 152). What is interesting here is the uncanny resemblance between the woman's and the worker's supposed greater access to truth: they are both seen as marginal cases that can lead us to the reality that the (normative) middle-class male misses.

15 Even before the advent of feminist theory in the early-1960s a critic such as Pierre Leprohon was intelligently pointing out that in Antonioni's films "the woman has become an autonomous character; she is no longer designed to serve as a complement to one or more partners: that is to say, deformed by the domination of a masculine figure" (Leprohon, *Michelangelo Antonioni*, p. 30). Leprohon does not at this early moment have the critical concepts with which to probe this dynamic further, but his suggestion that Antonioni's early films were not financially successful precisely because they were dominated by women is a trenchant one.

16 Interestingly, what we hear the men murmuring on the sound track (not translated in the subtitles) is: "Is she a foreigner? Do you think she's French? She must be French."

17 One example of this is Antonioni's decision in *Red Desert* to paint parts of the landscape, literally, in order, as he said, to more clearly portray the interior feelings of his characters.

18 Further information on Antonioni's own career as a painter and the complex relation between painting and his films can be found in "Identification of a Filmmaker," an interview with Sophie Lannes and Philippe Meyer originally published in *L'Express* (August 9–15, 1985), and reprinted in Antonioni, *The Architecture of Vision*, pp. 245–56.

19 "A Talk with Michelangelo Antonioni on His Work," p. 36.

20 Antonioni also said in the *Film Culture* interview: "I think it is important at this time for cinema to turn towards this internal form of filmmaking, towards ways of expression that are absolutely free, as free as those of literature, as free as those of painting which has reached abstraction" ("A Talk with Michelangelo Antonioni on His Work," p. 26). Later in this same interview, the director testified to the great importance of painting in his life: "I have a great love for painting. . . . painting is something that moves me passionately" (p. 44).

It should be added that in his 1961 article, Richard Roud, in discussing several apparently gratuitous camera movements in one of Antonioni's early films, *La signora senza camelie* (The lady without camelias), was thinking along the same lines that I am trying to develop when he congratulated the director for giving us a "non-representational element for our pleasure . . . an experience in pure form" (Roud, "Five Films," p. 11).

Antonioni's films not only borrow a formalist visual aesthetic from modern painting but also quite consciously resemble the modern novel in ways that are too complex to go into here. See William Pechter's statement: "The best new novel I have encountered in the past few years is *L'Avventura*. And it is a film" (Pechter, "On *L'Avventura*" in *L'Avventura*, ed. George Amberg and Robert Hughes [New York: Grove Press, 1969], p. 287).

21 Relevant here is a remark that Antonioni is said to have made during a visit to the studio of famed abstract expressionist painter Mark Rothko in New York: "Your paintings are like my films – they're about nothing . . . with precision" (quoted in Seymour Chatman, *Antonioni: Or, the Surface of the World* [Berkeley: University of California Press, 1985], p. 54). Chatman goes on to quote an article by Richard Gilman, published contemporaneously with the encounter between the two artists, that elaborates on the quotation from Antonioni: "[Antonioni's films] are part of that next step in our feelings which art is continually eliciting and recording. We have been taking that step for a long time, most clearly in painting, but also in music, in certain areas of fiction, in anti-theatre. It might be described as accession through reduction, the coming into truer forms through the cutting away of created encumbrances" (Richard Gilman, "About Nothing – With Precision," *Theater Arts*, vol. 46, no. 7 [July 1962], p. 11; quoted in Chatman, *Antonioni*, p. 54).

22 For Antonioni, this notion of abstraction has always been obscurely tied up with the larger question of realism. He realized that, in principle at least, more details of a filmed reality were latent on the film stock than could be made visible through current photographic technology. Thus, in a sense, the cinematic image is always an abstraction.

23 Micciché, *Il cinema italiano*, p. 27.

24 "An In-Depth Search," interview with Alberto Ongaro, reprinted in Antonioni, *The Architecture of Vision*, p. 345. (This interview originally appeared in Italian in *L'Europeo*, December 18, 1975.)

25 "An In-Depth Search," interview with Ongaro.

26 Reprinted in *Cher Antonioni: 1988–89* (Rome: Ente Autonomo Gestione Cinema, 1988), p. 20.

27 Lorenzo Cuccu, *Antonioni: Il discorso dello sguardo: Da "Blow up" a "Identificazione di una donna"* (Pisa: ETS Editrice, 1990), p. 11.

28 "Making a Film Is My Way of Life," reprinted in Antonioni, *The Architecture of Vision*, pp. 14–15. (Originally published in *Cinema nuovo* in 1959.)

29 Carlo di Carlo, "Voir d'un oeil nouveau," in *Cher Antonioni*, p. 37.

30 "Preface to *Six Films*," in Antonioni, *The Architecture of Vision*, p. 66.

31 Spinazzola, *Cinema e pubblico*, p. 7.

32 Spinazzola, *Cinema e pubblico*, p. 12.

33 Guido Fink, unpublished lecture given at the University of California at Berkeley, April 1993.

34 "My Experience," in Antonioni, *The Architecture of Vision*, pp. 7–8. (Originally published in *Bianco e nero* in 1958.)

35 Brunetta, *Storia del cinema italiano*, vol. 2, p. 740.

36 Brunetta, *Storia del cinema italiano*, vol. 2, p. 147.

37 Spinazzola, *Cinema e pubblico*, p. 146.

38 Gian Piero Brunetta, "Il giardino delle delizie e il deserto: trasformazioni della visione e dei modelli narrativi nel cinema italiano del dopoguerra," in *Schermi e ombre: Gli italiani e il cinema nel dopoguerra*, ed. Marino Livolsi (Scandicci: La Nuova Italia, 1988), p. 65.

39 Provocatively, Brunetta insists on seeing Italian film of the 1960s – "whose importance is not less in the history of Italian cinema than neorealism" – as a *movement*. As such, it has its own formal differences from preceding cinema (in the use of montage and the long take); commercial differences (the director, as auteur, is removed as much as possible from the demands of the industry); and differences in subject matter (with the new treatment of taboo subjects such as Fascism, factory work, and the Republic of Salò) (Brunetta, "Il giardino delle delizie e il deserto," pp. 66–7).

40 In a recent, otherwise excellent book about Antonioni, critic Sam Rohdie uses the following "thoughtful" adjectives in characterizing the American critical reaction to *Zabriskie Point*: "vicious," "stupid," "uncomprehending," "insulting," "vulgar" (Rohdie, *Antonioni* [London: BFI, 1990], p. 137). Rohdie attacks Seymour Chatman for his "stodgy book" and, especially, for choosing not to like this failure of Antonioni's: "He [Chatman] dislikes *Zabriskie Point* because it is merely, pointlessly beautiful; narratively it is badly acted, unrealistic, inaccurate (no 'real,' 'true' American could accept it), unlikely, over-contrived" (pp. 137–8).

Pace Rohdie's intemperate remarks, few Italian critics thought more of the film than did we Americans. Goffredo Fofi, for example, attacked the director for his "megalomania" and said that Antonioni always failed when he attempted the "grand historical-philosophical-sociological vision" (Fofi, *Cinema italiano: Servi e padroni* [Milan: Feltrinelli, 1971], p. 100). He called the film "a wagonload of commonplaces from the American 'analytic' cinema, youthful rebellion, and off-Broadway and off-Hollywood theater and film that provoke a horrible feeling of the already-seen and already-noted, with the difference that this operation of supposed synthesis is extremely more presumptuous and therefore more irritating than all the things that he is recording or manipulating" (p. 101).

41 *Look*, November 18, 1969, p. 40.
42 *New York Times*, September 30, 1982.
43 *Village Voice*, October 19, 1982.
44 *New Yorker*, September 30, 1996, p. 90.
45 *Variety*, December 8–14, 1997, p. 22.
46 Robin Woods, "Ideology, Genre, Auteur," in *Hitchcock's Films Revisited* (New York: Columbia University Press, 1989), p. 292.
47 "Antonioni Discusses *The Passenger*," in Antonioni, *The Architecture of Vision*, p. 334. (Interview originally appeared in *Filmmakers Newsletter* in 1975.)

Chapter 1: *L'avventura* (1960)

1 For more details of the film's production history, see Seymour Chatman and Guido Fink, eds., *L'avventura* (New Brunswick, N.J.: Rutgers University Press, 1989), pp. 173–5. Their account is based on that of Tommaso Chiaretti, "L'avventura dell'avventura," in *L'avventura* (Rome: Casa Editrice Cappelli, 1960). The bulk of Chiaretti's report has been translated as "The Adventure of *L'Avventura*," in the extremely useful but out-of-print *L'Avventura*, ed. George Amberg and Robert Hughes, pp. 185–208.
2 Penelope Houston, "L'Avventura," *Sight & Sound*, no. 30 (Winter 1960–1), pp. 11–12.
3 Ironically, it is with this film, which Vittorio Spinazzola puts in the "auteurist superspectacle" category along with *La dolce vita* and *Rocco and His Brothers*, both of which appeared the same year, that the director for the first time became *more* accessible to the average Italian filmgoer: "Antonioni remolded the intimacy of his behavioral investigations according to the model of a lively emotional adventure, which was able to involve a relatively larger number of spectators than in the past" (Spinazzola, *Cinema e pubblico*, p. 240). Spinazzola also points out that *L'avventura* grossed 92 million lire in its initial release, which, while hardly substantial (*La dolce vita* grossed 768 million lire in its first release, and 2.2 billion after five years), was nevertheless four times more than *Il grido* had grossed three years earlier.
4 Antonioni, "A Talk with Antonioni on His Work," pp. 25–6. That Antonioni's method consists of the kind of cutting away favored by Michelangelo, rather than the additive method, is attested to by the fact that the shooting ratio in this film (the amount of footage shot versus the amount used in the final film) was abnormally high, 12:1. (On the shooting ratio, see the editor's note to the partial reprint of the original *Film Culture* interview, in *L'Avventura*, ed. George Amberg and Robert Hughes, p. 219.)
5 Chatman also speaks of "contingency" rather than causality as being the ordering principle behind the plot in modernist works such as *L'avventura*. He does admit, however, that "sequence, of course, necessarily remains, for narrative must preserve chronology, the march of events, if it is to remain narrative and not become another kind of text—exposition, argument, description, or something else" (Chatman, *Antonioni*, p. 75). This distinction seems hard to maintain in actual practice, though, for it seems that a "sequence" must, by definition, always imply some sort of causality. Pierre Leprohon makes a similar point

when he says that *L'avventura*, like *La dolce vita*, rejects "any kind of arbitrary dramatic construction, preferring to be guided by the autonomous dictates of the crisis in question" (Leprohon, *The Italian Cinema*, p. 170). One wonders how Leprohon is able to distinguish between a plot that is somehow a product of the situation, or "crisis," itself, and one constructed in advance, however "arbitrary," by Antonioni the auteur.

6 But it can also be seen in such apparently minor, "irrelevant" moments as when the prostitute, at the end of the film, tries to pick up with her stockinged feet the money that Sandro has left her.

7 "*L'avventura* and the Critics," in *L'avventura*, ed. Chatman and Fink, p. 190.

8 Roland Barthes, *S/Z*, trans. Richard Miller (New York: Hill and Wang, 1974), p. 19.

9 Pascal Bonitzer, *Peinture et cinéma: Décadrages* (Paris: Cahiers du cinéma/Editions de l'étoile, 1987), p. 98. Seymour Chatman relates that several of Antonioni's collaborators urged him to account somehow for Anna's disappearance, and that he reluctantly did shoot a short scene in which Claudia receives a phone call informing her that Anna's dead body has been found. An alternative idea, apparently never filmed, was simply to have Anna show up at a party, with no explanation (*L'avventura*, ed. Chatman and Fink, pp. 165–6).

The director himself offered a typically cryptic "explanation" of Anna's disappearance:

> Everyone asks after seeing the film: what happened to Anna? There was a scene in the scenario, later cut (I don't remember why), in which Claudia, Anna's friend, is with the others on the island. They are speculating endlessly about the girl's disappearance. But there are no answers. After a silence someone says: "Perhaps she only drowned." Claudia turns suddenly. Everybody looks at each other in dismay. There: this dismay is the connotation of the film. (Antonioni, "About Myself and One of My Films," in *L'avventura*, ed. Chatman and Fink, p. 182)

10 Similarly, Aldo in *Il grido* is usually seen as suffering from a pervasive existential aloneness, when there is actually much more evidence for interpreting his behavior as the manifestation of a frustrated male ego, who simply refuses to believe he cannot have Irma, as he wishes.

11 Borrelli, *Neorealismo e marxismo*, p. 163.

12 Pascal Bonitzer gives an interesting reading of this ink-spilling scene that directly counters all other readings, for he finds something positive in it. Pointing out that the incident is constructed so as to be *neither* by accident nor design, he says that

> the gesture can also express a sort of aesthetic detachment, or perhaps even an aesthetic vertigo, the vertigo of the aleatory or random spot, which is more profoundly childish than the academic drawing which it destroys. As with anything to do with the random, there is ambiguity here, between destruction and creation, chaos and cosmos. To overturn an inkwell on a half-finished sketch is to destroy the sketch, but it is also to splatter on the paper, in place of the sketch (the dry academic copy), a wild ink-flower.

(Bonitzer, "The Disappearance (On Antonioni)," in *L'avventura*, ed. Chatman and Fink, p. 217.)

There is also a strange bit of business at the end of this sequence. Suddenly a group of what appear to be seminarians emerge from the church, distracting the two men from their dispute, and Sandro joins them. Again, it seems as though Antonioni is offering some sort of meaning encapsulated within, or beyond, the formal properties of the scene, without giving us enough clues to find out what it is. This does not stop John Simon, though, from offering what must be considered a very idiosyncratic reading of the scene: "He deliberately knocks over a bottle of India ink . . . the miniature black lava spreads malevolently across the innocent whiteness of the paper. The next moment, a group of priests ushers out of a church a phalanx of little seminarians in black garb, and an identically spreading black mass spills across the screen. (This seems to me a much stronger anticlerical touch than anything Fellini is supposed to have perpetrated.)" (Simon, "Thoughts on 'L'Avventura,' " in *L'Avventura*, ed. Amberg and Hughes, p. 268).

13 George Amberg, " 'But Eros Is Sick,' " in *L'Avventura*, ed. Amberg and Hughes, p. 250.

14 Amberg, " 'But Eros Is Sick,' " pp. 250, 251.

15 A great deal of formalist and psychoanalytic film theory is based on an assumption of the primacy of the shot/reverse shot system. Though it cannot be undertaken in the present work, it would be interesting to explore the ways in which these theories are necessarily altered by Antonioni's choice to include his character in many POV shots.

Chatman claims that the manner of including the character-spectator within the successive shot makes her or him into a "surrogate narrator, a telling-subject, no longer merely one of the told-objects. . . . [T]he person is an instrument or instance of the discourse, not just a component of the story" (Chatman, *Antonioni*, p. 92).

16 In any case, it is clear that the gaze or look is heavily thematized within the diegesis of the film itself, for the very act of looking at others is consistently underlined, especially in the last segment of the film, which takes place in the luxury hotel. This questioning of the nature of vision will become even more important in the later films.

17 The eminent abstract painter Willem DeKooning worked a similar thematic vein in his painting called *Woman as a Landscape*.

18 It is interesting that of his first film, the documentary *Gente del Po*, Antonioni once said "*Gente del Po* was a documentary on river life, fishermen; on *men*, that is, not on things or places" (quoted in Penelope Houston, "Michelangelo Antonioni," in *Cinema: A Critical Dictionary*, ed. Richard Roud [New York: Viking Press, 1980], p. 89). Things seem to have gotten more complicated in the intervening years.

Though he dates its beginning from *L'eclisse*, the late French philosopher Gilles Deleuze provocatively describes Antonioni's interest in the relation of human and landscape when he says we have moved "to the point of dehumanized landscapes, of emptied space that might be seen as having absorbed characters and actions, retaining only a geophysical description, an abstract inventory of them" (Deleuze, *Cinema 2: The Time-Image*, trans. Hugh Tomlinson and Robert Galeta [Minneapolis: University of Minnesota Press, 1989], p. 5).

19 See Anne Friedberg, *Window Shopping* (Berkeley: University of California Press, 1992), for a cogent critique of the way in which feminist film theory has uncritically adopted the Panopticon model of the centralizing gaze from French philosopher Michel Foucault. Friedberg argues instead for conceptualizing the cinematic gaze, since it is a historical development of the nineteenth-century experience of the diorama, panorama, and the shopping arcade, as primarily virtual and mobile.

20 Leprohon, *Michelangelo Antonioni*, p. 66.

21 One such gesture, common also to neorealism (though usually unconscious), lasts but a moment. It occurs when Sandro has run to catch the train that Claudia has already taken. A boy, clearly a nonprofessional actor, comes running in the other direction, toward the camera, kicks something and then for a crucial second looks straight into the camera before disappearing out the left side of the frame. (It should be admitted that this moment is brief, but during it the illusion is utterly destroyed.)

22 Equally unconventional, what seems to arise from such intense, inordinately lengthy concentration is a realization of powerful physical *emotion* rather than, strictly speaking, sexual arousal, as would perhaps be more typical. Is it too much to claim that the length of this kissing scene makes it "female" precisely for that reason? In any case, this scene must have meant a lot to Antonioni, as Chiaretti reports that it took ten days to film, especially since the director was forced to wait for the train to pass each morning to get it in the shot. "For ten days," he reports, "the railroad workers watched, with ever increasing curiosity, the couple who made love always at the same time, surrounded by so many people" (Chiaretti, "The Adventure of *L'Avventura*," in *L'Avventura*, ed. Amberg and Hughes, pp. 207–8).

23 Here and elsewhere in this book, I use a theoretical vocabulary that I think Antonioni himself would recognize. Clearly, this denaturalizing effect I am attempting to analyze could also be described in Lacanian psychoanalytic terms, which would have the subject being jarred out of his or her imaginary relationship with the images on the screen into an (unconscious) awareness of the ever-present threat of castration. In the Lacanian paradigm, this awareness of the madeness and contingency of what is otherwise offered fully and unproblematically to our view makes us aware of an Other, the speaking subject, the initiator of the discourse.

24 Chatman, *Antonioni*, p. 99.

25 Throughout the film, the music, especially during the credits, is driven and nervous, but it also mixes the modern with southern mandolin sounds, evoking the clash of regional cultures that is a staple of the music of such Italian films as Rossellini's *Voyage to Italy*. At another time, bits of Chopin can be heard as part of a perky sound track that otherwise can sound very Hitchcockian, and later still, something like Ravel's "Bolero": all in all, a kind of a proto-postmodern quoting and pastiche.

26 Sam Rohdie offers an intriguing, if somewhat confusing alternative description of this opening shot:

The background moves forward at a level with Anna herself (it is no longer her ground, or her context, but her equal) while Anna moves slightly back to join up with it. The realignment and confounding of figure and ground to the point of figures becoming lost in a landscape or absorbed in a surface, becoming themselves surface, not a substance, but an effect of light or a meteorological consequence, is persistent in all of Antonioni's films. (Rohdie, *Antonioni*, p. 102)

27 Paintings – this time representational rather than abstract – appear explicitly again at the end of the film.

28 "Remarks on *L'avventura*," in *L'avventura*, ed. Chatman and Fink, pp. 196–7.

29 Marie-Claire Ropars-Wuilleumier, *L'écran de la mémoire: Essais de lecture cinématographique* (Paris: Editions du Seuil, 1970), p. 82.

Antonioni's space is also complexly layered in a way that is strangely reminiscent of the deep focus of the films of Orson Welles. This is especially evident in his penchant for the gigantic heads and torsos that often occupy the foreground of his shots while other things are going on, always in focus, in the background. The effect is strange, but it is never grotesque. What is produced, rather, is a kind of juxtaposition of different orders of presence that seems to call the conventional relationship of entities (both people and things) into question.

30 At one point, someone mutters, "Come m'irrita la vitalità della gente" (The vitality of people really irritates me), a theme in which the modernist Antonioni exactly follows the modernist T. S. Eliot of *The Waste Land* (1922),

31 The deathlike imagery of this abandoned or never-inhabited town is underlined when Sandro thinks he sees another town just like it on the next hill. Claudia says, "It isn't a town, it's a cemetery."

32 Frederic Jameson, "Postmodernism and Consumer Society," in *The Anti-Aesthetic: Essays on Postmodern Culture*, ed. Hal Foster (Port Townsend, Wash.: Bay Press), 1983, p. 125.

33 Quoted in Chiaretti, "The Adventure of L'Avventura," in *L'Avventura*, ed. Amberg and Hughes, p. 208.

34 "A Talk with Michelangelo Antonioni on His Work," p. 34.

35 Quoted in Houston, "Michelangelo Antonioni," p. 91. Antonioni elaborated on the notion of a "shared pity" in an interview with a French critic:

These are men and women who, without being normal themselves, try to lead their lives and their loves in a normal manner. But during the story they encounter so many difficulties that they are unable to avoid the final catastrophe. They are rescued to the extent that between them a hyphen based on reciprocal pity, on understanding, can be established, a resignation which is not weakness, but the sole force allowing them to remain together, to be linked to life, to be opposed to catastrophe. . . . They have recourse to this because both of them want to live and do not want to die. So they grab whatever life they can find. (*Les lettres françaises*, no. 826, May 26, 1960; quoted in Joëlle Mayet Giaume, *Michelangelo Antonioni: Le fil intérieur* [Crisne, Belgium: Editions Yellow Now, 1990], p. 124)

Resignation as the sole method of avoiding catastrophe: obviously a highly attenuated cast of characters.

36 Giorgio Tinazzi, *Michelangelo Antonioni* (Florence: La Nuova Italia, 1974), p. 83.

37 Tinazzi, *Michelangelo Antonioni*, p. 84.

38 The complete text of the statement can be found in *L'avventura*, ed. Chatman and Fink, pp. 177–9.

Chapter 2: *La notte* (1961)

1 This new accessibility seems also to have translated into increased box office receipts. *La notte* actually did much better than *L'avventura* in its initial release, a healthy 158 million lire, which put it in eighth place for the year. Spinazzola gives three reasons for the commercial success of the film: (1) heavy-handed threats of bureaucratic censorship, which galvanized public opinion in favor of the film; (2) the huge publicity surrounding the "discovery" of Antonioni at Cannes in 1960; and (3) the presence of well-known stars, Marcello Mastroianni and Jeanne Moreau, as headliners. By March 31, 1961, the film had grossed 301 million lire, and two years later the figure stood at 457 million. As Antonioni's fame grew, *L'avventura* as well continued to bring in substantial sums of money after its initial release.

With a limited, but secure audience established, Antonioni's films continued to do fairly well during this period. *L'eclisse*, for example, earned 100 million lire in initial release, and after a year, the figure stood at 280 million. *Red Desert* grossed 154 million in its initial release, about the same as *La notte*, but ticket prices had increased in the meantime. By June 1965, nine months later, its gross stood at 367 million (Spinazzola, *Cinema e pubblico*, p. 240).

2 "A Talk with Michelangelo Antonioni on His Work," p. 35.

3 Tinazzi, *Michelangelo Antonioni*, p. 89.

4 "The Disappearance (On Antonioni)," in *L'avventura*, ed. Chatman and Fink, p. 215.

5 Quoted in Rohdie, *Antonioni*, p. 52.

6 To demonstrate more concretely the contingency of interpretation I have been talking about, one might consider two other wildly differing readings of this opening sequence. Here is a distinctly minority interpretation that, given a different set of basic hermeneutic premises, seems as plausible as the "neutral" reading I have proposed:

> *La Notte* starts with hope. The first shot tilts up from the overcrowded streets of Milan in the rush hour to the tall Pirelli building. The cool beauty of Gio Ponti's architecture is an image of the possible future environment, a triumph of art and science working together. It embodies a perfection to which man in his personal relationships can only aspire. (Ian Cameron and Robin Wood, *Antonioni*, rev. ed. [New York: Praeger, 1971], p. 74).

At the opposite pole, Seymour Chatman sees the architecture of *La notte* and the films that follow as an aspect of the dysfunctionality of the characters and the modern era in general:

> The city planning and architecture of Milan in *La notte* or of Rome in *L'eclisse* did not cause Lidia's and Vittoria's problems. But personal problems and bad architecture and misused public space are all parts of a vaster network of problems facing Western man. Bad architecture is simply one visible, concrete manifestation of the *malattia dei sentimenti* [disease of the emotions]. (Chatman, *Antonioni*, p. 103)

7 Tinazzi, *Michelangelo Antonioni*, p. 89.
8 Michelangelo Antonioni, *Sei film* (Turin: Giulio Einaudi, 1964), p. 302. This description is not found in the English-language version of these screenplays, which differs widely from the Italian. It should be said, however, that the Italian version is literary in nature and contains highly subjective descriptions – written by Antonioni after the films were made? – which may or may not actually be borne out visually in the films.
9 There are at least two versions of this scene in the various prints in circulation in the United States, one much shorter (and less graphic) than the other.
10 When he first announces that "I have to tell you something that you won't like," the emotionally deadened Lidia responds: "Is it really necessary?"
11 These are the two figures that have been identified by various Italian critics. It is quite possible, of course, that, with the exception of Giovanni and Lidia, *all* the figures at the party are "real" people. For a discussion of the theoretical implications of this kind of mixing, see my *Roberto Rossellini* (Berkeley: University of California Press, 1996).
12 Tinazzi, *Michelangelo Antonioni*, p. 96.
13 This review by James Stoller, which originally appeared in the *Columbia Daily Spectator,* is excerpted in Leprohon, *Michelangelo Antonioni*, p. 171. It may seem unfair to quote from what is obviously a student review, but since it was included in Leprohon's book it is, I think, fair game, and probably rather typical to boot.
14 Cameron and Wood, *Antonioni*, pp. 80–1.
15 Chatman, *Antonioni*, p. 70.
16 Quoted in Cesare Biarese and Aldo Tassone, *I film di Michelangelo Antonioni* (Rome: Gremese Editore, 1985), p. 105.
17 Years ago, some feminist experimental filmmakers proposed eliminating the female body from the film image, on the grounds that by definition it could no longer ever be seen in a nonsexual way, but only as an object for the male gaze. It soon became clear, however, that the complete evacuation of women from the screen was not a viable response to the tyranny of patriarchal viewing codes.
18 Tinazzi, *Michelangelo Antonioni*, p. 90.
19 Tinazzi usefully points out that despite the similarities, there are huge differences between the two party scenes. In the Fellini film, he says, we get the typical baroque quality that stems from a Catholic sense of deformity. With Antonioni, on the other hand, what strikes the viewer is "an attempt to objec-

tify, to reduce, to clearly posit the dialectic" (Tinazzi, *Michelangelo Antonioni*, p. 88).

20 Biarese and Tassone, *I film di Michelangelo Antonioni*, p. 107.
21 Rohdie, *Antonioni*, p. 52.
22 *La notte*, in Antonioni, *Sei film*, p. 355. Further references to this screenplay will be found in the text.
23 Biarese and Tassone, *I film di Michelangelo Antonioni*, p. 112.
24 Tinazzi also raises the important question of whether the focus on the intellectual in this film (and on the intellectual named Steiner in Fellini's *La dolce vita*) is really part of a serious study of the role of the intellectual in Italian society, or whether the directors are just continuing to talk about themselves, as part of a self-referential modernism (pp. 88–9). To me, the two possibilities are not mutually exclusive, since what is at stake is also the role of the filmmaker as intellectual in Italian society.
25 Biarese and Tassone, *I film di Michelangelo Antonioni*, p. 112.
26 At one point, Giovanni echoes the traditional artist's complaint that he must content himself with mere representations, telling the industrialists that he envies them because they can "tell stories . . . with real men, real houses, real cities" (p. 335).
27 Leprohon, *Michelangelo Antonioni*, p. 76.
28 "A Talk with Michelangelo Antonioni on His Work," p. 39. Seymour Chatman reductively says that Giovanni does what he does in this scene because he is "addicted to sex" (*Antonioni*, p. 58).
29 Quoted in Biarese and Tassone, *I film di Michelangelo Antonioni*, p. 112.

Chapter 3: *L'eclisse* (1962)

1 The film's title refers to an eclipse that Antonioni went to Florence to film. He reports wondering whether there could also be something such as an "eclipse of the feelings." He says that he left this sequence out of the film, however, because it overliteralized the title and was just too obvious ("Preface to *Six Films*," in Antonioni, *The Architecture of Vision*, p. 59). The result of this decision, though, is a title that provides another ambiguous (non-) clue, pointing everywhere and nowhere at once.
2 Rohdie, *Antonioni*, p. 116.
3 Vitti is also the star of the director's next film, *Red Desert*. It would be interesting to try to plot the effect of her "intertextuality" across these four films. How does her presence in all of them alter our perception of the individual meanings of each?
4 For a full discussion, see Brunette and Wills, *Screen/Play*, esp. chap. 4.
5 Tinazzi, *Michelangelo Antonioni*, p. 97.
6 Biarese and Tassone, *I film di Michelangelo Antonioni*, p. 115.
7 Thus it is astonishing that critics such as Biarese and Tassone (and they are not alone) can describe, scene by scene and purely on the basis of visual information, exactly what Vittoria is thinking and feeling.
8 Once again, Chatman insists on a nostalgic reading that clashes with Antonioni's own often-expressed heavily ambivalent views of modern life. Hence, ac-

cording to Chatman, much of the characters' difficulties in the film can be traced to the fact that this pedestrian crossing has replaced the organic quality of the piazza, a traditional Italian urban topographical feature that is fast disappearing in this new world. "Vittoria and Piero's affair is in a sense already doomed simply by their meeting there" (Chatman, *Antonioni*, p. 110). Referring to the reappearance of the pedestrian crossing at the end of the film, after the characters are gone, Chatman gets even more apocalyptic: "By having both characters disappear, Antonioni insists on the banal intersection, makes us contemplate it with such dreary intensity that we sense, if not completely understand, the ferocious relationship between the urban humdrum and the prospect of worldwide technological self-destruction" (p. 112). This seems, ultimately, rather too much meaning to ascribe to a pedestrian crosswalk.

9 In the preface to the English version of Antonioni's middle-period screenplays, the director claims that, at least during the shooting of one scene, the "screenplay was of value to me only as a psychological note" (Antonioni, *Screenplays of Michelangelo Antonioni* [New York: Orion Press, 1963], p. xvii). The scene he discusses is the one in which Piero and Vittoria enter the home of Piero's parents, a scene that is quite different from the one in the original screenplay. However, the Italian version of the screenplays, *Sei film*, which came out a year after the English version, and which includes *Red Desert*, is itself quite different from the English version and appears to have been altered to reflect, to some extent at least, the way the films were actually shot. In the preface to *Sei film*, Antonioni does say that there are parts that no longer "coincide" with the finished films, and that the parts that are still correct tend to be "pseudoliterary." What appears to be his final judgment on the question is something that should clearly be heeded: "A movie not imprinted on film doesn't exist. The scripts presuppose the film. They don't have autonomy; they are dead pages" (Antonioni, *The Architecture of Vision*, p. 68).

10 Seymour Chatman quite rightly disagrees with those critics who want to claim these moments as symbolic, as, for example, when Philip Strick says the breeze symbolizes "the agitation of her own thoughts" (Strick, *Antonioni* [London: Motion Publications, 1963], p. 12; quoted in Chatman, *Antonioni*, p. 68). As noted in chapter 2, Chatman more plausibly argues for their function as *metonymic* instead, so that when a rustling tree is seen in the film's finale, for example, we think "Where is Vittoria?" rather than "these are symbolic of the agitation of Vittoria's thoughts" (ibid.; he also gives very good examples here of critics who have tended to read these "symbols" overliterally then complained that Antonioni was too obvious in his use of symbols). Nevertheless, seeing these various moments as specifically *metonymic* also seems, to my mind, too literal-minded and thus too limiting. Rather, they seem to be representative of various, nonspecific, nonlocalized emotionally suggestive states that resonate in the viewer on some prediscursive level.

11 "The Night, the Eclipse, the Dawn," in Antonioni, *The Architecture of Vision*, p. 289.

12 This dialogue is not printed in the English version of the screenplay.

13 Tinazzi points out the interesting dissonance created within the fiction film by having this "minute of silence" actually last one minute. A similarly masterful

handling of sound to make a thematic point comes near the end of the film, when all the phones, one after the other, begin ringing again after Piero has replaced the receivers (Tinazzi, *Michelangelo Antonioni*, p. 96).

14 Tinazzi, *Michelangelo Antonioni*, p. 94.

15 Its description in the screenplay: "She has a package in her hand and begins to unwrap it with great care. The object inside the package seems to interest her enormously. It's a stone 20 centimeters by 40 on which a small twig is painted, or so it seems. Looking at it closely, one realizes that it's not painted, it's like a sign of a branch that has been flattened on the stone, faded, delicate, as if moved by the wind or the water. It's a fossil" (p. 375).

16 There is also a curious, tentative interest here in the question of visual representation that looks forward to the concerns of *Blow-up*, since so much footage in this scene from *L'eclisse* is devoted to filming the photographs of Africa that adorn Marta's walls. Here, Antonioni seems to be underlining the mediation that always accompanies the entrance of the exotic into Western culture.

17 At this point, the evidence provided by the screenplay is much more precise and explicit than the evidence of the film itself and is perhaps worth quoting. For one thing, when they part for the last time, we are told that Vittoria hugs Piero "desperately" and that "she is serious, the expression on her face is almost one of fear, it seems almost as if she's trembling" (p. 429). When she exits the front door, she bumps into a passerby, and the script tells us that "this very banal incident is enough to cause all of her decisiveness to disappear instantly," and then goes on to point out that the shop she stops in front of is the same one we saw earlier in the film, in the scene of Piero's ugly treatment of his former girlfriend (p. 430). Again, though, it is difficult to know to what extent to defer to the screenplay for meanings that are perhaps not clearly perceptible in the film.

18 Chatman, *Antonioni*, p. 80.

19 Tinazzi, *Michelangelo Antonioni*, p. 95.

20 Quoted in Biarese and Tassone, *I film di Michelangelo Antonioni*, p. 121.

21 Quoted in Chatman, *Antonioni*, p. 80.

22 Geoffrey Nowell-Smith, "Shape around a Black Point," *Sight & Sound*, vol. 33 (Winter 1963–4), p. 19; quoted in Chatman, *Antonioni*, p. 250, n. 19.

23 "The Disappearance (On Antonioni)," in *L'avventura*, ed. Chatman and Fink, p. 218.

Chapter 4: *Red Desert* (1964)

1 Quoted in Biarese and Tassone, *I film di Michelangelo Antonioni*, p. 127.

2 Ropars-Wuilleumier, *L'écran de la mémoire*, p. 86.

3 Actually, the innovative power of Antonioni's handling of color is that it is *not* always vibrant. Seymour Chatman usefully distinguishes between Hollywood's use of color, which is primarily in the form of saturated hues, and Antonioni's, which contrasts these saturated hues "with muted, almost monochromatic effects. . . . [I]n the process . . . he constructs color rhythms and orchestrations of an intricacy that Eisenstein dreamt of" (Chatman, *Antonioni*, p. 131).

4 Giaume, *Le fil intérieur*, p. 68; original quotation from *La revue du cinéma*,

no. 298 (September 1975). For a detailed discussion of color symbolism in this film, see Ned Rifkin, *Antonioni's Visual Language* (Ann Arbor, Mich.: UMI Research Press, 1982). For an explanation of the implications of Antonioni's attempts to manipulate color in *Red Desert*, see Rohdie, *Antonioni,* pp. 161–9. Rodhie also analyzes a fascinating treatment for a film, proposed by Antonioni as early as 1940, that already shows the director's obsession with the question of color.

The original working title of *Red Desert* was "Celeste e verde" (Pale blue and green), but Antonioni dropped it, he told Godard, because it was not "virile enough" (p. 295; translation modified). Again, the connection between abstraction and masculinity is evoked, as it was, continually, in the work of the abstract expressionist painters in the 1950s; Antonioni's attitude toward masculinity is obviously a complicated, even conflicted, one.

5 In the interview with Godard, Antonioni said that Giuliana prefers cool colors for her shop because they put more emphasis on the objects she is selling. "I was interested in the contrast between cool and warm colors: there was orange, yellow, a brown ceiling – and Giuliana realizes that for her it is no good" (pp. 294–5).

6 An elaborate, even brilliant, example of this exercise in futility can be found in William Arrowsmith, *Antonioni: The Poet of Images*, ed. Ted Perry (New York: Oxford University Press, 1995), pp. 96–9. Although most critics have pointed to the obvious importance of red, Biarese and Tassone insist that it is the cold, white colors that predominate (p. 127). Chatman seriously misunderstands the scene in Corrado's hotel room by reading the color too literally: Giuliana has had "relief" sexually, he says, because the colors in the hotel change from white to "blushing pink" (Chatman, *Antonioni,* p. 59). Ropars-Wuilleumier, on the other hand, helpfully places *Red Desert* in the larger context of the many filmmakers, such as Alain Resnais, who began using color in the early 1960s. "It's not an accident that the move to color accompanies, both in the films of Resnais and Antonioni, a break with the search for time and the development of an invading space. With color, space in the cinema becomes important in itself rather than just representing the decor of the drama or the reflection of a human being" (Ropars-Wuilleumier, *L'écran de la mémoire,* p. 168).

7 For an extensive analysis of *Red Desert* from a pictorial perspective, see Angela Dalle Vacche, *Cinema and Painting: How Art Is Used in Film* (Austin: University of Texas Press, 1996), pp. 43–80.

8 The composition of this shot strongly recalls the painting by Edvard Munch, *Evening on Carl Johan Street, Oslo* (1892), an early expression of faceless alienation, especially given that the emphasis is on Giuliana's back, which is toward us in the shot.

9 A brilliant modern example of this rigorous use of the extreme long shot to enhance the expressivity of both interiors and exteriors can be found in Todd Haynes's recent film, *Safe* (1995).

10 Quoted in Ropars-Wuilleumier, *L'écran de la mémoire,* pp. 168–9; original quotation is from *Les nouvelles littéraires*, April 15, 1965.

11 Rohdie, *Antonioni,* p. 160.

12 Rohdie, *Antonioni,* p. 175. Earlier, Rohdie offers a more global view of the

dynamic relation between figural image and narrative that is similar to the one I have been developing throughout this book. In certain scenes, he says, it seems "as if the film hesitates between the image serving a function in the narrative, and the image detaching itself from the narrative, becoming purely pictorial, as if these patches of colour were simultaneously narrative signs and purely relations of colour. But the fascination of these images is that they are neither completely the one nor the other: the narrative seems to fade out, as the colour of it fades in, or it is the reverse of this, in either case a kind of shimmering effect between significance and its loss" (p. 157). I would amend this analysis in two ways: first, the opposition is not between "significance and its loss," but between two different *kinds* of significance; second, the terms of this analysis need to include *character* (and the attendant problem of audience identification) as well as narrative, strictly speaking.

13 Michelangelo Antonioni, "Red Desert," in *The Architecture of Vision*, pp. 285–6. In the light of this argument for consideration of painterly abstraction as an important element of this and other films of Antonioni, it is only fair to mention that the director specifically denies, in the interview with Godard, that this is what he is doing:

> In my film, the methods of the painter are not used; we are very far from the exercise of painting—or at least, so it seems to me. And of course certain pictorial needs, which in painting do not have any narrative content, find this content in cinema. That is where the novel and painting come together (p. 296).

Yet what he says here is contradicted elsewhere in this discussion with Godard and in other interviews, as when he told Philip Strick that in *Red Desert* "I want to paint the film as one paints a canvas; I want to invent the colour relationships, and not limit myself by photographing only natural colours" (quoted in Chatman, *Antonioni*, p. 131).

14 "Red Desert," in Antonioni, *The Architecture of Vision*, p. 285. Translation modified.

15 "Antonioni dans 'Il deserto rosso,'" interview with Michèle Manceaux, in *Michelangelo Antonioni: Entretiens et inédits 1950/1985*, ed. Carlo di Carlo and Giorgio Tinazzi, vol. 5 of *L'oeuvre de Michelangelo Antonioni* (Rome: Cinecittà International, 1992), p. 184. (Many of the interviews in that volume have been reprinted in English in Antonioni, *The Architecture of Vision.*)

16 "Antonioni dans 'Il deserto rosso,'" p. 185.

17 "Red Desert," in Antonioni, *The Architecture of Vision*, p. 283.

18 The theme of the past that is ironically compared to the present is also found in this film, but, as the industrial present seems so totally regnant here, it is much sketchier than in the other films we have been discussing. Thus the chair seen in Giuliana's hallway during her psychological crisis recalls those chairs based on Renaissance models that are a staple of Italian homes; her shop is in the via (Dante) Alighieri; and the action itself takes place in Ravenna, a city, as pointed out earlier, especially rich in history and early artifacts.

19 "Red Desert," in Antonioni, *The Architecture of Vision*, p. 285.

20 Or at least this is my reading of the body language, camera placement, and dialogue of these two scenes. The director himself apparently intended that the audience take Giuliana's side in her sexual encounter with Corrado, but not in the one with her husband:

> I would like to emphasize one moment in the film which is intended as a criticism of the old world. When the woman, in the middle of her crisis, needs help, she meets a man who takes advantage of her and her insecurity. They are the same old things that overwhelm her. Somebody like her husband would have acted differently: first he would have tried to help her then perhaps later – but as it is, she's betrayed by her own world. ("The Night, the Eclipse, The Dawn," pp. 291–2)

I read Corrado and Giuliana's husband as versions of each other, whereas Antonioni seems to have intended them as contrasts. Italian critics, however, have tended to view Corrado more positively than does Antonioni, though it seems clear – even in the dialogue! – that Corrado is part of the problem for Giuliana, and not part of the solution. Sam Rohdie, too, says that after Corrado and Giuliana make love, "the entire room takes on a rose-pink tint, the same colour as the sand on the Sardinian beach in the fairy tale Giuliana composes for her son" (p. 157), implying complete approval of Corrado's actions here. (Cf. Chatman's similar remark [note 6] that the change of color in this scene from white to "blushing pink" signifies Giuliana's sexual "relief.")

21 Similarly, note that when Giuliana sits down next to the peddler's cart, the peddler seems to be there more as a transparent backdrop to her middle-class anxieties than for his own sake.

22 However, in a strange remark that Antonioni made to a French interviewer – repeated, to my knowledge, nowhere else – the director said: "A new class is born in this fascinating decor and my heroes belong to this working-class bourgeoisie" ("Antonioni dans 'Il deserto rosso,' " p. 183).

23 Biarese and Tassone, *I film di Michelangelo Antonioni*, p. 124.

24 According to various interviews that Antonioni has given, we are meant to understand Giuliana's earlier auto "accident" as, in fact, a suicide attempt, although the dialogue itself in no way indicates this. In one interview, the director admitted that perhaps he failed to make it clear that Giuliana had tried to kill herself by crashing into a truck ("Red Desert," in Antonioni, *The Architecture of Vision*, p. 284).

Chapter 5: *Blow-up* (1966)

1 It is now difficult to appreciate how "scandalous" the film seemed when it came out in 1966. In response to the perhaps predictably obsessive questioning of a *Playboy* interviewer, Antonioni insisted that "eroticism has nothing to do with *Blow-up*." The director went on to say that he was not aware of the pubic hair that the interviewer says he noticed ("Apropos of Eroticism," in Antonioni, *The Architecture of Vision*, p. 148).

The other "shocking" aspect of the film – still being hyped today, on the box notes of the cassette tape – was its depiction of the swinging London scene. The "decadent" party that takes place about halfway through seems almost laughably tame thirty years later, but its subversive power at the time of the film's release should be kept in mind for a proper historical appreciation. A silly, but indicative bit in which the film tries to display its rebellious hipness comes when Hemmings gets Redgrave to smoke a cigarette (or joint?) *against* the pounding beat of the music.

2 Most critics, if they mention the Cortàzar story at all, discuss the (slight) connection between the plots of fiction and film. But what they actually share is an intangible feeling of openness, a tone of vivacious experimentation, and a splitting of perspective between the first and third person, which parallels a theoretical concern in the film that will be discussed later in this chapter. An article by Henry Fernandez ("From Cortazar to Antonioni: Study of an Adaptation") in the collection edited by Roy Huss (*Focus on Blow-up* [Englewood Cliffs, N.J.: Prentice-Hall, 1971], pp. 163–7) stresses the parallelism of Cortàzar's comparison between photography and fiction to Antonioni's comparison between photography and film, but the analysis is not convincing.

3 These figures have been called mimes, clowns, and a host of other names by various critics. William Arrowsmith more precisely identifies them as " 'ragging' students": "Everywhere in Europe matriculating freshmen, usually at the end of March, celebrate Ragweek, *la festa delle matricole*. Dressed in costumes akin to those of the commedia dell'arte, they run about the streets performing improvised games and tricks, cadging money for charity" (Arrowsmith, *Antonioni: The Poet of Images*, p. 108).

4 In all subsequent references to the main characters of the film, those played by David Hemmings and Vanessa Redgrave, I will use the actors' names, as the characters' names are never actually mentioned in the film. Italian critic Lorenzo Cuccu believes that the widespread practice of calling the photographer Thomas originally stemmed from publicity material surrounding the film, but this name is not used in the film itself.

5 Miccichè, *Il cinema italiano*, p. 27.

6 Antonioni told an interviewer as early as 1964, while filming *Red Desert*, that "the next film I shoot will almost surely have a man as main character" ("Antonioni dans 'Il deserto rosso,' " p. 186). He did not elaborate.

7 Rohdie, *Antonioni*, p. 184.

8 Rohdie continues: "In these later, 'male' films, political, sociological, even philosophic conclusions are less easily concluded, less securely held, than they might have been in the earlier 'female' films . . . out of which a whole host of existential meanings were generated, not, happily, by Antonioni, but certainly by critics, and especially by some on the Italian left, of the alienation-under-capitalism kind" (Rohdie, *Antonioni*, p. 184). Presumably for Rohdie these films then are to be credited with having only a kind of evanescent formal meaning, rather than a political or philosophical one, but he seems not to realize that a reading that emphasizes formal elements at the expense of political ones is itself the product of a political choice.

9 Quoted in Biarese and Tassone, *I film di Michelangelo Antonioni*, p. 138.

10 Roland Barthes has also spoken provocatively of the power of the gaze in Antonioni, but in a completely ungendered, and positive, way:

> Another kind of fragility for the artist, paradoxically, is the firmness and insistence of his gaze. Power, in whatever form, because it is violence, never looks; if it looked a minute longer (a minute too long), it would lose the essence of power. But the artist stops and looks a long time, and I imagine that you became a filmmaker because the camera is an eye, constrained, because of its technical nature, to look. What you add to this disposition, which is common to all filmmakers, is to look at things radically, until they are used up. . . . This is dangerous, because looking longer than is asked (I insist on this extra intensity) upsets all established orders, whatever they are, to the extent that, normally, the time of the gaze is controlled by society: hence, when the work escapes this control, the scandalous nature of certain photographs and films: not the most indecent or the most combative, but simply the most "posed." (Barthes, "Cher Antonioni," in *Cher Antonioni: 1988/1989*, pp. 20–1)

11 "Le cinéma italien parle: Michelangelo Antonioni," interview by Aldo Tassone, in *Michelangelo Antonioni: Entretiens et inédits 1950/1985*, ed. di Carlo and Tinazzi, p. 108.

12 Chatman, *Antonioni*, pp. 152–3.

13 Arrowsmith, *Antonioni: The Poet of Images*, p. 124.

14 "Michelangelo Antonioni," in *Cinema: A Critical Dictionary*, p. 93.

15 The trenchant critic Andrew Sarris, in an early review of the film, describes the brightly colored bus and truck that pass Hemmings in a way that bolsters my argument for a graphic, figural understanding of Antonioni's films: "That sudden splash of blue and yellow defines Antonioni's mood and milieu better than any set of speeches ever could" (Sarris, "Antonennui," in *Focus on Blow-up*, ed. Huss, p. 32).

16 There is also, occasionally, a glimpse of an unmotivated aspect of "raw reality" in something like a shot of the little boy behind bars in a driveway whom we see briefly as Hemmings walks briskly past him, a "fact" that has nothing, ostensibly, to do with the narrative.

17 Miccichè, *Il cinema italiano*, p. 241.

18 Semiotician Juri Lotman sees in the film's insistence on the need to *interpret* reality a kind of paradigm of the operations of semiotics itself. Thus, when Hemmings hangs up his enlargements, he takes them out of their temporal context (what happened before and after) and out of their causal context, which was a three-dimensional situation that also included the photographer, who was the cause of the anger that the couple manifests in the photos. The semiotic "message" is thus impoverished and made more incomprehensible, but this latter operation, according to Lotman, is an important step in giving it a *new* meaning. Hemmings creates *another* context for the woman (one that excludes him) by giving an alternative explanation for her emotion – something that is in the bushes. We thus have to forget what we thought we knew in order to see the elements arranged into a new explanation. What is strange, says Lotman, is that we see both versions at the same time. When Hemmings spots the photos

after his sex frolic with the "birds," he suddenly realizes he has to change the temporal context as well. Thus what Antonioni shows is that reality must be interpreted, that what seems obvious is not necessarily so. For Lotman, this is the same as the work of the semiotician who cuts up representations into units (like the photographic blowups), then considers them as signs to be deciphered, using both the paradigmatic and syntagmatic axes. Thus what I and others do when we analyze this film on our VCRs is similar, according to Lotman, to what Hemmings is trying to do with his enlargements (Juri Lotman, "Les problèmes de la sémiotique et les voies du cinéma contemporain," in *Michelangelo Antonioni 1966/1984*, ed. Lorenzo Cuccu, vol. 2 of *L'oeuvre de Michelangelo Antonioni* [Rome: Ente Autonomo di Gestione per il Cinema, 1988], pp. 199–205).

19 For a totally opposite reading of the ending of the film, see Arrowsmith, *Antonioni: The Poet of Images,* pp. 125–6. For him, the mimes represent the power of the group to stifle individual growth (and thus they stand in for all of the inauthentic, "swinging London" that we have seen throughout the film). For a critic who regards the photographer favorably, as the supreme creative artist in the mold of the masculinist individualists of the abstract expressionism of the 1950s, this view is perhaps not a complete surprise. "Here [when he retrieves the ball], if he succumbs it is only briefly, perhaps because he is stronger, more loyal to his perceptions and experience, by virtue of having been so overwhelmingly tested and tempted" (p. 126).

20 "Apropos of Eroticism," p. 149.

21 Notice to what extent this film, like *L'avventura,* is a film about disappearances: the woman played by Redgrave, the body, and finally, at the very end, even the photographer.

22 In this, it is reminiscent of the "signature effect" that Jacques Derrida has linked with the question of the frame (note that this signature occurs near the end or "outer frame" of the film, just as an artist's signature usually appears near the edge or frame of a painting). See Derrida, *The Truth in Painting,* trans. Geoff Bennington and Ian McLeod (Chicago: University of Chicago Press, 1987); and Brunette and Wills, *Screen/Play.*

23 All quotations of dialogue in this chapter have been taken directly from the sound track of the film.

24 "Preface to *Six Films,*" Antonioni, *The Architecture of Vision,* p. 63.

25 "Apropos of Eroticism," p. 149.

26 "Le cinéma italien parle: Michelangelo Antonioni," p. 108. The problematic relation between reality and representation is also established more trivially (and more humorously) elsewhere in the film when Hemmings keeps trying out different lines about his former wife in response to Redgrave's questions. After speaking to someone on the telephone, Hemmings variously tells Redgrave that it is my wife; she is not my wife, we just have some kids; no, we do not have any kids; she is easy to live with; no she is not, that is why I do not live with her. After all these conflicting representations, we obviously know nothing about his "wife."

27 Reprinted in *Michelangelo Antonioni 1966/1984,* ed. Lorenzo Cuccu, p. 208.

28 Ropars's description of the "presence" of death as produced only through the

trace coincides nicely with Roland Barthes's idea, developed in *Camera Lucida* (New York: Hill and Wang, 1981), that the referent of every photograph (which is itself always established as a kind of trace), its "subject," is always death, in addition to whatever else it ostensibly shows.

29 Ropars-Wuilleumier, "L'espace et le temps," pp. 214–15.
30 Cuccu, *Antonioni: Il discorso dello sguardo*, p. 12.
31 Biarese and Tassone, *I film di Michelangelo Antonioni*, pp. 136–7.

Chapter 6: The *Passenger* (1975)

1 "The World Is Outside the Window," in Antonioni, *The Architecture of Vision*, p. 183.
2 "An In-Depth Search," in Antonioni, *The Architecture of Vision*, p. 347. Translation modified.
3 The original script of *The Passenger* was written by the director Mark Peploe and the noted experimental filmmaker and semiotician Peter Wollen. Antonioni told Gideon Bachmann that he had felt a little distanced because of this circumstance, but he accepted because the script seemed to speak to him. "For the first time, I felt like I was working more with the brain than, let's say, with the stomach" ("Talking of Michelangelo," in Antonioni, *The Architecture of Vision*, p. 242).
      Peter Wollen has told me in private conversation that though he and Peploe had no idea when they wrote the screenplay that it would ultimately be filmed by Antonioni, both writers revered the Italian director, knew his films well, and were, in effect, conscious of writing an "Antonioni film," albeit one heavily influenced by *Easy Rider*, which had appeared in 1969. Truffaut's *Wild Child* and Werner Herzog's *The Mystery of Kaspar Hauser* and, more distantly, Hitchcock's *North By Northwest*, were also mentioned by Wollen as important cinematic influences.
      Wollen said that he and Peploe rented a car and drove to all the locations they were interested in and wrote the script to accord with those locations; some of these were later altered by Antonioni. According to Wollen, the script as written lacked directions for camera technique, all of which, including the famous penultimate long take – discussed later – were supplied by the director.
4 The only 35-millimeter print of the film that is now available in the United States (owned by Jack Nicholson) is an English version that is quite similar to the original Italian version and thus different from the available cassette tape. I saw this print at the Virginia Film Festival in November 1996, in the company of Peter Wollen, with whom I conducted an onstage interview after the screening.
      The title of this print is the English version of the European title, "Profession: Reporter," and it contains the scenes missing from the American version on cassette, which I discuss more fully later in the chapter. When an audience member asked Peter Wollen about the genesis of the title *The Passenger*, he replied that the character who plays the Woman was originally intended to do all the driving, highlighting the notion of Locke's essential passivity. When

shooting began, though, it was discovered that Maria Schneider, who plays the Woman, could not drive.

5 All dialogue is taken directly from the sound track of the film.

6 *Encyclopedia of Philosophy*, ed. Paul Edwards (New York: Macmillan, 1967), vol. 4, p. 495; vol. 6, p. 97. Locke also claimed that someone is the same person who did X if he remembers doing X, but critics have pointed out the difficulty of distinguishing between a genuine and an apparent memory. Also, of course, people forget. Locke's detractors have maintained that memory is not enough to constitute personal identity since it *presupposes* it (vol. 6, p. 98).

7 The narrative reticence of *The Passenger* seems to have been a purposeful decision on the director's part. Antonioni told Alberto Ongaro that

> in this film I have instinctively looked for narrative solutions that are different from my usual ones. It's true, the basic format may be the same, but as I was shooting, every time I realized that I was moving on familiar grounds, I tried to change direction, to deviate from the norm, to resolve in some other way certain moments of the story. Even the way in which I had these realizations was strange. I noticed a sudden lack of interest in what I was doing, and that was the sign that I had to move off in another direction. (Antonioni, "An In-Depth Search," p. 346; translation modified)

Sam Rohdie provides a perhaps overelaborate but provocative exploration of Antonioni's treatment of narrative in this film:

> The estrangement between characters and their contexts, bodies and fictions, which is a constant in Antonioni's films, is doubled over in *The Passenger* by the gaze of the narrative upon its own fiction as it unfolds, as if the body of the film was estranged from the fiction included in it, hence that sense in *The Passenger* of a fiction and the fiction being watched, but these two positions, these two perspectives never meeting. . . . It is an odd sensation: a fiction made unreal by the film which registers it, not only doubled characters in an Antonioni film, but a doubled film: the fiction and the record of it. (Rohdie, *Antonioni*, pp. 145–6)

Rohdie says that the best example of this technique is found in the famous long-take sequence, the penultimate shot of the film, which is discussed at the end of this chapter.

8 Antonioni seems so intent on withholding narrative information that at one point he even indulges in a little self-reflexive joke. Late in the film, Locke and the Woman proceed toward the Plaza de Iglesia, mentioned several times in the dialogue, where Robertson was supposed to meet someone. When they arrive, the camera uncharacteristically gives us a close-up of a street sign that says "Plaza de Iglesia," thus for once clearly spelling out the location. The punchline of the in-joke comes when Locke self-consciously says, "Ah, here we are, the Plaza de Iglesia."

9 "An In-Depth Search," p. 346.

10 In a 1975 interview, he said, "I no longer want to employ the subjective camera, in other words the camera that represents the viewpoint of the character" (quoted in Chatman, *Antonioni*, p. 196).

11 Chatman, *Antonioni*, p. 197. In any case, while Chatman is certainly right to claim that "the strategy of the camera shots is constantly to undermine any sense that Locke's point of view is central and constantly adhered to" (p. 199), he goes too far when he says: "We do not experience a traditional identification with the hero. Just as Locke himself suffers from a kind of detachment from the world, the camera keeps us detached from him" (p. 199). As the critic Robin Wood has shown in his work on Hitchcock, "The power of the POV shot in constructing identification has been greatly exaggerated. . . . [T]he construction of audience identification with a character goes far beyond camerawork and visual point of view positioning, and depends at least as much on narration itself, on whether or not the actor is a star (in which case we automatically identify with him or her), and so on" (Wood, "Star and Auteur: Hitchcock's Films with Bergman," in *Hitchcock's Films Revisited*, p. 308).

12 Explaining his handling of actors in this film to some American interviewers, Antonioni said: "I watch them through the camera and at that moment tell them to do this or that. But not before. I have to have my shot and they are an element of the image – and not always the most important element" ("Antonioni Discusses *The Passenger*," p. 336).

13 By the way, this scene does not take place on the roof of La Sagrada Familia, Gaudí's famous unfinished cathedral in Barcelona, as some critics have mistakenly pointed out, perhaps unconsciously harkening back to the scene on the church roof in *L'avventura*.

14 "Antonioni Discusses *The Passenger*," p. 335.

15 "Profession Against," interview with Luigi Vaccari, in Antonioni, *The Architecture of Vision*, p. 218.

16 An interesting exploration could be made of the influence of an American star (who was well known even in 1975) on Antonioni's working methods and even on his script. For one thing, *The Passenger* seems to have much more humor than the usual Antonioni film – Locke muttering "Christ" while alone in church, then apologizing, presumably to God, or depositing his fake moustache on the lamp in the restaurant – and one wonders whether these were features of Peploe and Wollen's script or of Nicholson's improvisations.

17 "Antonioni Discusses *The Passenger*," p. 340.

18 The critic William Arrowsmith describes these two scenes in some detail. This glimpse of Moravia's book, especially, becomes the basis of Arrowsmith's rather involved reading of the film that relates it to "Tecnicamente dolce," the project that Antonioni never filmed (see Arrowsmith, *Antonioni: The Poet of Images*, pp. 155–6).

19 "Antonioni Discusses *The Passenger*," p. 342.

20 "An In-Depth Search," p. 348. For Lorenzo Cuccu, who regards all of Antonioni's films as explorations of the problematics of vision, it is not merely activity that Locke seeks, but rather an escape from *looking*: "Locke does not know how to live precisely because he looks" (Cuccu, *Antonioni: Il discorso dello sguardo*, p. 80).

21 Sam Rohdie offers a suggestive description of this shot, saying that it flattens "both figure and ground, as if the girl were being projected onto the screen of the landscape, the figure turning into ground, being dissolved by it, fullness and

depth becoming surface, substance and figuration turning into an image" (Roh-die, *Antonioni*, p. 125). It should be remembered, though, that we have seen this same dynamic of flattening – especially with women – throughout the films discussed in this study.

22 "Talking of Michelangelo," in Antonioni, *The Architecture of Vision*, p. 330. Biarese and Tassone have also pointed out the many personal connections be-tween Locke and the director: both work on ephemeral material; Antonioni had also just finished a frustrating documentary, the film on China; both are globe-trotters; and – at least according to Biarese and Tassone – Jenny Runacre, the British actress who plays Rachel, strongly resembles Monica Vitti (Biarese and Tassone, *I film di Michelangelo Antonioni*, p. 156).

23 "Talking of Michelangelo," p. 330.

24 Seymour Chatman usefully points out the gap between Locke's video view of the African ruler and what Antonioni's camera shows us, especially since the latter does a complete 360-degree pan around the narrative space. Antonioni's camera is obviously seeing more of the picture than Locke's narrow camera view – once again, the foregrounding of different subjectivities – but it is hard to agree with Chatman's rather naive statement that Antonioni's full pan im-plies "that now the full story has been told" (Chatman, *Antonioni*, p. 192).

25 Cuccu, *Antonioni: Il discorso dello sguardo*, pp. 67–8.

26 "Antonioni Discusses *The Passenger*," p. 333.

27 "An In-Depth Search," pp. 348–9. Translation modified.

28 A view that is apparently not shared by William Arrowsmith, who, in his insis-tence on a putative religious vision in the film, seems to believe that visual data can be discussed factually, independently of assigning interpretations to them: "With *The Passenger*, the religious theme is, however tentative, tangibly, pow-erfully present; the film will inevitably be underread or misread if the viewer imposes his own expectations or fails to confront the *fact* of the visual text" (Arrowsmith, *Antonioni: The Poet of Images*, p. 14).

29 "Antonioni Discusses *The Passenger*," p. 335.

30 "The World Is Outside the Window," p. 183.

31 Nevertheless, even this interpretation seems plausible when compared with Sey-mour Chatman's religious reading of the long-take: "Is it too fanciful to suggest that its function is to bear Locke's soul out of the room?" (Chatman, *Antonioni*, p. 189).

32 Antonioni explained that the final shot was done with a special camera from Canada, mounted on a series of gyroscopes so that the image wouldn't be bumpy ("Antonioni Discusses *The Passenger*," p. 338). Since the camera had been designed for use in filming 16-millimeter commercials, Antonioni had to convince the technicians that 35-millimeter would also work, and the apparatus was subsequently recalibrated. Antonioni wanted 600 meters of film, the tech-nicians thought that more than 120 meters was not feasible, so they compro-mised by aiming for 300 meters. (The director complained that if he had had 600 meters he could have started the shot sequence much earlier in the scene.) It took eleven days to film this sequence, partly because the wind was disturbing the camera, but also because the imbalance of interior and exterior lighting conditions only allowed them to shoot between 3:30 and 4:30 each afternoon.

Apparently an early forerunner of the Steadicam, the device allowed the camera to hang in the air and thus is not, technically speaking, a tracking shot. But the only time the zoom lens was used, according to the director, was just at the moment that the camera seems to penetrate the grill on the window. The director, stationed in a truck in front of a monitor, controlled everything; at the time of the interview, he maintained that he would continue to work this way in the future, since he did not want to be surprised, in the editing room, to discover that the director of photography had shot things differently than he wanted him to ("The World Is Outside the Window," p. 182).

The best or at least the most detailed discussion of the long take can be found in Rohdie, *Antonioni*, pp. 146–8. See also Antonioni's article, "La penultima inquadratura," translated as "Antonioni on the Seven-Minute Shot," in Antonioni, *The Architecture of Vision*, pp. 125–6.

33 "Antonioni Discusses *The Passenger*," p. 338.
34 Rohdie, *Antonioni*, p. 148.
35 Biarese and Tassone, *I film di Michelangelo Antonioni*, p. 154.

Selected Bibliography

Works in English

Amberg, George, and Robert Hughes, eds. *L'Avventura*. New York: Grove Press, 1969.

Antonioni, Michelangelo. *The Architecture of Vision: Writings and Interviews on Cinema*. Edited by Carlo di Carlo and Giorgio Tinazzi. American edition edited by Marga Cottino-Jones. New York: Marsilio Publishers, 1996.

Screenplays of Michelangelo Antonioni. New York: Orion Press, 1963.

Arrowsmith, William. *Antonioni: The Poet of Images*. Edited by Ted Perry. New York: Oxford University Press, 1995.

Chatman, Seymour. *Antonioni: Or, the Surface of the World*. Berkeley: University of California Press, 1985.

Chatman, Seymour and Guido Fink, eds. *L'avventura*. New Brunswick, N.J.: Rutgers University Press, 1989.

Leprohon, Pierre. *The Italian Cinema*. Trans. Roger Greaves and Oliver Stallybrass. New York: Praeger, 1972.

Michelangelo Antonioni: An Introduction. Trans. Scott Sullivan. New York: Simon & Schuster, 1963.

Rohdie, Sam. *Antonioni*. London: BFI, 1990.

Works in Other Languages

Antonioni, Michelangelo. *Sei film*. Turin: Giulio Einaudi Editore, 1964.

Biarese, Cesare, and Aldo Tassone. *I film di Michelangelo Antonioni*. Rome: Gremese Editore, 1985.

Cuccu, Lorenzo. *Antonioni: Il discorso dello sguardo: Da "Blow-up" a "Identificazione di una donna."* Pisa: ETS Editrice, 1990.

La visione come problema: Forme e svolgimento del cinema di Antonioni. Rome: Bulzoni, 1973.

di Carlo, Carlo, and Giorgio Tinazzi, eds. *Michelangelo Antonioni: Entretiens et inédits 1950/1985*. Vol. 5 of *L'oeuvre de Michelangelo Antonioni*. Rome: Cinecittà International, 1992.

Miccichè, Lino. *Il cinema italiano degli anni '60*. 3d ed. Venice: Marsilio, 1975.

Tinazzi, Giorgio. *Michelangelo Antonioni*. Florence: La Nuova Italia, 1974.

Index

Antonioni, Michelangelo (*cont.*)
interpretation, question of, in, 2–5, 31, 75, 76, 93–4, 109, 164–6
language theme in, 47, 61
lesbianism in, 34–6
male behavior, critique of, in, 11, 32–4, 55, 62, 80, 82–3, 99–100, 113–15, 160n10, 171n20
marriage, depiction of, in, 33–4, 70–2, 80–1, 115
Marxist view of, 6–7
memory in, 131–2
men, focus on, in, 99, 102, 111
metonymy, use of, in, 59
music in, 41, 48, 74, 87, 88, 98, 162n25
narration in, 29–30, 64–5, 95–6, 106–7, 119, 123, 133, 176n7
nature/culture dichotomy in, 116
object, the, in, 13–14, 17, 88–9, 93–5, 97, 116
past, theme of the, in, 47–8, 63, 83–4, 170n18
politics in, 7, 12–13, 82, 100–1, 110–11, 139–40, 155n7
reality in, 104, 119–21, 124–6, 138–9, 141, 173n16
regionality in, 33
self and subjectivity in, 14, 102–8, 129–31, 133, 136–7, 141, 162n23
self-reflexivity in, 39, 40, 42–4, 93, 104, 106, 111–14, 118, 124–6, 134, 139
sexuality in, 6, 46, 55, 70–2, 81–2, 100, 105, 171n20
social construction of meaning, theme of, in, 117–18, 121
sociopolitical critique in, 7–11, 31, 56–7, 63–4, 66–9, 80–5, 100–1, 110–11, 166n24
sound, ambient, meaning of, in, 41, 73–4, 79, 98, 142
space in, 45, 163n29
symbolism in, 57–9, 77–8, 88–9, 92, 98–9

technology theme, in, 13, 50–1, 55, 83, 96–8
vision in, 14, 77, 104, 119–26, 132, 161n16, 177n20
visual metaphors in, 2, 58–9
visual storytelling in, 30
women, focus on, in, 8–10, 19, 20, 22–3, 32, 34, 36, 42–4, 56, 66, 100–1
women and the "natural" in, 37, 156n14
Ardant, Fanny, 25
Arrowsmith, William, 114–15, 116, 169n6, 172n3, 174n19, 178n28
art films, 1
auteurism, 26–7
Avventura, L', 2, 5, 9, 22, 26, 28–51, 52–3, 54, 59–60, 62, 70, 80, 91

Bachmann, Gideon, 138
Baigneuse, La, 36
Barthes, Roland, 4, 7, 13–14, 26, 31, 40, 48, 123, 173n10, 174n28
Bazin, André, 91
Bergman, Ingmar, 1, 33, 57–8
Bergman, Ingrid, 8, 29
Beyond the Clouds, 25, 138
Biarese, Cesare, 61, 64, 68, 77, 143–4, 166n7, 178n22
Bicycle Thief, The 18, 21
Blow-up, 4, 23, 26, 32, 34, 39, 74, 109–26, 127, 133, 139, 140
Bonitzer, Pascal, 11, 31, 89, 160n9
boom, il, 6, 45, 82
Borelli, Armando, 6–7, 32
Bosè, Lucia, 19
Broch, Hermann, 63–4
Brunetta, Gian Piero, 5, 19, 22, 158n39
Butor, Michel, 53

Cabinet of Dr. Caligari, The, 95
Calvino, Italo, 45
Cameron, Ian, 58, 164n6
Cannes Film Festival, 28–9
Canby, Vincent, 25
Carné, Marcel, 16